Genealogy
Software Guide

Genealogy
Software Guide

Marthe Arends

Cover design courtesy of Karen McClelland

To my husband, Michael, for all of his love, support, and patience.

Contents

Illustrations

Due to space restrictions, some reports have titles, headers, and footers omitted, containing information such as page number, the date the report was generated, preparer/submitter information, and report title.

Figures

Preface

The goal of this book is to provide a complete reference for genealogy software. When I started this project, I had visions of a volume listing details and reviews for every existing genealogy-related program; after surveying current software, and coming to grips with the reality of just how impractical and confusing such a book would be, I narrowed my plan down to supported genealogy-related software. Over the last few years, many programs have been orphaned with outdated and clumsy interfaces, inadequate features, and no author support. For this reason, my book will feature only software that is still supported by the author or the publisher.

Genealogy software has changed quite a bit in the last few years; as users demand more features and more power, software publishers comply with "bigger, better, faster" programs. New users are easily confused by the barrage of software claims and endorsements by a number of genealogy experts.

A variety of software is included for review: commercial and shareware databases, and utilities. Unfortunately, software changes rapidly with new versions and frequently released updates; I have attempted to keep this book as up-to-date as possible, with information being correct at the time of review. Some software is not included, and I apologize if your favorite program was left out; only programs that are currently supported are included.

I began research into each program by asking companies and authors to fill out a questionnaire with specific details about their program, support, and update policy. Most companies responded to my request for information, although I was unable to review a few programs (generally due to an availability problem). Information about those programs that are not reviewed can be found in Appendix E.

It would be impossible to provide detailed reviews of each program. Rather than just list features, I've tried to provide a sense of what the program feels like through screen shots and sample printouts. Of course, major features and functions are listed, as are details on common characteristics. I was as objective as possible when reviewing the software, and made no comparisons between similar programs.

Just as it was not reasonable to review obsolete software, reviews for all of the other computer platforms were not feasible. While Commodore 64s, Amigas, Ataris, and other computers are still in use, there are very few existing programs for them. The original plan for this book included Macintosh program reviews, as well as IBM compatible reviews, but time, space, and computer restraints have limited the reviews to IBM compatible only. Macintosh and other OS software are listed; however, Macintosh software infor-

xvi

There are many people to whom I am very grateful for their help with this book: my heartfelt appreciation and thanks go to the many software companies and authors for their assistance and support. Throughout this project, I encountered only courtesy, generosity, and endless patience with my many questions.

My husband and family offered many ideas, and gave endless support. The Genealogical Publishing Company assigned me a wonderful editor, Christina Schaefer, who deserves much praise for the excellent job she did simultaneously editing the book, and keeping me sane as I travelled the labyrinth of publishing my first book. Christina went above and beyond the call of editorial duty, and I appreciate the time she spent working with me.

I'm grateful for the support of many friends and students who gave freely of their advice: George Archer was especially helpful with many excellent suggestions; Deb Cruze, Wendy Garner, and Barb Butler all maintained an interest in the project and kept me working when I would rather have been playing.

Marthe Arends

Chapter 1

Genealogy and Computers

Why Use Genealogy Software?

Imagine you are at a family reunion and 20 people are interested in your genealogy data. You want to share it with them, so you run to the local photocopy store and make 20 copies of your:

- Family Group Sheets
- Pedigree Charts
- Notes
- Sources
- Family photos
- First 3 chapters of your family history book

This sounds tedious, tiring, and very expensive! Now imagine sending the same 20 people the identical information, but this time, all you have to do is click a few buttons in your genealogy program. Family data, notes, sources, photos, and the chapters from your family history book are all placed on a couple of floppy disks, or printed as hard copies. This sounds much easier and a lot less expensive.

Computers were created to take mundane, tedious work, and free up the user to spend his or her time on more important matters. Genealogists look to computers to crunch the numbers, store information, organize data, calculate relationships, and create a variety of reports and charts; in short, to do all the hard work so you can concentrate on research.

Genealogy software allows you to share your information easily and quickly, with little or no cost. You can place your data online and share it with the world, or export a GEDCOM file and exchange your data with a new-found cousin. You can print charts, reports, graphs, graphic images, and family history maps, and send them to friends and families without computer capability.

Multimedia capabilities allow you to create computer "scrapbooks" with images, sound clips, and even video. Books, complete with index, table of contents, and graphics can be easily generated by many genealogy databases from the information you enter into the program. Other programs will create a book from PAF or GEDCOM files.

The features of today's genealogy database programs vary, but most include multimedia capabilities, problem-solving functions such as relationship calculators, the ability to print customized charts and reports, events which can be sourced and documented, notes for individuals and families, useful organizational charts and forms, and the ability to create a Web page.

Used wisely, genealogy software can further your research by attending to all of the record-keeping tasks, and allow you to spend your time and energy tracing your family history.

Why Use a Genealogy Program?

- convienent
- data shared easily
- organization
- material won't decay
- liven up your research with photos, sound, and video clips
- let the computer do the hard work

GEDCOM (**GE**nealogy **D**ata **COM**munication): The specification which allows data to be exchanged between different programs

 Notes

What Equipment Do You Need?

Hardware

It's an unhappy fact that the older and slower your computer is, the harder it will be to run the latest versions of software. Although there are DOS programs available—some of which are still supported by the authors—the majority of software is available for IBM compatible computers running Windows 3.x, Windows 95, or later.

There are several Macintosh programs available as well; most of them are written for System 7.0 and later. Users of the Psion palmtop have a choice of a few programs, and if you own an obsolete computer such as a Commodore Amiga, you may be able to find older software online or through user groups.

Each program review in this book will list the minimum hardware requirements needed to successfully run that software, as specified by the manufacturer. As a rule, most IBM compatible programs require a 386 or better processor, with a 486 or better recommended. A hard drive is a must-have peripheral in today's world of genealogy; with the size of current commercial programs, the larger your hard drive, the better off you'll be. Some of the newer programs can take up a hefty chunk of your hard drive; I try to have 100MB of hard drive space free for data files and graphics. If you are limited by hard drive space, consider purchasing a larger one (as you add individuals to your database, you'll be thankful for the extra space), or use a program that does not demand a large amount of drive space.

Mac vs IBM

Nothing can fire up a heated argument faster than the IBM vs Macintosh debate. Both platforms have advantages, both have disadvantages; in the end, it all boils down to a matter of personal preference. Traditionally, Mac genealogists have had less software from which to choose, but recently Macintosh versions of popular IBM compatible software have entered the market and given Mac users more options.

Operating Systems

The second biggest argument I've seen break out among computer genealogist is regarding the Windows 3.1 vs Windows 95 debate. Should you upgrade, or should you wait? What about incompatibilities between Windows 95 and older DOS programs? With the release of Windows 98, the debate will get that much hotter.

Again, the choice comes down to personal preference. Most IBM compatible software today is being written for Windows 95 specifically, or a combination of Windows 95 and Win 3.x. There are still many programs which are Windows 3.x specific, and even some that are DOS- based. Personally, I haven't discovered a genealogy program (DOS, or Win 3.x) that does not run under Windows 95.

Likewise, most new Macintosh software will run under the older System 7 OS, although some programs now require a Power Mac and/ or System 8 OS.

If you are concerned about your system's performance, consult the software company or author before you make a purchase.

Hardware:
The computer equipment.

Software:
The programs which run on a computer.

Windows Family:
❖ Windows 3.1
❖ Windows NT
❖ Windows 95
❖ Windows 98

Operating System:
The software that runs a computer, e.g., Windows 3.x, Windows 95, Macintosh System 7.1, Unix, DOS.

Peripherals

If your budget allows, there are many peripherals that will enhance your computer genealogical abilities. Scanners (hand or flatbed), digital cameras, laser printers, color printers, modems, microphones, and removable media storage devices can enrich your data.

Of the above list, a good printer is a must. Inexpensive inkjet printers are readily available, as well as good-quality laser printers. The recent drop in price makes color inkjet printers within the reach of most genealogists, although they are not required.

CD-ROM drives are also very useful and becoming a necessity to researchers as more and more CDs are being released. Recommended minimum CD-ROM speed is 8x (8 times); faster drives are preferred and are becoming more reasonable as their prices continue to drop. Most software which comes on a CD requires at least 2x (double-speed) CD-ROM speed.

A removable media storage device, such as a Zip drive, is an excellent investment. Their high-capacity disks (100MB) can be used to back up data as well as store large graphics, freeing up valuable hard drive space.

Fast modems are also becoming less expensive; if you are planning to be on either the Internet or a BBS, invest in a modem with at least 56.6K speed.

Color flatbed scanners have recently undergone a dramatic drop in price; what was once out of the reach of all but a professional genealogist is now available at reasonable cost. Flatbed scanners allow you to place an object on a glass screen (very similar to a photocopier) while the scanner passes under it. A hand-held scanner is usually less expensive, but you must guide the smaller-sized scanner over the object.

If you have a limited genealogy budget, plan for an inkjet or inexpensive laser printer, CD-ROM drive and modem. If you have a bit more freedom, add a flatbed scanner, color inkjet printer, and a removable media storage device.

Peripherals Useful To Genealogists:

- **modem**
- **laser printer/color inkjet printer**
- **CD-ROM drive**
- **color flatbed scanner**
- **digital camera**
- **removable media drive**
- **large hard drive**
- **recordable CD-ROM drive**

Peripherals:
Computer components such as modems, printers, extra drives, etc.

CD-ROM Drive:
Plays Compact Disks (aka CD-ROM or CD), which can hold information from 100+ floppy disks; most genealogy data is released on CDs.

Removable Media Devices:
A special disk drive which takes disks up to 1 gigabyte (GB) in size, and can be used as an additional hard drive, or as a very large-capacity floppy drive; such devices are useful for backups and storage.

Flatbed Scanner:
Similar in appearance, although smaller, to a photocopy machine, a scanner takes a digital picture of an item placed on its "face"; the image is stored as a graphics file, and can be imported into many genealogy programs.

Hand-held Scanner:
A smaller and less expensive version; you must manually pass the scanner over the item to be scanned.

 Notes

Questions to Ask Yourself Before Purchasing Genealogy Software

- ◆ **What sort of research will you be doing?**
- ◆ **Will your computer run the software you want?**
- ◆ **What is the level of your expertise?**
- ◆ **Do you have budget limitations?**
- ◆ **Is extensive product support an issue?**
- ◆ **Do you want to publish your research?**
- ◆ **How much flexibility (customization) do you require?**

The type of software which will serve you best depends on your research needs and resources. If you are a family historian who is gathering information on a family for your own satisfaction, you may want a program that is geared to hobbyists. If you are a professional researcher, or are preparing a submission for a lineage society, you may be happier with software geared for the advanced researcher.

Read the system requirements for the software in which you are interested; will it run on your computer, or do you need to purchase more RAM, install a CD-ROM drive, speed up your processor, or add a bigger hard drive? Is the program compatible with your operating system? Does it have the functions that you want? Is the program geared to your level of expertise?

If you are a computer novice, you will probably want to purchase a program that is easy to use, has good technical help and support, and a tutorial or guidance in getting started. Likewise, researchers who are new to genealogy will probably want a program that is easy to use, and has a good manual which explains the program features in detail. Computer veterans can skip entry-level programs and should not be daunted by more complex software.

Does your budget allow you to purchase a program without consideration of price, or are you limited to a specific price range? Will you need to purchase other software (add-ons)? Does the software company or author charge for minor upgrades and "bug" fixes, or just major upgrades when new features are added?

If you are a new user, or a computer technophobe, you might need to rely on help from the software company. If you require voice help for installing the program or assistance getting it working, be sure there is adequate technical support. If a printed manual is important, think twice before purchasing a program with only online help.

If you are planning on publishing your research in book format, choose a program that has a variety of reports, particularly one that meets your format requirements. Look for a program that permits you to customize reports, print photos, create an index and table of contents, and print your sources and notes.

Flexibility is built into most new programs, giving you options to customize general preferences, reports, and other features. If you are looking for the ability to personalize the program to your needs, be sure the software supports customization.

Tutorial:
Some programs have a **tutorial** either within the program, or in the manual; the tutorial can give you valuable assistance using the software.

Technophobe:
Person afraid of technology; in computer terms, technophobe refers to one who is hesitant about installing new software or hardware for fear of damaging their computer.

Opinions

Part of your software research plan should involve seeking opinions on various programs. Other people's opinions of a program can give you an insight to what is important to them, but keep in mind that their needs may not match your own. Search out program reviews, but be wary of those reviews where lots of personal opinions are expressed: the best reviews detail features and functions, explain limitations and abilities, and leave it up to the reader to decide if the program is right.

While it is good to ask people what program they use, take your line of questioning a bit further. Some questions you might want to ask someone when discussing their favorite program:

- Why do you like the program?
- What features do you find especially valuable?
- Did you try other programs before you chose this one?
- With what function or feature are you not happy?
- What sort of technical help is available?
- Does the program have a steep learning curve?
- Is the manual helpful?
- Does the program have a tutorial?
- Given my software needs, would you recommend the program to me?

If you read the soc.genealogy.computer newsgroup, you've probably seen people recommending and comparing programs; such discussions can be useful when they detail specific functions, but all too often they end up being a "my program is better than your program" argument. Read everything you can find about the various programs, but reserve your judgment until you've had a chance to see the program, or have ruled it out due to other factors.

Software Review and Information Resources
- **Genealogy magazines**
- **Computer magazines (usually feature the larger commercial programs)**
- **Society newsletters**
- **User groups**
- **Genealogy newsgroups and mailing lists**
- **Genealogy computer books**
- **Author or product Web sites**
- **Software sites, such as the Software Springboard http://www.toltbbs.com/~kbasile/software.html**

Choosing the Program

There are 5 steps to choosing the right genealogy program:

1. **Decide** what type of program you want (beginner, intermediate, expert), and what you want from a program.
2. **Choose** the items which are important to you. If you want to print a book from the program, make sure it supports a book report function, or has the charts and reports you desire.

Notes

 Notes

3. **Investigate** programs by reading reviews, soliciting opinions, and noting a program's limitations and abilities. Make a list of the programs in which you are interested.
4. **Weed** out any programs which don't fit your profile: programs that are beyond your budget, require a more powerful system than what you have, run in an undesirable operating system, don't have the features you require, etc.
5. **Evaluate** the programs you have remaining on your list by downloading and trying demo copies.

Evaluating a Program

Evaluating a genealogy program gives you the chance to explore the program in a hands-on manner. Most programs have a demo copy available for experimentation, and although many programs have limited features, you have a chance to get a feel for the program by entering in some names, sources, etc.

When evaluating a program, you'll want to ask yourself:

- Does the sourcing ability meet with your requirements?
- Does the program have the reports you want?
- Is the interface intuitive and easy to use?
- Can the program be customized to fit your needs?
- Are multimedia objects supported?
- Can you search for items in a manner that makes sense to you?
- Does the program have the features, functions, and bells and whistles that *you* want?

Play with the program by entering as many names, dates, locations, events, sources, etc. as you can (most demos have limits). See how the program handles difficult situations: multiple parents, re-ordering children, conflicting evidence, aliases, etc. Review your research and apply any special problems or circumstances which you face (non-traditional marriages, surname problems, name changes, etc.).

Software reviews and recommendations can be helpful, but don't let yourself be brow-beaten into purchasing a program that offers too much or too little. Try programs, read reviews, and seek opinions, then weigh the evidence and make an informed decision.

Checklist for Genealogy Database Software

 Notes

Many people have found that purchasing software takes a big chunk out of a genealogy budget. For this reason, it's important to investigate a program as thoroughly as possible before purchase. It's also a good idea to create a checklist of items which are important to you. Items you may want to check:

Program Support:
- ❑ separate edit screen for each individual, or for a family?
- ❑ customizable events
- ❑ hot keys and macros for repeat information
- ❑ tutorial
- ❑ printed manual
- ❑ demo version
- ❑ technical support
- ❑ multiple sets of parents
- ❑ merge, delete, and unlink functions for individuals
- ❑ date conversion
- ❑ multiple dates
- ❑ mailing addresses for individuals
- ❑ automatic birth order
- ❑ foreign characters and language
- ❑ father's surname automatic for children
- ❑ name change/alternate names
- ❑ multimedia scrapbooks
- ❑ Web page creation
- ❑ GEDCOM import and export

Program performance:
- ❑ quality of data check
- ❑ computation of relationships
- ❑ universal changes for a particular location or source
- ❑ automatic save of data upon exit

Program limitations:
- ❑ number of people in database
- ❑ number of sources
- ❑ number of notes
- ❑ number of events per person and per family
- ❑ number of multimedia objects per person or family

Program Resources:
- ❑ reports
- ❑ sources and documentation
- ❑ manual

Chapter 2

What to Expect in Genealogy Software

What Are the Types of Software?

Generally speaking, genealogy software is divided into 2 basic types: databases and utilities. A **genealogy database** stores and manipulates family data, such as names, dates, relationships, sources, and notes. It can create charts and reports from the data you input, import and export information, and handle assorted tasks related organizing, recording, and displaying your family information.

A **utility program** usually performs 1 specific task, or a collection of related tasks with 1 objective. A utility program can create an index, produce a book from your data, create specialized charts and forms, or map geographic information.

Software comes in 2 categories: commercial and shareware. A commercial program is one you must purchase to use; however, some commercial programs have demos available with limited capabilities, so you can see what the software looks like before you buy it. Shareware programs also allow you to try out the program before you purchase (or "register") it. Like commercial demos, some shareware demo programs have limited features until they are registered. You are obliged to register any shareware program you use; if you don't, you will be in violation of the program's license. Individuals write most of the genealogy shareware programs; it is important to support the program by registering it if you are going to use it.

What to Look for in Software

When shopping for a genealogy database program, there are several things to keep in mind. Demo versions let you to roll up your sleeves, dive into the program, and investigate its qualities and flaws, ease of use, features, and functions.

When trying out genealogy database programs, keep a mental checklist of features: ask yourself if the program suits your particular research needs.

◆ GUI

Graphical User Interface (GUI) translates to how the program screens appear. Does the program look visually pleasing? Will you be comfortable working with that GUI? Does the layout make sense to you? If you prefer to not use a mouse, does the program support keyboard commands and shortcuts?

◆ Edit Screen

Is the edit screen intuitive? Are the fields easily accessed? Are you comfortable entering data? Does the layout make sense? Can you customize the fields?

Database:
Family data entered and manipulated, reports generated, assorted functions.

Utility:
Program which performs one specific task or set of tasks.

Shareware:
Try before you buy; you must register a shareware program if you continue to use it.

Commercial:
Buy before you try; some commercial programs have demo copies available for download.

Demo:
Demonstration version of a program; generally free or very low cost, demos offer a good way to evaluate a program before you purchase it.

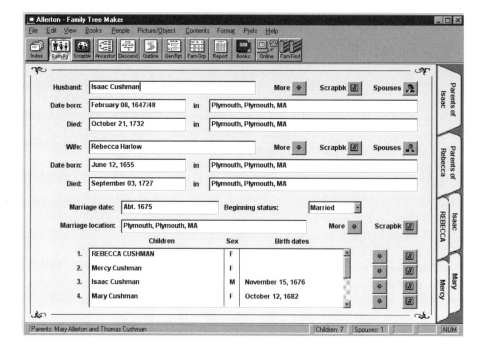

Figure 2.1
Edit Screen from
Family Tree Maker

◆ Sources

What sourcing functions does it have? Can you
source all the events and fields? What level or sourcing
do you need? What are the notes limitations? Can you
create notes for just individuals as well as families?

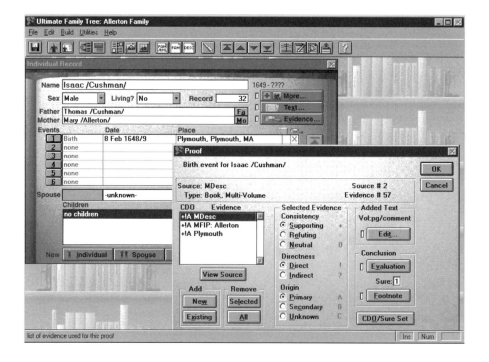

Figure 2.2
Source Entry Screen
from Ultimate Family
Tree

◆ Multimedia Support

Does the program allow you to incorporate scanned images, photos, sounds, and video clips? Can you create an electronic scrapbook? Can photos be included in printed charts and reports?

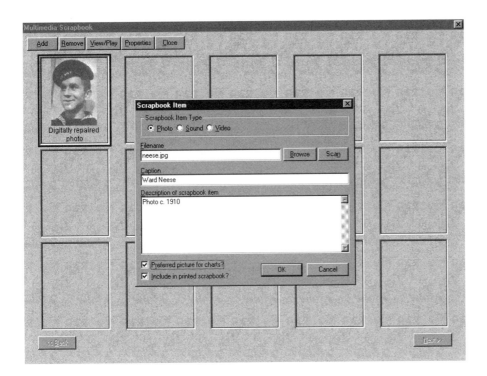

Figure 2.3
Multimedia Entry
Screen from Family
Origins

◆ GEDCOM

The GEDCOM (**GE**nealogy **D**ata **COM**munications) import and export ability is a very important item software. Without it, you have no way of sharing your data without printing reports (most genealogy programs store data in proprietary data forms that cannot be read by other programs). If you wanted to add data from a friend's database, you would have to type it in manually. GEDCOM support allows you to import data from other sources and incorporate the information into your own database, or into a new one. You can also export the information contained in your database and share it with interested researchers.

GEDCOM specifications were created by The Church of Jesus Christ of Latter-day Saints to standardize the encoding of information such as names, dates, locations, relationships, events, etc., to permit the exchange between different software programs. The latest version of GEDCOM is 5.5, but new standards are being developed. Be wary about purchasing a program that does not support GEDCOM transfers.

A GEDCOM is a specially formatted text file; each GEDCOM file consists of a **Level** (each level 1 line refers to the previous level 0 line, level 2 lines refer to the previous level 1 lines, etc.), a **Tag** (such

Why Use GEDCOM?
Most genealogy programs store data in proprietary data forms which cannot be read by other programs. If you want to share your data with someone using a different program, you need to export it in a standardized format that can be recognized by most other programs. That standardized specification is called **GEDCOM.**

Notes

as INDI for indivdual, HUSB for husband, BIRT for birth), and a **Value** (the actual data). There are 6 sections that make up a GED-COM file: header, submitter, individuals, families, sources, and a trailer. You can see an example of a GEDCOM in Appendix F.

◆ Reports

A popular and useful function of genealogy database is the ability to create a variety of charts, lists, and forms referred to generally as **reports**. Some programs support only standard reports, such as Family Group Sheets and Pedigree (Ancestor) Charts, while others support detailed and customizable reports. Report options often include font type and size, borders, the way surnames are printed (all uppercase or not), and whether to include notes and sources. Some software titles allow you to select information you'd like included, such as dates, locations, and individuals. The following are examples of reports from various programs. Keep in mind that the exact appearance and format of the reports may be different with each program.

Figure 2.4
Report Menu from Legacy

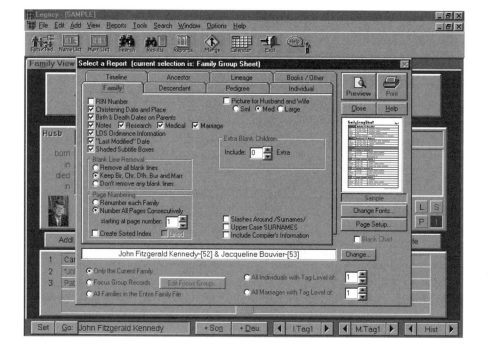

Family Group Sheet (FGS)

Probably the most commonly-used form, the FGS lists information regarding a specific family. Information on husband, wife and children is included with dates and locations. Some forms are more detailed than others and list the parents of each spouse, spouses of children, or other events and notes. See page 21 for an example of an FGS.

Pedigree or Ancestors Chart

The second most widely-used chart, the Pedigree Chart, displays the ancestors of an individual. Most charts display 3 to 5 generations, and can include dates, locations, and record numbers. The format of a Pedigree Chart is:

Notes

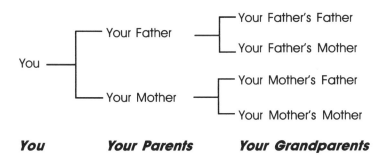

You   Your Parents   Your Grandparents

Pedigree Chart:
Displays a person's ancestors by generation in a graphic format.

Some programs support **Cascading Pedigree Charts**: charts that display several generations over multiple pages. Individuals whose lines continue on another page are referenced, allowing you to follow a line back quickly and easily. **Wall Charts** are produced by multiple sheets of paper taped together to form 1 huge chart, or by the use of large paper and a specialty plotter. A sample Pedigree Chart can be see on page 22.

Ahnentafel

Ahnentafel (German for "ancestor table") is, in essence, a fully detailed pedigree chart without the graphic layout. If you add numbers to the Pedigree Chart above, you'll see:

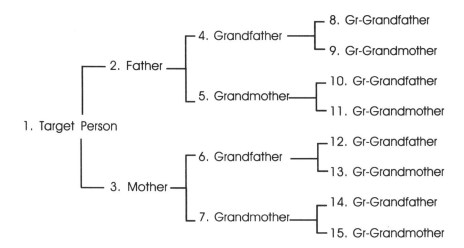

The numbers next to each relationship are always the same, number 5 is always the paternal grandmother; number 15 is always the maternal great-grandmother. An Ahnentafel uses these numbers and presents the information in a text form:

1. Target Person

2. Father

3. Mother

4. Paternal Grandfather

5. Paternal Grandmother

6. Maternal Grandfather

7. Maternal Grandmother

8. Paternal Great-Grandfather

9. Paternal Great-Grandmother

10. Paternal Great-Grandfather

11. Paternal Great-Grandmother

12. Maternal Great-Grandfather

13. Maternal Great-Grandmother

14. Maternal Great-Grandfather

15. Maternal Great-Grandmother

Ahnentafel:
Also shows family information by generation, in text format.

Notice that each generation contains twice as many individuals as the previous generation in a geometric progression. The number of the first person in any specific generation is equal to the number of individuals in that generation. So, the great-grandfather generation begins with number 8, and there are 8 ancestors in that generation. The great-great-great-grandfather generation begins with number 32, and there are 32 ancestors in that generation.

Each even-numbered person is male, each odd-numbered person female. To find a specific person's father, simply multiply the person's number by 2. Add 1 to find the person's mother. A sample Ahnentafel can be seen on page 23.

Descendants Chart

A Descendants Chart lists all the descendants, by generation, of a specific individual. Most programs allow you to choose how many generations you want displayed, and what type of information to include. A generation is indicated by indentation; each generation is indented in the same manner so you can tell in which generation a person belongs at a glance. The children of each person are listed below them in birth order. All of the descendants of the first child will be listed before the remaining children are listed. You can see an example of a Descendants Chart on page 24.

Register Report

Register reports, Modified Register, and Henry style reports are all commonly used as **book reports**—e.g., the format best suited when printing a family history book. The New England Historic Genealogical Society set the standard for the Register system, and you will find that most publications use it, or a variation: an individual is listed with dates and places for events, such as birth, death, and marriage. Information on the individual's spouse (including biographical details) is listed next, followed by listings of children and their information. Biographical information is created by incorporating notes, sources, and other text files. A sample Register Report can be found on page 25.

Blank Charts

Most programs will generate various blank forms for recording research data. Pedigree Charts, Family Group Sheets, Research Log, Census Extract Sheets, Correspondence Log, Calendars, and many other types of blank forms can be printed. Sample blank forms can be seen on pages 26 and 27.

Graphics Scrapbook

Some programs have the ability to include photos in various printed reports, and some can print a "scrapbook" showing photos and identifying remarks.

Photos in Charts

Photos liven up any report. Scanned or digitized images included in forms let you to share fragile and valuable photos with other members of the family and interested persons. Many programs allow you to select a preferred photo for an individual, or which photos you would like included in reports.

Kinship Reports

A Kinship Report lists the relationship between every person in the database and a selected individual. This report is very useful when you have many collateral lines and would like to know exact relationships. See page 28 for a Kinship Report.

Other Reports and Lists

The types of reports and lists will vary among the different programs, but many offer additional items, such as: Individual Summary, Address List, Duplicate List (list of duplicate persons in the database), Unlinked Individuals, Problem List, Sources List, Birthdays and Anniversaries List, Calendar, Place Name List, Timeline, Events List, Database Statistics.

Register Report:
Also called "Book Report" is used when creating a book or family history.

Research Tip:
Rather than purchase expensive forms to record information when you are researching in libraries, archives, etc., make use of the blank forms function available in many genealogy programs.

Graphics Programs:
Allow you to manipulate graphical images such as scanned photographs. Popular titles include *Adobe Photoshop*, and *Paint Shop Pro*.

NOTES

Customizable Reports

A powerful function in many programs is the ability to customize reports, charts, and lists. The appearance of most reports can be customized by font, style, colors, and other graphic choices. Some programs allow you to further customize reports by creating your own (selecting which fields of information will be included), others just allow you to specify whether to add notes and sources, and which individuals to include.

◆ Support

Support is an important factor when choosing a product; be wary of purchasing one which has very limited or no support. Will you need a printed manual? Is technical help available for installation? Is voice help available for questions about operating the software? Is online help available? Does the software company or author welcome suggestions and "wish lists" from users?

◆ Cost

Often the most important factor when choosing a program, initial cost can range from a few dollars for a shareware program, to $100.00 or more for a professional-level program. Keep in mind, many companies charge for significant upgrades; bug fixes and minor upgrades are often distributed for little or no charge. When purchasing a program, make sure it is the latest version available.

Husband	Patrick KENNEDY - 46	
Born	1823	Dunganstown, Ireland
Died	22 Nov 1858	Boston, MA
Occupation	Cooper, Ward Boss	
Religion	Roman Catholic	
Married	28 Sep 1849	Holy Cross Cathedral, Boston, MA

Wife	Bridget MURPHY - 47	
Born	1821	
Died	20 Dec 1888	Boston, MA
Buried		Cathedral Of The Holy Cross, MA
Religion	Roman Catholic	

Children

1	F	Mary KENNEDY - 60	
Born		9 Aug 1851	Boston, MA
Spouse		Laurence KANE - 66	
Married		1883	Boston, MA

2	F	Johanna KENNEDY - 61	
Born		4 Dec 1852	
Spouse		Humphrey MAHONEY - 64	
Married		22 Sep 1872	Boston, MA

3	M	John KENNEDY - 62	
Born		4 Jan 1854	Boston, MA
Died		24 Sep 1855	

4	F	Margaret KENNEDY - 63	
Born		18 Jul 1855	Boston, MA
Spouse		John T. CAULFIELD - 65	
Married		1882	Boston, MA

5	M	Patrick Joseph KENNEDY - 44	
Born		14 Jan 1858	Boston, MA
Died		May 1929	
Occupation		Dockhand, Saloonkeeper, Senator, Bank President[1]	
Religion		Roman Catholic	
Spouse		Mary Augusta HICKEY - 45	
Married		1887	

Husband's Notes

The potato famine of 1845-48, plagued the country of Ireland and pushed many Irishmen to flee to the land of promise, the USA. Patrick Kennedy was among those to leave his home in Wexford County, Ireland, in 1848, in hopes of finding a better life in the US. Once he arrived in the US, he settled in East Boston, where he remained for the rest of his life.[1]

Upon Patrick's arrival in Boston, he immediately became involved in politics. He was known as a Ward Boss in Boston, looking out for the other Irish immigrants and trying to improve the conditions in the community.[1]

Husband's Medical

He died of an outbreak of Cholera.

Husband's Residences

Duganstown, Ireland
Liverpool St., East Boston, MA

Wife's Notes

After her husband died, she opened up a "Notions Shop" to provide for her family.

Wife's Medical

Suffered from heart trouble in her old age (67).

Her death was caused by a cerebral hemorrhage.

Ancestors of Joseph Patrick Kennedy

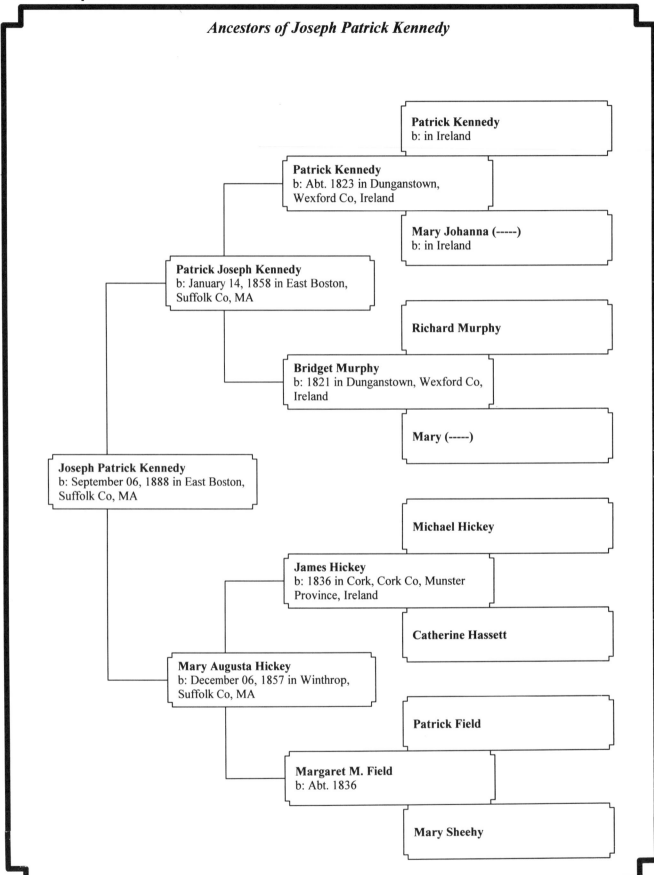

Patrick Kennedy
b: in Ireland

Patrick Kennedy
b: Abt. 1823 in Dunganstown,
Wexford Co, Ireland

Mary Johanna (-----)
b: in Ireland

Patrick Joseph Kennedy
b: January 14, 1858 in East Boston,
Suffolk Co, MA

Richard Murphy

Bridget Murphy
b: 1821 in Dunganstown, Wexford Co,
Ireland

Mary (-----)

Joseph Patrick Kennedy
b: September 06, 1888 in East Boston,
Suffolk Co, MA

Michael Hickey

James Hickey
b: 1836 in Cork, Cork Co, Munster
Province, Ireland

Catherine Hassett

Mary Augusta Hickey
b: December 06, 1857 in Winthrop,
Suffolk Co, MA

Patrick Field

Margaret M. Field
b: Abt. 1836

Mary Sheehy

Family Tree Maker Pedigree Chart (2-2)

FIRST GENERATION

1. **Mary Ann Whitney**: born on 22 Mar 1807

SECOND GENERATION

2. **Nathan Whitney**: born on 8 Apr 1772; died in 1816

3. **Sarah Cox**

THIRD GENERATION

4. **Nathan Whitney Capt.**: born on 30 Apr 1742 in Biddeford, Maine

5. **Patience Barnard (Bernard)**: born in 1742 in Greenland, New Hampshire; died in 1840

FOURTH GENERATION

8. **Nathan Whitney**: born on 10 Jan 1706/7 in Maine; married on 12 Nov 1730

9. **Lydia Young**

FIFTH GENERATION

16. **Nathaniel Whitney**: born on 14 Apr 1680 in York, York Co. Maine; died about 1768 in Maine

17. **Sarah Ford**: born in 1685 in Kittery, Maine

SIXTH GENERATION

32. **Benjamin Whitney**: born on 6 Jun 1643 in Watertown, Middlesex Co. Massachusetts; married about 1668 in York, York Co. Maine; died on 26 Mar 1723 in Sherburne, MA/or Maine

33. **Jane Poor**: born about 1647; died on 14 Nov 1690

SEVENTH GENERATION

64. **John Whitney**: born on 20 Jul 1592 in Isleworth, Middlesex, England/or Westminster, Eng.; married in 1618 in London, London, Middlesex, England; died on 1 Jun 1673 in Watertown, Middlesex Co. Massachusetts

1 Joseph Patrick Kennedy, Male, B: 06 September 1888, East Boston, Suffolk Co, MA
  2 Joseph Patrick Kennedy Jr., Male, B: 25 July 1915, Hull, Plymouth Co, MA
  2 John Fitzgerald Kennedy, Male, B: 29 May 1917, Brookline, Norfolk Co, MA
    3 Caroline Bouvier Kennedy, Female, B: 27 November 1957, New York City, NY
    3 John Fitzgerald Kennedy Jr., Male, B: 25 November 1960, Washington, DC
    3 Patrick Bouvier Kennedy, Male, B: 07 August 1963, Falmouth, Barnstable Co, MA
  2 Rosemary (Rose Marie) Kennedy, Female, B: 20 February 1920, Brookline, Norfolk Co, MA
  2 Kathleen "Kick" Kennedy, Female, B: 20 February 1920, Brookline, Norfolk Co, MA
  2 Eunice Mary Kennedy, Female, B: 10 July 1921, Brookline, Norfolk Co, MA
    3 Robert Sargent Shriver III, Male, B: 28 April 1954, Chicago, Cook Co, IL
    3 Maria Owings Shriver, Female, B: 06 November 1955, Chicago, Cook Co, IL
    3 Timothy Perry Shriver, Male, B: 29 August 1959, Boston, Suffolk Co, MA
    3 Mark Kennedy Shriver, Male, B: 17 February 1964, Washington, DC
    3 Anthony Paul Shriver, Male, B: 20 July 1965, Boston, Suffolk Co, MA
  2 Patricia Kennedy, Female, B: 06 May 1924, Brookline, Norfolk Co, MA
    3 Christopher Kennedy Lawford, Male, B: 29 March 1955, Santa Monica, Los Angeles Co, CA
    3 Sydney Maleia Lawford, Female, B: 25 August 1956, Santa Monica, Los Angeles Co, CA
    3 Victoria Francis Lawford, Female, B: 04 November 1958, Santa Monica, Los Angeles Co, CA
    3 Robin Elizabeth Lawford, Female, B: 02 July 1961, Santa Monica, Los Angeles Co, CA
  2 Robert Francis Kennedy, Male, B: 20 November 1925, Brookline, Norfolk Co, MA
    3 Kathleen Hartington Kennedy, Female, B: 04 July 1951, Greenwich, Fairfield Co, CT
      4 Meaghan Anne Kennedy Townsend, Female, B: 07 November 1977, Santa Fe, Santa Fe Co, NM
      4 Maeve Fahey Kennedy Townsend, Female, B: 01 November 1979, New Haven, New Haven Co, CT
      4 Rose Katherine Kennedy Townsend, Female, B: 17 December 1983, Weston, Middlesex Co, MA
    3 Joseph Patrick Kennedy II, Male, B: 24 September 1952, Boston, Suffolk Co, MA
      4 Joseph Patrick Kennedy III, Male, B: 04 February 1980, Boston, Suffolk Co, MA
      4 Matthew Rauch Kennedy, Male, B: 04 October 1980, Boston, Suffolk Co, MA
    3 Robert Francis Kennedy Jr., Male, B: 17 January 1954, Washington, DC
      4 Robert Francis Kennedy III, Male, B: 02 September 1984, Mt. Kisco, Westchester Co, NY
    3 David Anthony Kennedy, Male, B: 15 June 1955, Washington, DC
    3 Mary Courtney Kennedy, Female, B: 09 September 1956, Boston, Suffolk Co, MA
    3 Michael LeMoyne Kennedy, Male, B: 27 February 1958, Washington, DC
      4 Michael LeMoyne Kennedy Jr., Male, B: 09 January 1983, Charlottesvlle, Albemarle Co, VA
      4 Kyle Frances Kennedy, Male, B: 06 July 1984, Washington, DC
    3 Mary Kerry Kennedy, Female, B: 08 September 1959, Washington, DC
    3 Christopher George Kennedy, Male, B: 04 July 1963, Boston, Suffolk Co, MA
    3 Matthew Maxwell Taylor Kennedy, Male, B: 09 January 1965, New York City, NY
    3 Douglas Harriman Kennedy, Male, B: 24 March 1967, Washington, DC
    3 Rory Elizabeth Katherine Kennedy, Female, B: 12 December 1968, Washington, DC
  2 Jean Ann Kennedy, Female, B: 20 February 1928, Boston, Suffolk Co, MA
    3 Stephen Edward Smith Jr., Male, B: 28 June 1957
    3 William Kennedy Smith, Male, B: 04 September 1960, Boston, Suffolk Co, MA
    3 Amanda Mary Smith, Female, B: 30 April 1967
    3 Kym Marie Smith, Female, B: 29 November 1972, Vietnam

Family Heritage Outline Descendants Chart (2-4)
The information on this chart may not be correct and is for demonstration purposes only.

Descendants of Bridget Murphy

First Generation

1. **Bridget Murphy** was born 1821 in Dunganstown, Wexford Co, Ireland. She died 20 Dec 1888 in Boston, Suffolk Co, MA. Bridget was buried in Malden, Middlesex Co, MA.

    ATTR HCrCem

    Research: Birth Surety:1

    >Death note: Death Surety:2

    >Burial note: Burial Surety:2

    Noted events in her life were:

    1. Immigration; Abt 1847; Boston, Suffolk Co, MA. Immigration Surety:1

    Bridget married Patrick Kennedy, son of Patrick Kennedy and Mary Johanna (-----), 26 Sep 1849 in Boston, Suffolk Co, MA.

    They had the following children:

    +   2   F   i.   **Mary L. Kennedy** was born 9 Aug 1851 in East Boston, Suffolk Co, MA. She was christened 10 Aug 1851 in East Boston, Suffolk Co, MA. Mary died 7 Mar 1926 in Boston, Suffolk Co, MA. She was buried Mar 1926 in Malden, Middlesex Co, MA. Mary married Lawrence M. Kane, son of Philip Kane and Margaret Murphy, 1 Jan 1883 in Boston, Suffolk Co, MA.

    +   3   F   ii. **Joanna L. Kennedy** was born 27 Nov 1852 in East Boston, Suffolk Co, MA. She was christened 4 Dec 1852 in East Boston, Suffolk Co, MA. Joanna died 23 Feb 1926 in Revere, Suffolk Co, MA. She was buried Feb 1926 in Malden, Middlesex Co, MA.
    Joanna married Humphrey Charles Mahoney 22 Sep 1872 in Boston, Suffolk Co, MA.

    +   4   M   iii. **John Kennedy** was born 4 Jan 1854 in East Boston, Suffolk Co, MA. He was christened 5 Jan 1854 in East Boston, Suffolk Co, MA. John died 24 Sep 1855 in Boston, Suffolk Co, MA. He was buried in Cambridge, Middlesex Co, MA.

    +   5   F   iv. **Margaret M. Kennedy** was born Jul 1855 in East Boston, Suffolk Co, MA. She was christened 22 Jul 1855 in East Boston, Suffolk Co, MA. Margaret died 2 Apr 1929 in Revere, Suffolk Co, MA. She was buried in Malden, Middlesex Co, MA. Margaret married John Thomas Caulfield 21 Feb 1882 in Boston, Suffolk Co, MA.

    +   6   M   v.   **Patrick Joseph Kennedy** was born 14 Jan 1858 in East Boston, Suffolk Co, MA. He was christened 16 Jan 1858 in East Boston, Suffolk Co, MA. Patrick died 18 May 1929 in Boston, Suffolk Co, MA. He was buried in Malden, Middlesex Co, MA. Patrick married Mary Augusta Hickey, daughter of James Hickey and Margaret M. Field, 23 Nov 1887 in Boston, Suffolk Co, MA.

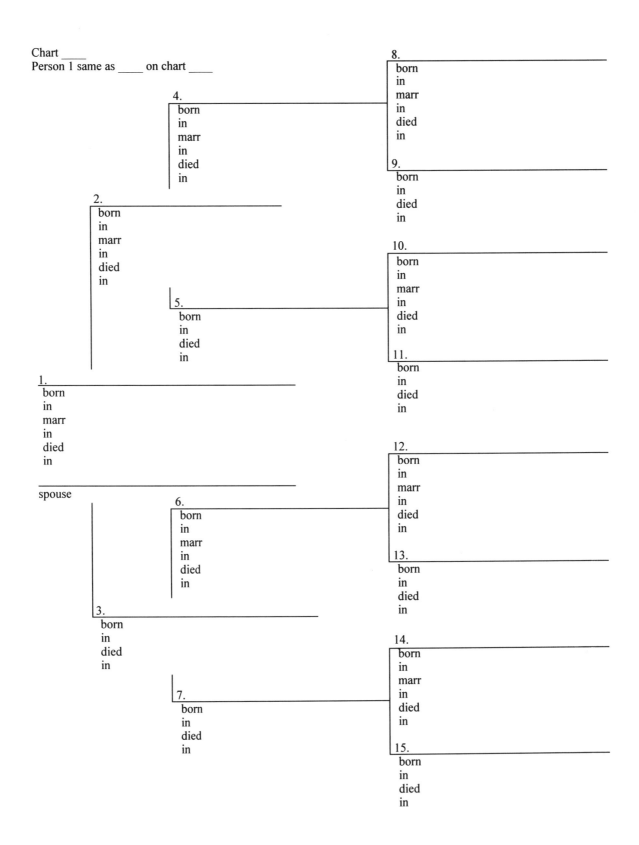

Chart _____
Person 1 same as _____ on chart _____

8. _____
born
in
marr
in
died
in

4. _____
born
in
marr
in
died
in

9. _____
born
in
died
in

2. _____
born
in
marr
in
died
in

10. _____
born
in
marr
in
died
in

5. _____
born
in
died
in

11. _____
born
in
died
in

1. _____
born
in
marr
in
died
in

spouse _____

12. _____
born
in
marr
in
died
in

6. _____
born
in
marr
in
died
in

13. _____
born
in
died
in

3. _____
born
in
died
in

14. _____
born
in
marr
in
died
in

7. _____
born
in
died
in

15. _____
born
in
died
in

Ultimate Family Tree (blank) Pedigree Chart (2-6)

Husband:		
Born:	in:	
Married:	in:	
Died:	in:	
Father:		
Mother:		
Other Spouses:		

Wife:		
Born:	in:	
Died:	in:	
Father:		
Mother:		
Other Spouses:		

	CHILDREN	
1	Name:	
	Born:	in:
	Married:	in:
	Died:	in:
	Spouse:	
2	Name:	
	Born:	in:
	Married:	in:
	Died:	in:
	Spouse:	
3	Name:	
	Born:	in:
	Married:	in:
	Died:	in:
	Spouse:	
4	Name:	
	Born:	in:
	Married:	in:
	Died:	in:
	Spouse:	
5	Name:	
	Born:	in:
	Married:	in:
	Died:	in:
	Spouse:	
6	Name:	
	Born:	in:
	Married:	in:
	Died:	in:
	Spouse:	
7	Name:	
	Born:	in:
	Married:	in:
	Died:	in:
	Spouse:	
8	Name:	
	Born:	in:
	Married:	in:
	Died:	in:
	Spouse:	

Family Tree Maker (blank) Family Group Sheet (2-7)

starting person

Nathan Whitney

children

Abel Whitney

Anna Whitney

Asa Whitney

David Whitney

Ebenezer Whitney

John Whitney

Lydia Whitney

Matthias Whitney

Nathan Whitney Capt.

Sarah Whitney

parents

Nathaniel Whitney

Sarah Ford

siblings

Abel Whitney

Amos Whitney

Isaac Whitney

Joanna Whitney

John Whitney

Lydia Whitney

Lydia Whitney

Nathaniel Whitney

Sarah Whitney

aunts/uncles

Benjamin Whitney

Jane Whitney

John Whitney

Jonathan Whitney

Joshua Whitney

Mark Whitney

Timothy Whitney

grandchildren

Abigail Whitney

Anna Whitney

Benjamin Whitney

Betty Whitney

Daniel Whitney

Daniel Whitney

Eliphalet Watson

Elizabeth Watson

Elsie Whitney

Eunice Whitney

George Whitney

Hannah Whitney

Hannah Whitney

Jeremiah Whitney

Jesse Whitney

John Watson

John Whitney

Joseph Watson

Joseph Whitney

Joseph Whitney

Joshua Whitney

Levi Whitney

Lucy Whitney

Lydia Whitney

Lydia Whitney

Lydia Whitney

Martha Whitney

Mary Whitney

Mary Whitney

Nathan Whitney

Nathan Whitney

Nathan Whitney Watson

Nathaniel (twin) Whitney

Patience Whitney

Reuben Whitney

Roxanna Whitney

Samuel Watson

Samuel Whitney

Sarah (twin) Whitney

Ultimate Family Tree Kinship Chart (2-8)

How the Programs Were Reviewed

NOTES

Each database program is reviewed with a specific checklist of items arranged in 5 sections: Basic Information, Program Information, Reports, Sources, and Bells and Whistles. Comments are added as needed.

The **Basic Information** section contains:
* purchase price
* system requirements
* contact info
* Internet addresses (where applicable)

The **Program Features** section contains:
* information about the GUI (interface)
* standard features
* functions
* limits and restrictions (if any)

The **Reports** section contains:
* specifics about the reports
* limits and restrictions (if any)
* sample reports are shown for many programs

The **Sources** section contains:
* information about the program's sourcing and documenting abilities

The **Bells and Whistles** section contains:
* especially notable functions
* abilities not found in similar programs

The **Comments** section contains:
* information regarding different program versions
* miscellaneous information about the program
* Web page features and items

Additionally, screen shots and sample printed reports are provided for many programs. The checklist of items for the utility programs varies; since each program has a different function, each requires a different set of questions. For consistency, each utility review includes basic information (name and address of the author, Internet information, if a copy is available for download, etc.), as well as details of features and functions; screen shots and sample reports are included for a variety of programs.

 NOTES

Common Database Features

I have listed commonly-included features found in most genealogy programs in a list below. These features are found in almost all of the programs; if you are unsure if a feature has been included in the program of your choice, contact the author or company.

Common features found in most genealogy programs:

- GEDCOM import and export
- Relationship calculator
- Date calculator
- Soundex calculator
- Mailing labels
- LDS ordinances
- Unlink an individual without deleting
- Submitter information
- Foreign characters
- Specify display font
- Select font for printed reports
- Backup and restore functions

Chapter 3

Locating Genealogy Software

Where To Obtain Software

Once you've decided what type of genealogy database you need, you have to locate a source for such programs. A computer or software store will carry some programs, but the fact is that most mainstream software stores do not carry a wide variety of genealogy software. In addition, most computer store employees are unfamiliar with genealogy software, and may not be able to answer questions about those programs which they do carry.

Resources for Software

- **Software companies and authors**
  This is often the best source for obtaining the latest version of the software. You can find advertisements and reviews for genealogy software in many genealogy periodicals; shareware is almost exclusively available only from the author or shareware distributor.

- **Genealogy stores**
  Mail order and online stores, such as Ancestry, Appleton's, and Lineages carry a variety of genealogy software.
  If you are purchasing online, be sure the site has a secure server when using credit cards. See Appendix B for a list of software-purchasing resources.

- **Genealogy societies and groups**
  Many software companies offer group members special prices on their software. Some vendors also make presentations to groups, to display their programs' features.

- **Genealogy conventions and conferences**
  This is often *the* place to go to find bargains and special discounts on software. Visiting a vendor at a convention also offers you a hands-on opportunity to try the software and ask questions.

- **Demo copies on BBSs or Internet**
  Demonstration copies of many programs can be downloaded from Web sites, BBSs, or online software archives. Demos let you to try a version of the program before you purchase.

Downloading Software

A file **download** is the transfer of a file from a remote computer via a modem to your own computer. You save the file on your hard drive, or a floppy disk (preferably a hard drive). The time it takes a file to transfer depends on the connection, size of the file, and modem speed.

Genealogy files can be many types: simple plain-text data files, genealogy programs, graphics, sound clips, video clips, etc. You can tell what type a file is by its extension (the last 3 letters of the file name).

Notes

Online Hint:
If you are the adventuresome type and have a knowledge of your computer, you may be eligible to be a **Beta Tester** (someone who tests versions of software before they are released to the public); contact your favorite program's author and ask about beta testing policies.

What You Need to Download a File:
- ❖ Computer
- ❖ Modem
- ❖ Phone line
- ❖ Terminal program (for a BBS)
- ❖ Web browser or FTP client (for Internet files)
- ❖ Hard drive (recommended)

Notes

Some Popular File Types:

.exe	executable file
.dat	data file
.txt	text file
.ged	GEDCOM file (actually, a GEDCOM is a text file)
.zip	zipped (archived) file
.wav	wave (sound) file
.avi	movies for Windows (video) file
.jpg	graphic file
.gif	graphic file (different format from a .jpg)
.sit	stuffit (Mac archive) file
.hqx	BinHex (archive) file
.sea	self-extracting archive

Archivers

Many files you find online will be archived, that is, the files which make up a complete program will be compressed together into 1 easily downloaded file.

The concept of archived files can be easily described using the following analogy: picture yourself standing with a handful of paper clips, and an envelope on 1 side of a street. A paper clip holder lies on the other side of the street. Your job is to transfer the paper clips to the holder. Which would be more efficient, taking each paper clip across the street one at a time, or placing all of the paper clips in an envelope and taking it to the paper clip holder?

Just as it's easier to put all the paper clips in 1 container and transfer them at the same time, it is also easier to place all the related files that make up a program in 1 archived file for an efficient "1 time" download. All that remains for you to do upon download completion is to un-archive the file into its original many files.

Popular File-Archiving Software:

PKZip (PC)
WinZip (PC)
Stuffit (Mac)
BinHex (Mac)

There are several different types of archivers, but the most popular for the IBM is PKZip. Zipped files have file extension of .zip, and can be un-archived using PKZip, PKUnzip, or WinZip. Macintosh users frequently use the archiver Stuffit.

Some files are archived and you may not know it. If you execute a downloaded .exe file, you may be surprised to find it un-archiving itself. Such files are known as self-extracting archives, and they require no further action on your part.

Many file archives now come with easy-to-use interfaces which make archiving and un-archiving easy. These programs can be found on any shareware or online file collection such as Shareware.com (http://www.shareware.com) or via the Filez (program file) search engine at http://www.filez.com.

Computer Viruses and You!

True or False:
  · **You can catch a computer virus from an e-mail message.**
  · **You can catch a computer virus from software you download.**
  · **You can't catch a computer virus from commercial software.**

The Answers:
    false (with a notation), true, and false

Any time you run a downloaded file or insert a disk into your computer you run the risk of acquiring a virus. While it is possible to get a virus from commercial software (it is extremely rare and happens only in a very, very small percentage of disks and CDs sold), it is impossible to get a virus from an e-mail message *unless* you execute a file infected with a virus that was *attached* to a piece of e-mail. Just reading e-mail will not give you a virus. Running programs attached to a piece of e-mail *can* infect your computer. The moral? Check any and all files you download before running them.

How To Avoid Computer Viruses
  ♦ **Check all disks new to your computer with virus detection software**
  ♦ **Before running a program, scan the file with a virus detection program**
  ♦ **Schedule your virus-detecting software to periodically scan your hard drive and data disks**
  ♦ **If you suspect you have a virus, run a virus detection and virus-killing program**

The solution is to be cautious about *any* new software you acquire. Keep current backups of your hard drive, in case a file is infected. If you do suspect you have a virus, there are several good commercial anti-virus and virus-scanning programs available. The most popular for IBM compatibles are Norton AntiVirus, McAfee's VirusScan, and Thunderbyte Software's Thunderbyte. Symantec also produces the Norton AntiVirus for the Macintosh.

In addition, there are freeware and shareware anti-virus programs available. The Internet mailing list Virus-L archives includes publicly distributed programs and information.

Norton AntiVirus	http://www.symantec.com/avcenter/
VirusScan	http://www.mcafee.com/
Thunderbyte	http://www.thunderbyte.com/

Types of Viruses:
❖ Trojan Horse
❖ Worm
❖ Mail Bomb

What a Computer Virus Can Do:
❖ format your hard drive or floppy drive
❖ corrupt data and program files
❖ damage your computer's operating system

Don't Panic!
While it's possible to contract a computer virus, there's no need to construct a computer "bomb shelter."

❖ Use common sense and be cautious with any software.
❖ Make frequent and *complete* backups of your hard drive.
❖ Make multiple backups of particularly valuable files (such as your genealogy data).
❖ Invest in a good virus detector/killer, and register it.
❖ Use current virus killers. New viruses are popping up all the time; out-of-date virus software may give you a false sense of security.

Chapter 4

Genealogy Database Programs

The information listed in this, and subsequent chapters, was accurate to the best of my knowledge at the time the program was reviewed.

You may find that some functions are not listed in a review; although I was as thorough as possible, I found that not all functions are readily apparent, or are listed in the product documentation. For instance, many programs include a Soundex conversion function, but it is often not described or evident.

Since new versions of software are released frequently, the information may not reflect the latest version of the program. If you have questions about a program's version number, features, functions, price, or system requirements, contact the author.

To review programs, I used either the demo database that was included with the program, or I imported a test GEDCOM. Any incorrect information or discrepancy in the data itself is due to the test GEDCOM, and should not reflect upon the program.

There are a few instances where reports are not available for some programs, generally due to a program not printing reports (i.e., some demo programs had the print function disabled).

A-Gene
Version 2.0.36 for Windows

Basic Information

Mike Simpson
20 Palace Green
Berwick-upon-Tweed, Northumberland
TD15 1HR England
Voice: 011-441-289-304560
e-mail: mike.simpson@btinternet.com
http://www.btinternet.com/~genealogy/
agene.htm
Shareware fee: £20
Demo available for download

System requirements: 486 or higher IBM
    compatible
RAM: minimum 4MB, 8MB recommended
Hard drive: 5MB required
CD-ROM: not required

Program Information

Individuals per database: unlimited
Spouses per individual: 10
Children per relationship: 30
Children reordered: yes
Multiple parents allowed: no
Field sizes: note (32,000 characters), name
    (25 characters), date (15 characters), place
    name (4 lines of text)
Note options: general, birth, death, burial,
    and marriage detail notes
Multimedia options: 3 files per individual
    allowed (1 image, 1 video in .AVI format,
    and 1 sound file in .WAV format)
Program options: 4 user-defined fields
    supported, text editor built-in
Date options: perpetual calendar in
    Gregorian dates only
Search options: individual's name, birth
    place, birth and death years, and Record
    Information Number (RIN); search also by
    Soundex, and for duplicate individuals
Certificate feature: birth, marriage, and
    death can be entered and printed

Database maintenance and options:
    backup, restore, compare, merge, repair,
    compact, basic disk-maintenance functions

Reports

View reports before printing: yes
Customized reports
• Options: specify individuals to include
Sources included on reports: some
Ahnentafel
Descendants Chart
Family Group Sheet
Migrant Ships
Marriage Details
Pedigree Chart
Persons Detail
Unique Surnames
Timeline
Search Notes
Lists
• Family
• Marriage Detail
Persons Narrative Story
• Ancestor format
• Descendants format

Bells and Whistles

• Data can be imported from the
   International Genealogical Index (IGI)
• Graph function allows you to display
   information in graphical (pie chart, bar
   chart, etc.) format
• Included A-Locate program (can be
   accessed via the A-Gene menu) allows you
   to display and print parish and other
   location information
• Browser function allows you to view and
   edit any supported database
• A-Census program module is available

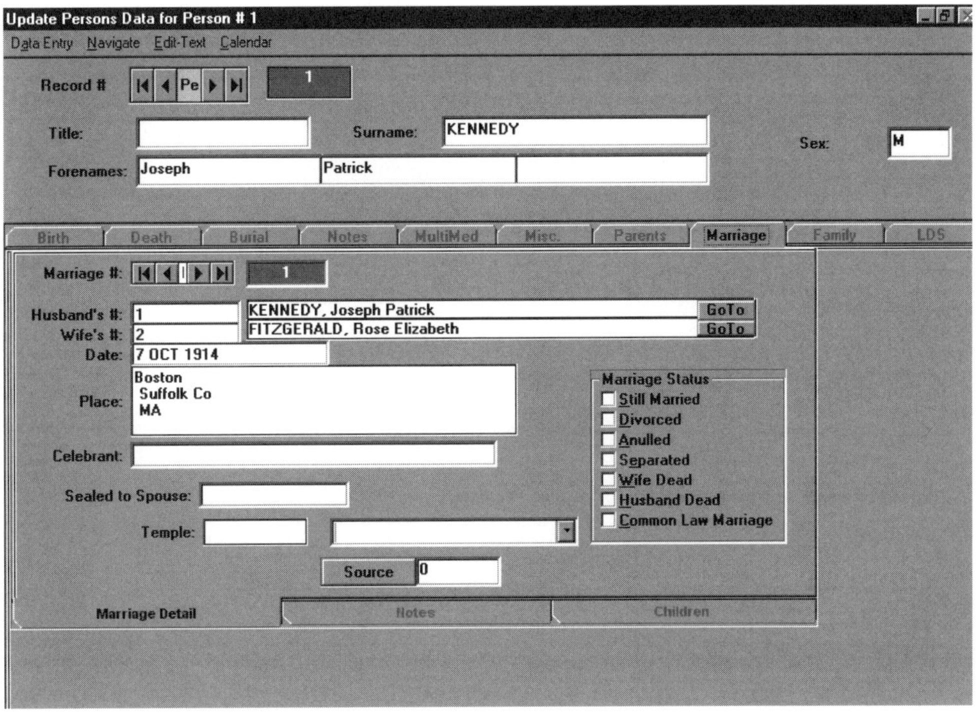

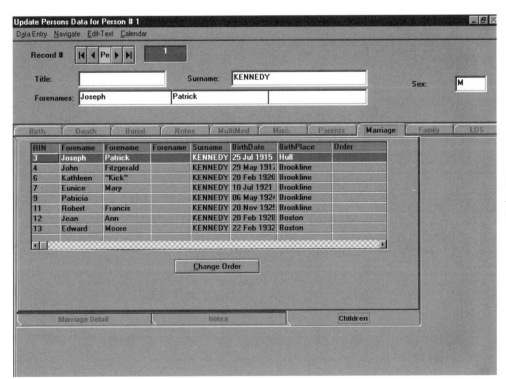

Figure 4.1
A-Gene Edit
Marriage Screen

Figure 4.2
A-Gene Edit
Children Screen

A-Gene - Family Group Sheet:-   **Page 1**   **Printed: Thursday, July 30, 1998**

Husband:	Wife
ANTHONY SMITH (2)	**LYDIA WILLETS (3)**

Marriage Details:	
16 MAY 1746 Monmouth County NEW JERSEY (NJ Lic.)	
Born: 26 Jul 1723 CAPE MAY NEW JERSEY	Born: 16 Jan 1726 LAKEWOOD TWP MONMOUTH NEW JERSEY
Baptised:	Baptised:
Died: 01 Feb 1809 Age At Death: 85 yrs 7 mths GREENE COUNTY PENNS.	Died: 1810 Age At Death: Approx. 84 yrs GREENE COUNTY PENNSYLVANIA
Buried: 01 Feb 1809	Buried:
Jefferson Twp GREENE COUNTY Pa.	Smith Cem GREENE COUNTY PENNSYLVANIA
Father: THOMAS, SR. SMITH (4)	Father: TIMOTHY WILLETTS (6)
Mother: Mary (Wells) ALLEN (5)	Mother: Judith WILLIAMS (7)

Children	Born	Died	Married
Timothy SMITH (2027)	25 Jan 1747 Monmouth County NEW JERSEY	ABT 1822 Age At Death: Approx. 75 yrs GREENE COUNTY Pa.	Sarah WILLETS (2045) ABT 1767
			Hannah WILLIAMS (2053) AFT 1806
Thomas SMITH (2028)	09 Dec 1748 Monmouth County NEW JERSEY	17 Aug 1839 Age At Death: 90 yrs 8 mths (age 90 years 8 mos.)	Deborah LAING (2054) 1771
Judith (Burge) SMITH (2029)	09 May 1751 Monmouth County NEW JERSEY	05 Mar 1836 Age At Death: 84 yrs 10 mths Columbiana County Ohio	Jacob BURGE (2065) BEF 1769
			JOHN HANK (2072) 25 APR 1801
Anthony, Jr. SMITH (2030)	10 Feb 1753 Monmouth County NEW JERSEY	11 Aug 1835 Age At Death: 82 yrs 6 mths Monroe County Ohio	Hannah SOOY (2073) ABT 1783
Noah SMITH (1)	20 Mar 1756 NEW JERSEY	01 Dec 1835 Age At Death: 79 yrs 9 mths GREENE COUNTY PE	Mrs. Noah SMITH (10693) ABT 1776
			Mrs. Sarah SMITH (10694) 1792
			Anne HOGE (1946) AFT 1793
James SMITH (2031)	09 May 1758 Monmouth County NEW JERSEY	AFT 1798 Greene co. Pa. (named in Father's will)	

A-Gene Family Group Sheet (4-1)

Descendant Story:-   Page 1   Printed: Thursday, July 30, 1998

Descendant story for *Sr. Timothy WILLETTS *Sr.   (6)

Timothy was born 25 Dec 1687 at HEMPSTEAD, LONG ISLAND, NEW YORK
Timothy died AFT 1755 at Monmouth County ? NEW JERSEY

His parents were:-
Hope WILLETTS (25) who was born ABT JUL 1652 at Hempstead, Long Island and died 10 Mar 1702 at
Jerusalem, LONG ISLAND, NEW YORK age at death: approx. 50 yrs and Mercy (Mary or Marcy) LANGDON
(24) who was born ABT 1652 at American Colonys - dtr of Joseph and died AFT 1721 at Cape May, New Jersey?
(Widow Townsend)

Timothy had the following siblings:-
Joseph WILLETTS (5020) who was born 1677
Mary WILLETTS (5021) who was born 1679
Elizabeth WILLETTS (5022) who was born 1680
Richard WILLETTS (5023) who was born 1683 and who died 1759 aged At Death: Approx. 76 yrs
Hester WILLETTS (5024) who was born 1686
Hope WILLETTS (5025) who was born 1689
Phebe WILLETTS (5026) who was born 1690 and who died AFT 1722
James WILLETTS (5027) who was born 1694 and who died 1743 aged At Death: Approx. 49 yrs
Abagail (Triplet) WILLETTS (5030) who was born 03 Aug 1696 and who died AFT 1716
Patience (Triplet) WILLETTS (5029) who was born 03 Aug 1696
Hannah (Triplet) WILLETTS (5028) who was born 03 Aug 1696

Timothy 's Marriage(s):-
Timothy was married to Judith   WILLIAMS (7) 1714 at NEW JERSEY

Generation 1 - Wife ?* Judith WILLIAMS ?*   (7)

Judith was born ABT 1690
Birth Notes:-
Her maiden name unknown. Could have been Judith Williams, of a Quaker
family, who live in New Jersey at the time Timothy Willetts was
 married.
Need to search further in New Jersey and in Quaker records for that
period. She was heir to George Williams of Shrewsbury Township,
 Monmouth
County New Jersey (est June 1751).

Her parents were:-
George? WILLIAMS (5031) and died ABT 1751 at Shrewsbury, Monmouth, New Jersey and   UNKNOWN
(11981)

General Notes regarding Judith :-
Her maiden name unknown. Could have been Judith Williams, of a Quaker
family, who live in New Jersey at the time Timothy Willetts was
 married.
Need to search further in New Jersey and in Quaker records for that
period. She was heir to George Williams of Shrewsbury Township,
 Monmouth

10 Generation Ahnentaefel Chart for Ippolita SFORZA

    1   8169   Ippolita SFORZA   ABT 1442   Milan - dtr of Francesco Sforza

Generation 2 Parents _____

    2   7252   Francesco SFORZA   1401   Milan

    3   8125   Bianca Maria VISCONTI   1423   Milan - dtr of Flippo Maria Duke of Milan

Generation 3 Grandparents _____

    4   8127   Giacomuzzo (Muzio) ATTENDOLO   1369   Romagna

    5   12940   UNKNOWN

    6   8126   Filippo Maria VISCONTI   ABT 1380   Milan - son of Gian Galeazzo

    7   10452Maria Of SAVOY   ABT 1395   Savoy

Generation 4 Great-Grandparents _____

   12   6034   Gian Galeazzo VISCONTI   1351   Milan - son of Galeazzo II

   13   8170   Catharine De VISCONTI   Milan? dtr of Bernabo

   14   10858Amadeus Vii SAVOY   ABT 1362   Savoy

   15   10862Dtr Of The BERRY

Generation 5 Great-Grandparents * 2 _____

   24   8171   Galeazzo Ii MILAN   Milan - son of Stefano

   25   10451Bianca Of SAVOY

   26   6378   Bernabo VISCONTI   1309   Milan - son of Stefano

   27   12120   UNKNOWN

   28   10836Amadeus Vi SAVOY   1334   Savoy

   29   10863Dtr Of BOURBON

   30   4096   John Duke BERRI   1341   Duchy of Berri/Berry of France

   31   13138   UNKNOWN

Generation 6 Great-Grandparents * 3 _____

   48   8172   Stefano Of MILAN   Miland - son of Matteo I Visconti

   49   12411   UNKNOWN

   50   10806Amadeus V SAVOY   1249   Savoy

   51   13134   UNKNOWN

   52   8172   Stefano Of MILAN   Miland - son of Matteo I Visconti

   53   12411   UNKNOWN

   56   10806Amadeus V SAVOY   1249   Savoy

   57   13134   UNKNOWN

   58   9967   Louis Ii BOURBON   ABT 1338   France

   59   13139   UNKNOWN

   60   2221   Jean (John) FRANCE   1319   Mans

   61   4196   Bona Of LUXEMBOURG & BOHEMIA   ABT 1320   Bohemia - dtr of John of Luxembourg

Generation 7 Great-Grandparents * 4 _____

   96   8173   Matteo I VISCONTI   Milan?

   97   12412   UNKNOWN   **A-Gene Ahnentafel Report (4-3)**

Ancestors and Descendants
Version 1.40

Basic Information

Adventures in Ancestry, Inc.
10714 Hepburn Circle
Culver City, CA 90232-3717
Voice: 800-237-5333
Fax: 310-842-7443
e-mail: dan@aia-and.com
http://www.aia-and.com/
Price: $87.00

System requirements: IBM or compatible,
640K (or more) recommended, running
DOS, Windows 3.x, Windows 95, Windows
NT, or OS/2; 2 floppy drives (1 must
hold 720K or more)
Hard drive: recommended
Monitor: can be used on older laptops
without color
CD-ROM: not required
Mouse: not required

Program Information

Individuals per database: 9,999; before
using, you must estimate the size of the
database (number of individuals) which
can be modified later; 9 (independent or
interlinked) databases can be active
Spouses per individual: 36
Children per relationship: 36
Multiple parents allowed: yes
Non-traditional relationships: supported
Name options: nicknames, aliases, honorific
prefixes, suffixes
Field sizes: name (80 characters), location
(17 characters), address (more than 100
characters)
Field options: more than 200 fields supported;
individuals have 76 data fields on 4
screens
Note options: 252 allowed for each
relationship
Program options: record numbers supported
(for individuals, relationships,

households, and sources), global change
for place names supported
Ditto-key entry: supported
Date options: double dates, date-entry
format (DDMMMYYYY), date modifiers
(Aft, Bef, Cir, Exa, Fam, Abo, Abt, Est,
Cal, Liv, See), 3 letter only month abbreviate;
Julian, Gregorian, and Jewish calendars
supported
Search options: individual's name, number,
or alias, relationship number, husband or
wife's name or number, household number,
source number; also different printed
reports which search the various fields
Household record options: categories
(current business, current household,
current other addresses, historic business,
historic household, other historic
addresses); links to individual and
relationship records
Types of individual records: basic,
independent, long, secondary; info entered
in relationship records is copied from
individual records
Database maintenance and options:
backup and restore supported, information
is saved when a new or existing record is
changed

Reports

Name Index (alphabetical listing of
individuals in the database)
Ancestors Report (Pedigree Chart)
- 12 fields options to include or exclude
- Number of generations to print: 3, 4, or 5
- Cascading (continuous) report
- Customize the lines and boxes (no
boxes, single-line boxes, boxes with
shadows, and double-line boxes) as well as
outside page borders and data content of
the boxes

Descendants Report
- 12 field options to include or exclude
- Number of descendants to include in a report: no limit

Special Reports
- Options: custom listings, profiles, summaries, or diagrams with data from 20 different fields

Family Group Sheets
- Maximum number of children: 36
- Maximum number of source citations: 40

Notes
- Printing options: can be printed with Family Group Sheets

Basic Records and Basic Lists
- Types: individual, relationship, household, and source

Summary Reports
- Types: cause of death, kind of evidence, health conditions, and more

Diagrams
- Types: disease or death, adoption/lineage, occupation, military, and more

Profile Reports
- Types: fraternal, LDS Temple, relationship ended by, and more

Sources

Creation: can be created for every reference item; can add, browse, change, and delete source records

Options: can be referenced in individual, relationship, and household records without having to be re-entered; can search for additional information

Multiple sources for each event: yes

Number of source category types: more than 100

Print options: source records, forms, numbers, and labels

Entry options: the source type, description, cost (e.g. fees), and kind of evidence

Bells and Whistles

- 5 user manuals give comprehensive support to the program with lots of details, illustrations, and a complete index
- Supports a dictionary; entries can be printed
- Online help is available
- Translation tables can be customized
- Keyboard templates are included (standard keyboard and laptop)

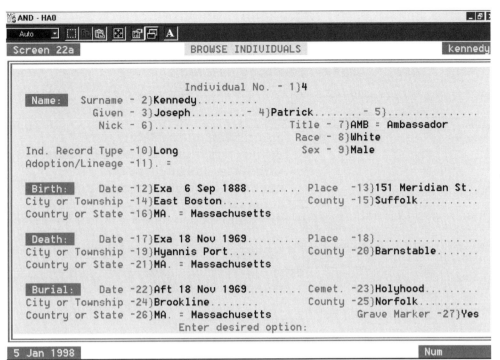

Figure 4.3
Ancestors and
Descendants
Browse Individual
Information

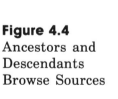
Figure 4.4
Ancestors and
Descendants
Browse Sources

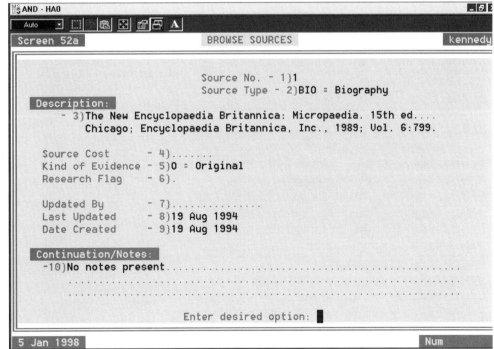

Ancestral Quest

Version 2.0 (CD)

Basic Information

Incline Software
PO Box 17788
Salt Lake City, UT 84117-0788
Voice: 800-825-8864
Voice: 801-278-5886
Fax: 801-273-1535
e-mail: ancquest@ancquest.com
http://www.ancquest.com
Price: $44.95 CD, $39.95 disk
Demo available for download
Orders accepted online

System requirements: Windows 3.1, Windows 95 or higher
RAM: 2MB
Hard drive: 2.5MB space
Monitor: EGA, Hercules® or higher resolution display (VGA recommended)
CD-ROM: required for CD version
Optional hardware: scanner, sound card, speakers, microphone, and video capture hardware

Program Information

Individuals per database: 30,000, unlimited databases allowed, more than 1 database can be active at the same time
Children and spouses reordered: yes
Multiple parents allowed: yes
Name options: honorific prefixes supported, can specify surnames capitalized
Field sizes: surname (16 characters), given name (16 characters)
Note options: general notes, tagged notes (for a specific field, which can be accessed quickly), event notes, and source notes (references sources); address, family contact, and telephone note tags can be exported in list form
Multimedia options: unlimited items (scanned images, audio, and video clips)
per individual, items can be modified, default photo can be specified, image slide show available, images stored in a separate database, interactive scrapbook supported
Program options: select screen colors and fonts, identification field can be customized, can import a partial GEDCOM file
Date options: automatic date conversion, date modifiers (Abt, Bef, Aft), 4 digit year required
Search options: partial name; browse list (search by name, individual number, or marriage number)
Merge options: duplicate records, records with identical custom IDs
Database maintenance and options: can password protect database; database repair, backup, and restore supported

Reports

View reports before printing: yes
Customized reports
- Options: individuals to include
Pedigree Report
- Number of generations to print: 4, 5, or 6
- Photos included
- Cascading report
- Blank report
- Index
Family Group Record
- Photos included
- Specify which notes included
- Print single copy
- Cascading (continuous) report
- Print blank form
- Layout option: condensed
Ancestry Chart
- Photos included
- Format options: standard or wall chart
- Specify font
- Select box style

Descendants Chart
- Format options: standard or wall chart

Lists
- Unlinked Individuals
- Duplicate Individuals
- Individuals by RIN
- Individuals by Alpha
- Possible Problems
- Family Reunion Contacts

Book Reports
- Format options: Ahnentafel and Modified Register Report
- Include notes
- Include photos
- Indexes

Scrapbook
- Options: photos and descriptions for each individual

Sources

Creation: recorded as notes for individuals; standardized Tag Table assists in choosing tags (titles)

Create source tags: supported

Copy and paste in source notes: supported

Print options: indicate which notes are used when source notes option is selected

Source guidelines: examples available in online help

Bells and Whistles

- Ancestral Quest and PAF use the same data files, no need to import and export GEDCOMs when working with the 2 programs
- CD version comes with Hammond World Maps program
- Very comprehensive manual
- High-quality printed reports
- Birth, marriage, and death information pops up when you place the pointer over a individual in the main screen

Comments

Incline Software has licensed a version of Ancestral Quest to Infobases, Inc., who markets it under the name of *LDS Family History Suite.*

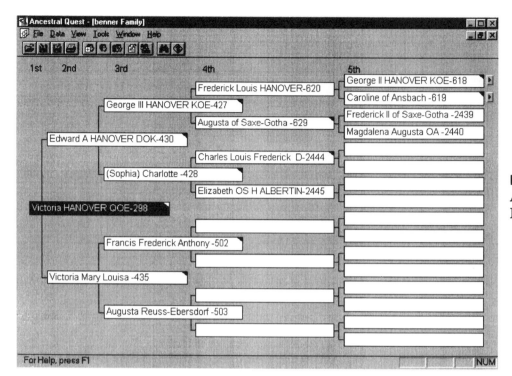

Figure 4.5
Ancestral Quest
Main Entry Screen

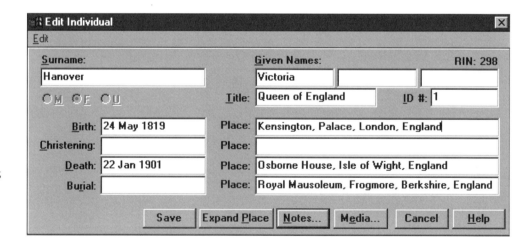

Figure 4.6
Ancestral Quest
Edit Individual
Screen

Family Group Record - 109

Husband	Edward Augustus HANOVER Duke of Kent-430			
Born	2 Nov 1767	Place Buckingham House, , London, England		
Christened		Place		
Died	23 Jan 1820	Place Sidmouth, Devon, , England		
Buried		Place		
Married	11 Jul 1818	Place Kew Palace		
Husband's father	George III HANOVER King of England-427		MRIN: 106	☒ Deceased
Husband's mother	(Sophia) Charlotte -428			☒ Deceased

Wife	Victoria Mary Louisa -435			
Born	17 Aug 1786	Place Coburg		
Christened		Place		
Died	16 Mar 1861	Place Frogmore House, Windsor, , England		
Buried		Place		
Wife's father	Francis Frederick Anthony -502		MRIN: 137	☐ Deceased
Wife's mother	Augusta Reuss-Ebersdorf -503			☐ Deceased

Children	List each child in order of birth.

1 Sex **F** Victoria HANOVER Queen of England-298

Born	24 May 1819	Place Kensington, Palace, London, England
Christened		Place
Died	22 Jan 1901	Place Osborne House, Isle of Wight, England
Buried		Place Royal Mausoleum, Frogmore, Berkshire, England
Spouse	Albert Augustus Charles Prince-299	MRIN: 68
Married	10 Feb 1840	Place Chapel Royal, St. James Palace, England

Sources of information

HUSBAND - Edward Augustus HANOVER Duke of Kent-430
Duke of Kent and Strathern, 4th son of George III. Because William IV had no legitimate children, his niece Victoria became heir apparent to the British crown upon his accession in 1830.

WIFE   - Victoria Mary Louisa -435
Widow of Emich Charles, 2nd Prince of Leiningen (1763-1814) and fourth dau. of Francis Frederick Anthony, Duke of Saxe-Coburg-Saalfeld and Augusta Reuss-Ebersdorf.

CHILD 1   - Victoria HANOVER Queen of England-298
Victoria, Queen of England, Empress of India; aka: Alexandrina Victoria Reign: 20 Jun 1837 - 22 Jan 1901; Crowned: Westminster Abbey 28 Jun 1838; She became queen at age 18. Her 63 year reign was the longest in the history of England. Her descendants, including 40 grandchildren, married into almost every royal family of Europe. With her personal example of honesty, patriotism and devotion to family life, Victoria became a living symbol of the solidity of the British Empire. The many years of her reign, often referred to as the Victorian age, witnessed the rise of middle

Descendants of Victoria HANOVER Queen of England

First Generation

1. Victoria HANOVER Queen of England was born 24 May 1819 in Kensington, Palace, London, England. She died 22 Jan 1901 in Osborne House, Isle of Wight, England and was buried in Royal Mausoleum, Frogmore, Berkshire, England.

> Victoria, Queen of England, Empress of India; aka: Alexandrina Victoria Reign: 20 Jun 1837 - 22 Jan 1901; Crowned: Westminster Abbey 28 Jun 1838; She became queen at age 18. Her 63 year reign was the longest in the history of England. Her descendants, including 40 grandchildren, married into almost every royal family of Europe. With her personal example of honesty, patriotism and devotion to family life, Victoria became a living symbol of the solidity of the British Empire. The many years of her reign, often referred to as the Victorian age, witnessed the rise of middle class and were marked by a deeply conservative morality and intense nationalism. She was obsessed with the collecting of memorabilia of her family. She mourned her late husband, Albert, for more than 40 years.

Victoria married (1) Albert Augustus Charles Prince, son of Ernest I of Saxe-Coburg- Saalfeld Duke and Louise of Saxe-Coburg- Altenburg on 10 Feb 1840 in Chapel Royal, St. James Palace, England. Albert was born 26 Aug 1819 in Schloss Rosenau, Near Coburg, Germany. He died 14 Dec 1861 in Windsor Castle, Berkshire, England.

> Prince Albert of Saxe-Coburg and Gotha, aka: The Prince Consort of Queen Victoria; Christened: (Francis) Albert Augustus Charles Emmanuel; He was an active and effective patron of the arts and sciences, organizing such enterprises as the epochal Great Exhibition of 1851 to stimulate the growth of British commerce, industry and national pride. Although regarded by many Britons as a meddling foreigner, Albert succeeded in strengthening the monarchy and in encouraging social progress. Overburdened with work, he succumbed to typhoid fever at the age of 42.

Albert and Victoria had the following children:

+   2 F   i.   Victoria Adelaide Mary Princess Royal was born 21 Nov 1840 and died 5 Aug 1901.

+   3 M   ii.   Edward VII WETTIN King of England was born 9 Nov 1841 and died 6 May 1910.

+   4 F   iii.   Alice Maud Mary Princess was born 25 Apr 1843 and died 14 Dec 1878.

+   5 M   iv.   Alfred Ernest Albert Prince was born 6 Aug 1844 and died 30 Jul 1900.

+   6 F   v.   Helena Augusta Victoria Princess was born 25 May 1846 and died 9 Jun 1923.

     7 F   vi.   Louise Caroline Alberta Princess was born 18 Mar 1848 in Buckingham, Palace, London, England. She died 3 Dec 1939 in Kensington, Palace, London, England and was buried in Frogmore, England.

> Titles: Princess Louise, Duchess of Argyll. Cremated at Golders Green Crematorium. Ashes buried in the Royal Burial Ground at Frogmore.

> Louise married (1) John CAMPBELL Duke of Argyll on 21 Mar 1871 in St. George Chap., Windsor, England. John was born 1845. He died 1914.

> John Campbell, 9th Duke of Argyll

+   8 M   vii.   Arthur William Patrick Prince was born 1 May 1850 and died 16 Jan 1942.

+   9 M   viii.   Leopold George Duncan Prince was born 7 Apr 1853 and died 28 Mar 1884.

+   10 F   ix.   Beatrice Mary Victoria Princess was born 14 Apr 1857 and died 26 Oct 1944.

1. Victoria HANOVER Queen of England-298 (b.24 May 1819 d.22 Jan 1901)

sp: Albert Augustus Charles Prince-299 (b.26 Aug 1819 m.10 Feb 1840 d.14 Dec 1861)

  2. Victoria Adelaide Mary Princess Royal-300 (b.21 Nov 1840 d.5 Aug 1901)

   sp: Frederick III German Emperor-317 (b.18 Oct 1831 m.25 Jan 1858 d.15 Jun 1888)

    3. William II German Emperor-318 (b.27 Jan 1859 d.4 Jun 1941)

     sp: Augusta of Schleswig- Holstein- -699 (b.22 Oct 1858 d.11 Apr 1921)

      4. William Crown Prince-717 (b.1882 d.1951/1952)

       sp: Cecilie of Mecklenburg- Schwerin -815 (b.1886 d.1954)

        5. William -816 (b.1906 d.1940)

         sp: Dorothea VON SALVIATI-822 (b.1907 d.1972)

          6. Dau. 1 -823

          6. Dau. 2 -824

        5. Louis Ferdinand of Prussia Prince-817 (b.1907)

         sp: Kira of Russia Grand Duchess-825 (b.1907 d.1967)

          6. Friedrich Wilhelm of Prussia Prince-1218 (b.1939)

           sp: Waltraud FREYDAG-1231

            7. Philip Prince-1232 (b.1968)

           sp: Ehrengard VON REDEN-1233

            7. Friedrich Prince-1234 (b.1979)

            7. Viktoria Princess-1235 (b.1982)

            7. Joachim Prince-1236 (b.1984)

          6. Michael of Prussia Prince-1219 (b.1939)

           sp: Jutta JORN-1228

            7. Micaela Prince-1229 (b.1967)

            7. Nataly Princess-1230 (b.1970)

          6. Marie-Cecile of Prussia Princess-1220 (b.1942)

          6. Louis Ferdinand of Prussia Prince-1221 (b.1944 d.1977)

           sp: Donata of Castell- Rudenhausen -1225

            7. Georg Friedrich Prince-1226 (b.1976)

            7. Corneilie-Cecile Princess-1227 (b.1978)

          6. Christian Sigismund of Prussia Prince-1222 (b.1946)

           sp: Nina zu Reventlow Countess-1223 (m.1984)

            7. Daughter -1224

          6. Dau. 2 -831

          6. Dau. 3 -832

        5. Hubertus -818 (b.1909 d.1950)

         sp: Maria-Anna VON HUMBOLDT-833 (b.1916)

         sp: Magdalene REUSS-834 (b.1920)

          6. Dau. 1 -835

          6. Dau. 2 -836

        5. Frederick -819 (b.1911 d.1966)

         sp: Brigid GUINNESS Lady-837 (b.1920)

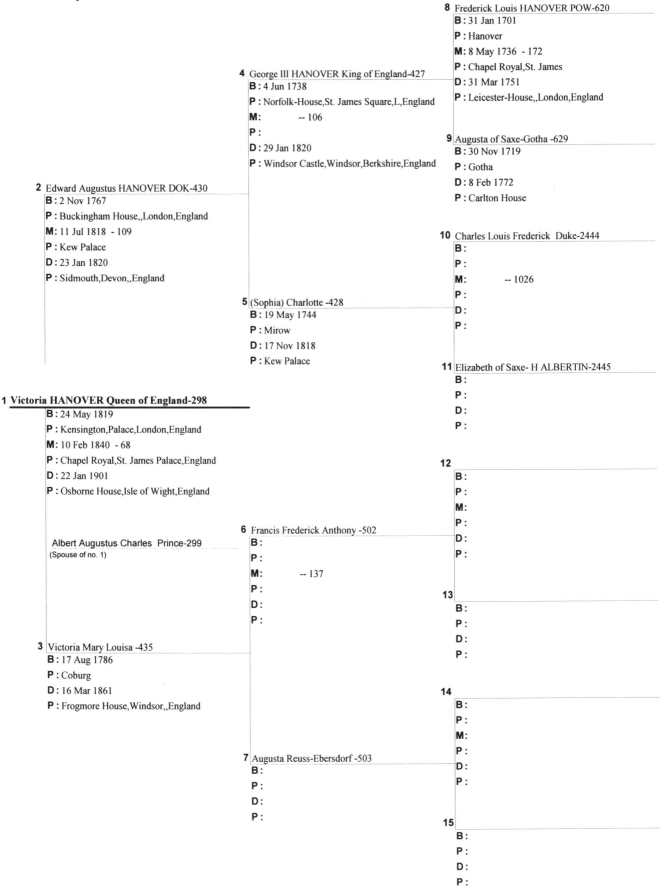

8 Frederick Louis HANOVER POW-620
B : 31 Jan 1701
P : Hanover
M : 8 May 1736 - 172
P : Chapel Royal,St. James
D : 31 Mar 1751
P : Leicester-House,,London,England

9 Augusta of Saxe-Gotha -629
B : 30 Nov 1719
P : Gotha
D : 8 Feb 1772
P : Carlton House

10 Charles Louis Frederick Duke-2444
B :
P :
M :   -- 1026
P :
D :
P :

11 Elizabeth of Saxe- H ALBERTIN-2445
B :
P :
D :
P :

4 George III HANOVER King of England-427
B : 4 Jun 1738
P : Norfolk-House,St. James Square,L,England
M :   -- 106
P :
D : 29 Jan 1820
P : Windsor Castle,Windsor,Berkshire,England

5 (Sophia) Charlotte -428
B : 19 May 1744
P : Mirow
D : 17 Nov 1818
P : Kew Palace

2 Edward Augustus HANOVER DOK-430
B : 2 Nov 1767
P : Buckingham House,,London,England
M : 11 Jul 1818 - 109
P : Kew Palace
D : 23 Jan 1820
P : Sidmouth,Devon,,England

12
B :
P :
M :
P :
D :
P :

13
B :
P :
D :
P :

6 Francis Frederick Anthony -502
B :
P :
M :   -- 137
P :
D :
P :

1 Victoria HANOVER Queen of England-298
B : 24 May 1819
P : Kensington,Palace,London,England
M : 10 Feb 1840 - 68
P : Chapel Royal,St. James Palace,England
D : 22 Jan 1901
P : Osborne House,Isle of Wight,England

Albert Augustus Charles Prince-299
(Spouse of no. 1)

14
B :
P :
M :
P :
D :
P :

15
B :
P :
D :
P :

3 Victoria Mary Louisa -435
B : 17 Aug 1786
P : Coburg
D : 16 Mar 1861
P : Frogmore House,Windsor,,England

7 Augusta Reuss-Ebersdorf -503
B :
P :
D :
P :

Ancestral Quest Pedigree Chart (4-7)

Birthwrite
Version 1.5 for Windows

Basic Information

Richard McDonald
12 Caronridge Crescent
Scarborough, ON
M1W 1L2 Canada
e-mail: rmcd@interlog.com
http://www.interlog.com/~rmcd/BirthWrite/
Shareware version available for download
Shareware fee: $30.00

System requirements: IBM 386 or compatible
(486 highly recommended)
RAM: 8MB minimum RAM (12MB strongly
recommended)
CD-ROM: not required

Program Information

Individuals per database: 2 billion
Spouses per individual: unlimited
Children per relationship: unlimited
Children and spouses reordered: no
(children are ordered by birth date or
order of entry)
Name options: honorific prefixes supported;
3 name fields (1 surname, 3 given names)
Non-traditional relationships: supported
Field sizes: name (30 characters), location
(50 characters), source (32,000
characters), note (32,000 characters)
Note options: can create notes for individuals
Multimedia options: 30 objects (graphics,
sound, video, or other OLE objects) per
individual, captions may be entered for
each graphic
Program options: SVGA display enables 5
generations of information on 1 screen
Date options: can specify date format (one
of four possible formats), specify dates
(exact, after/before, about, or unknown)
Search options: name fields, birth and
death information, sex, and cemetery
information

Database maintenance and options:
database repair and compact supported

Reports

View reports before printing: yes
Customized reports
+ Options: information to be included
Tree Charts (graphic chart which will print
either an Ancestor or Descendant Chart)
Tree Reports (text reports which will print in
Ancestor or Descendant format)
Lists
+ Ancestors
+ Descendants
+ All Individuals
+ Individuals (in table format)
Family Sheet Report
+ Will not print photos, but will print a
photo caption to indicate a photo is
attached to an individual
+ Ancestors and Descendants Family Sheet
Reports can be indexed

Sources

Creation: can source most event fields

Comments

A version of BirthWrite written for
Jewish researchers is available either
through the author (as Jewish
BirthWrite), or through The Douglas E.
Goldman Jewish Genealogy Center (under
the name Ilanot). The basic program of
the Jewish version is similar to BirthWrite,
but there are some significant changes.

+ **Calendars supported:** Hebrew, Islamic,
Gregorian, and Julian

Program attributes: Hebrew names, Jewish history, genetic diseases, Rabbi at marriage, migration information, death circumstances

Date attributes: Bar/Bat Mitzvah dates, circumcision date, Ketuba, and T'naim

Reports: Family Group Reports have been modified to handle the new data

Price: $30.00

For further details and information, contact:
The Douglas E. Goldman Jewish
    Genealogy Center
Beth Hatefutsoth
PO Box 39359
Tel Aviv 61329, Israel
Voice: 972-3-646-2061
Fax: 972-3-646-2134
e-mail: bhgnlgy@ccsg.tau.ac.il

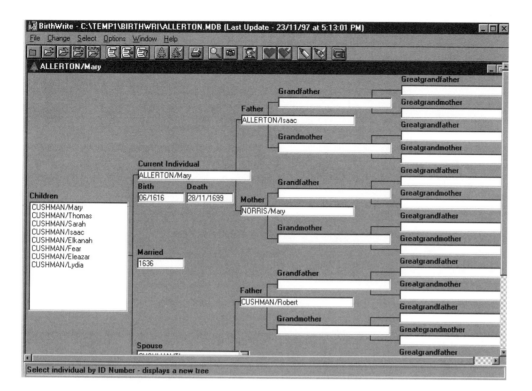

Figure 4.7
Birthwrite
Pedigree Screen

Figure 4.8
Birthwrite
Individual
Edit Screen

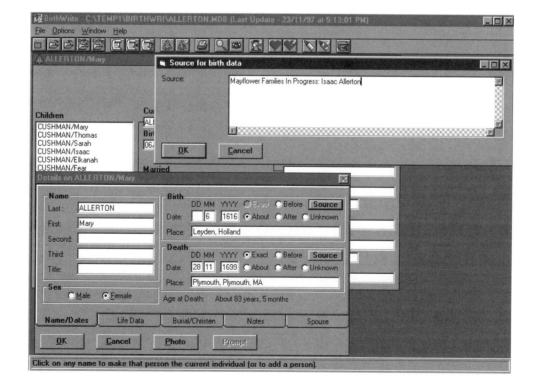

Listing report for ALLERTON/Isaac   and all descendents, sorted by Last Name.

Last Name	First Name	Birth Date	Death Date	Birth Place	Death Place	Cemetery	Age
ALLERTON	Unknown		05/02/1620		St Peters, Leyden, Holland		
ALLERTON	Isaac	22/05/1627	25/10/1702	Plymouth, Plymouth, MA	Wesmoreland Co, VA		75.4 Years
ALLERTON	Sarah	1627	<22/05/1627	Plymouth, Plymouth, MA	Plymouth, Plymouth, MA		
ALLERTON	Unknown	22/12/1620		Provincetown Harbour, Holland			376.9 Years
ALLERTON	Bartholomew	1612		Leyden, Holland			385. Years
ALLERTON	Remember	1614		Leyden, Holland			383. Years
ALLERTON	Mary	06/1616	28/11/1699	Leyden, Holland	Plymouth, Plymouth, MA		83.4 Years
ALLERTON	Isaac	1586	09/08/1900	England	New Haven, CT		314. Years
BREWSTER (Spouse)	Fear		<12/12/1634	England	Plymouth, Plymouth, MA		
COLCLOUGH (Spouse)	Elizabeth	1635	>04/1672				37. Years
CUSHMAN	Sarah	1641		Plymouth, Plymouth, MA			356. Years
CUSHMAN	Thomas	~09/1637		Plymouth, Plymouth, MA			360.2 Years
CUSHMAN	Isaac	08/02/1649		Plymouth, Plymouth, MA			348.8 Years
CUSHMAN	Elkanah	01/06/1651		Plymouth, Plymouth, MA			346.5 Years
CUSHMAN	Fear	20/06/1653		Plymouth, Plymouth, MA			344.4 Years
CUSHMAN	Eleazar	20/02/1657		Plymouth, Plymouth, MA			340.8 Years
CUSHMAN	Lydia	1662		Plymouth, Plymouth, MA			335. Years
CUSHMAN	Mary						
CUSHMAN (Spouse)	Thomas	08/02/1608	10/12/1691	Canterbury, England	Plymouth, Plymouth, MA		83.8 Years
FAIRFAX (Spouse)	Sarah		13/09/1678	prob. Rumbough, Co. Suffolk, Eng.	prob. Halesworth, Co. Suffolk, Eng.		
MAVERICK (Spouse)	Moses	03/11/1611	28/01/1686	Huish, Co. Devon, England	Marblehead, MA		74.2 Years
NORRIS (Spouse)	Mary		25/02/1621		Plymouth, Plymouth, MA		
SWINNERTON (Spouse)	Joanna						
UNKNOWN (Spouse)	Elizabeth		~1655		New Haven, CT		
UNKNOWN- (Spouse)	Margaret						

Birthwrite Descendants List (4-8)

Family Sheet set for CUSHMAN/Thomas   and 2 generations of known descendents.

Family Sheet for	**CUSHMAN/Thomas**			Sheet 1
Birth Date:	08/02/1608	Birth Place:	Canterbury, England	
Death Date:	10/12/1691	Death Place:	Plymouth, Plymouth, MA	
Christening Date:		Christening Place:		
Sex:	M			
Misc Info:				
Adopted?:	No			
Education:				
Residence:				
Occupation:				
Closest Friend:				
Characteristics:				
Burial:				
Cemetery:				
Section:				
Plot:				
Photo Caption:				
Notes:				

Spouse:	**ALLERTON/Mary**		
Birth Date:	06/1616	Birth Place:	Leyden, Holland
Death Date:	28/11/1699	Death Place:	Plymouth, Plymouth, MA
Christening Date:		Christening Place:	
Sex:	F		
Misc Info:			
Adopted?:	No		
Education:			
Residence:			
Occupation:			
Closest Friend:			
Characteristics:			
Burial:			
Cemetery:			
Section:			
Plot:			
Photo Caption:			
Notes:			

Marriage Information

Marriage Date:	1636
Marriage Place:	Plymouth, Plymouth, MA
Marriage End Date:	
Marriage Status:	

Children	BirthDate	Sheet Number
CUSHMAN/Mary		2
CUSHMAN/Thomas	~09/1637	3
CUSHMAN/Sarah	1641	4
CUSHMAN/Isaac	08/02/1649	5
CUSHMAN/Elkanah	01/06/1651	6
CUSHMAN/Fear	20/06/1653	7
CUSHMAN/Eleazar	20/02/1657	8
CUSHMAN/Lydia	1662	9

Birthwrite Family Sheet (4-9)

Ancestor Listing for CUSHMAN/Thomas

Ind	Par	GP	GGP

```
                                    / CUSHMAN/Robert
                    / CUSHMAN/Thomas   b. 08/02/1608 bp. Canterbury, England d. 10/12/1691 dp. Plymouth, Plymouth, MA
                    |                   \ REDER/Sarah
CUSHMAN/Thomas   b. ~09/1637 bp. Plymouth, Plymouth, MA Parents: m. 1636, mp. Plymouth, Plymouth, MA
                    |                   / ALLERTON/Isaac   b. 1586 bp. England d. 09/08/1900 dp. New Haven, CT
                    \ ALLERTON/Mary   b. 06/1616 bp. Leyden, Holland d. 28/11/1699 dp. Plymouth, Plymouth, MA Parents: m. 04/11/1611,
                    mp. Leyden, Holland
                                        \ NORRIS/Mary    d. 25/02/1621 dp. Plymouth, Plymouth, MA
```

Brother's Keeper
Version 5.2 for Windows

Basic Information

John Steed
6907 Childsdale Avenue
Rockford, MI 49341
Voice: 616-364-5503
Fax: 616-866-3345
BBS: 616-364-1127
e-mail: 75745.1371@compuserve.com
http://ourworld.compuserve.com/homepages/
Brothers_Keeper/
Shareware fee: $49.00 (Windows version)
Shareware version available for download

System requirements: IBM compatible 386
   MHz or higher, Windows 3.1 or higher
RAM: 4MB
Hard Drive: 3MB
CD-ROM: not required

Program Information

Individuals per database: 1 million
Children and spouses reordered: yes, in
   chronological order
Multiple parents: supported
Name options: aliases, father's surname
   automatically added to children's name
Field sizes: name (40 characters), message (7
   lines), location (40 characters), date (15
   characters); you can customize some of
   the fields
Ditto-key options: locations
Multimedia options: photos can be attached
   to individuals
Program options: global change for locations
   and sources supported, can specify word
   processor to use for text
Date options: convert dates entered as
   MMDDYYYY to standard format, global
   convert from one date format to another,
   date modifiers (Abt, Cir, Bef, Aft)
Search options: wildcard searches for
   individuals, define hot keys for frequently
   used words or phrases, field specific

(search for a word in a specific field or
multiple fields), marriage location and
date search, all-field search for a specific
word or phrase (exact match only), partial
or full name, Soundex match, and range of
dates
Database maintenance and options:
   quality check, backup, and restore
   supported; database split and merge
   supported

Reports

View reports before printing: yes
Customized reports
- Options: message lines, information to
  include, individuals to include, layout
- Types: Alphabetical Report, Numeric
  Report, Reference Order, and Ahnentafel
  Custom Report
Descendants Reports:
- **Tree Chart** (descendants of target
  individuals with parents and children
  connected by lines)
- **Box Chart** (descendants in boxes,
  connected by lines)
- **4 Family Box Chart** (descendants of gr-
  grandparents of a target individual)
  descendant chart (each generation of
  descendants; can indicate how each person
  is related to target individual)
- **Register Book** (report can be exported in
  Rich Text Format, can use 2 or 3
  column index)
- **Indented Book** (report can be exported in
  Rich Text Format, can use 2 or 3
  column index, can use Henry numbering
  system)
Ancestors Reports:
- **Ancestor (Pedigree) Chart** (cascading
  charts supported)
- **Collapsed Ancestor Chart** (shows up to
  50 generations of ancestors for target
  individual, you can specify whether or not

to show duplicate names; the report is called "collapsed" because there are no blank lines where an ancestor is unknown)

- **Timeline** (of target individual's ancestors; other events and individuals can be added by editing the events file)
- **Ahnentafel Book** (report can be exported in Rich Text Format, can use 2 or 3 column index)
- **Ahnentafel Custom List**

Family Group Sheet (FGS)
- Prints FGS to text
- Cascading reports
- Blank reports
- Includes photos

Relationship Chart
Reasonableness Check
Lists
- Alphabetical Report
- Numerical Report
- Reference Order
- Word Search
- Birthday/Anniversary
- Locations
- Sources
- Unconnected People Display

Sources

Creation: can be created for date and location fields; sources limited to 3 lines
Ditto-key entry: yes, using a pop-up screen
Quality of source data notation: yes
Print sources as footnotes: yes
Display and print alphabetical list: yes

Bells and Whistles

- Program is available in a variety of languages
- Databases from Brother's Keeper versions 4.5 and DOS version 5.0 can be converted

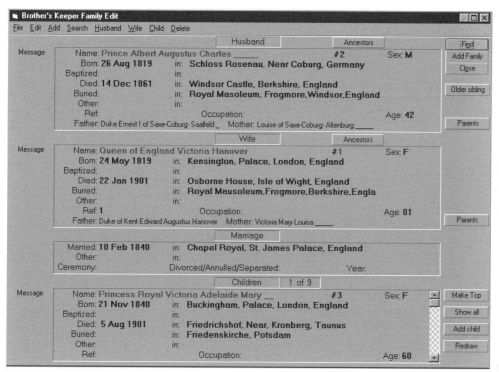

Figure 4.9
Brother's Keeper
Family Edit

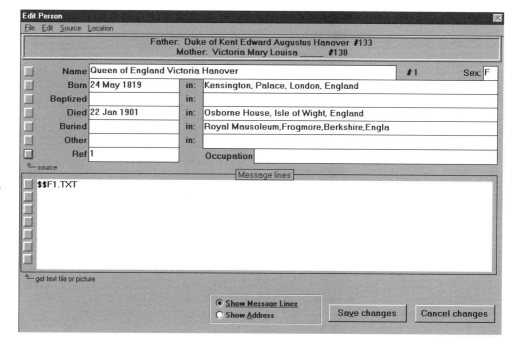

Figure 4.10
Brother's Keeper
Edit Person

Prince of Wales F. Hanover

Born 31 Jan 1701   #8
Hanover
Marr 8 May 1736
Chapel Royal, St. James
Died 31 Mar 1751
Leicester-House, London, England

King of England George Hanover

Born 4 Jun 1738   #4
Norfolk-House,St. James Square,London,En
Died 29 Jan 1820
Windsor Castle,Windsor,Berkshire,England

Augusta of Saxe-Gotha _____

Born 30 Nov 1719   #9
Gotha
Died 8 Feb 1772
Carlton House

Duke of Kent Edward A. Hanover

Born 2 Nov 1767   #2
Buckingham House, London, England
Marr 11 Jul 1818
Kew Palace
Died 23 Jan 1820
Sidmouth, Devon, England

Duke Charles Louis F. _____
                                    #10

(Sophia) Charlotte _____

Born 19 May 1744   #5
Mirow
Died 17 Nov 1818
Kew Palace

Elizabeth of Saxe- H. Albert
                                    #11

Queen of England V. Hanover

Born 24 May 1819   #1
Kensington, Palace, London, England
Died 22 Jan 1901
Osborne House, Isle of Wight, England
Spouse: Prince Albert Augustus Charles _____

Francis Frederick Anthony _____
                                    #6

Victoria Mary Louisa _____

Born 17 Aug 1786   #3
Coburg
Died 16 Mar 1861
Frogmore House, Windsor, England

Augusta Reuss-Ebersdorf _____
                                    #7

Brother's Keeper Pedigree Chart (4-11)

1. Queen of England Victoria Hanover b. 24 May 1819, Kensington, Palace, London, England, d. 22 Jan 1901, Osborne House, Isle of Wight, England, buried: Royal Mausoleum,Frogmore,Berkshire,Engla.

Parents

2. Duke of Kent Edward Augustus Hanover b. 2 Nov 1767, Buckingham House, London, England, m. 11 Jul 1818, in Kew Palace, Victoria Mary Louisa _____, b. 17 Aug 1786, Coburg, d. 16 Mar 1861, Frogmore House, Windsor, England. Duke died 23 Jan 1820, Sidmouth, Devon, England.

3. Victoria Mary Louisa _____ b. 17 Aug 1786, Coburg, d. 16 Mar 1861, Frogmore House, Windsor, England.

Grand Parents

4. King of England George III Hanover b. 4 Jun 1738, Norfolk-House,St. James Square,London,En, m. (Sophia) Charlotte _____, b. 19 May 1744, Mirow, d. 17 Nov 1818, Kew Palace, buried: St. George Chap., Windsor, England. King died 29 Jan 1820, Windsor Castle,Windsor,Berkshire,England, buried: St. George Chap.,Windsor Castle,Berkshir.

5. (Sophia) Charlotte _____ b. 19 May 1744, Mirow, d. 17 Nov 1818, Kew Palace, buried: St. George Chap., Windsor, England.

6. Francis Frederick Anthony _____ m. Augusta Reuss-Ebersdorf _____.

7. Augusta Reuss-Ebersdorf _____

Great Grand Parents

8. Prince of Wales Frederick Louis Hanover b. 31 Jan 1701, Hanover, m. 8 May 1736, in Chapel Royal, St. James, Augusta of Saxe-Gotha _____, b. 30 Nov 1719, Gotha, d. 8 Feb 1772, Carlton House. Prince died 31 Mar 1751, Leicester-House, London, England.

9. Augusta of Saxe-Gotha _____ b. 30 Nov 1719, Gotha, d. 8 Feb 1772, Carlton House.

10. Duke Charles Louis Frederick _____ m. Elizabeth of Saxe- Hildburghausen Albert.

11. Elizabeth of Saxe- Hildburghausen Albert

Great Great Grand Parents

16. King of England George II Hanover b. 30 Oct 1683, Herrenhausen, Palace, Hannover, Germany, m. 22 Aug 1705, in Herrenhausen, Caroline of Ansbach _____, b. 1683, d. 1737. King died 25 Oct 1760, Kensington, Palace, London, England, buried: Westminster, Abbey, London, England.

17. Caroline of Ansbach _____ b. 1683, d. 1737.

18. Duke Frederick II of Saxe-Gotha _____ m. Magdalena Augusta of Anhalt-Zerbst _____.

Wife:	**Queen of England Victoria Hanover** #1 died at age: 81

Born:	24 May 1819	in: Kensington, Palace, London, England
Baptized:		in:
Died:	22 Jan 1901	in: Osborne House, Isle of Wight, England
Buried:		in: Royal Mausoleum,Frogmore,Berkshire,Engla
Other:		in:
Ref:	1	Occupation:
Father:	Duke of Kent Edward Augustus Hanover #133	
Mother:	Victoria Mary Louisa _____ #138	

Victoria, Queen of England, Empress of India; aka: Alexandrina Victoria Reign: 20 Jun 1837 - 22 Jan 1901; Crowned: Westminster Abbey 28 Jun 1838; She became queen at age 18. Her 63 year reign was the longest in the history of England. Her descendants, including 40 grandchildren, married into almost every royal family of Europe. With her personal example of honesty, patriotism and devotion to family life, Victoria became a living symbol of the solidity of the British Empire. The many years of her reign, often referred to as the Victorian age, witnessed the rise of middle class and were marked by a deeply conservative morality and intense nationalism. She was obsessed with the collecting of memorabilia of her family. She mourned her late husband, Albert, for more than 40 years.

Husband:	**Prince Albert Augustus Charles _____** #2 died at age: 42		
Married:	10 Feb 1840	in: Chapel Royal, St. James Palace, England her age: 20 his age: 20	
Ceremony:		Divorced/Annulled/Separated: Year:	

Born:	26 Aug 1819	in: Schloss Rosenau, Near Coburg, Germany
Baptized:		in:
Died:	14 Dec 1861	in: Windsor Castle, Berkshire, England
Buried:		in: Royal Masoleum, Frogmore,Windsor,England
Other:		in:
Ref:		Occupation:
Father:	Duke Ernest I of Saxe-Coburg- Saalfeld _ #139	
Mother:	Louise of Saxe-Coburg- Altenburg _____ #140	

Prince Albert of Saxe-Coburg and Gotha, aka: The Prince Consort of Queen Victoria; Christened: (Francis) Albert Augustus Charles Emmanuel; He was an active and effective patron of the arts and sciences, organizing such enterprises as the epochal Great Exhibition of 1851 to stimulate the growth of British commerce, industry and national pride. Although regarded by many Britons as a meddling foreigner, Albert succeeded in strengthening the monarchy and in encouraging social progress. Overburdened with work, he succumbed to typhoid fever at the age of 42.

F Child 1	**Princess Royal Victoria Adelaide Mary __** #3 died at age: 60	
Born:	21 Nov 1840	in: Buckingham, Palace, London, England
Baptized:		in:
Died:	5 Aug 1901	in: Friedrichshof, Near, Kronberg, Taunus
Buried:		in: Friedenskirche, Potsdam
Other:		in:
Ref:		Occupation:
Spouse:	German Emperor Frederick III _____ #20	
Married:	25 Jan 1858	in: London, England
Ceremony:		Divorced/Annulled/Separated: Year:

M Child 2	**King of England Edward VII Wettin** #4 died at age: 68	
Born:	9 Nov 1841	in: Buckingham, Palace, London, England
Baptized:		in:
Died:	6 May 1910	in: Buckingham, Palace, London, England
Buried:		in:
Other:		in:

Brother's Keeper Family Group Sheet (4-13)

1. **Queen of England Victoria Hanover** b. 24 May 1819, Kensington, Palace, London, England, m. 10 Feb 1840, in Chapel Royal, St. James Palace, England, Prince Albert Augustus Charles _____, b. 26 Aug 1819, Schloss Rosenau, Near Coburg, Germany, (son of Duke Ernest I of Saxe-Coburg- Saalfeld _ and Louise of Saxe-Coburg- Altenburg _____) d. 14 Dec 1861, Windsor Castle, Berkshire, England, buried: Royal Masoleum, Frogmore,Windsor,England. Queen died 22 Jan 1901, Osborne House, Isle of Wight, England, buried: Royal Mausoleum,Frogmore,Berkshire,Engla. Victoria, Queen of England, Empress of India; aka: Alexandrina Victoria Reign: 20 Jun 1837 - 22 Jan 1901; Crowned: Westminster Abbey 28 Jun 1838; She became queen at age 18. Her 63 year reign was the longest in the history of England. Her descendants, including 40 grandchildren, married into almost every royal family of Europe. With her personal example of honesty, patriotism and devotion to family life, Victoria became a living symbol of the solidity of the British Empire. The many years of her reign, often referred to as the Victorian age, witnessed the rise of middle class and were marked by a deeply conservative morality and intense nationalism. She was obsessed with the collecting of memorabilia of her family. She mourned her late husband, Albert, for more than 40 years. Prince: Prince Albert of Saxe-Coburg and Gotha, aka: The Prince Consort of Queen Victoria; Christened: (Francis) Albert Augustus Charles Emmanuel; He was an active and effective patron of the arts and sciences, organizing such enterprises as the epochal Great Exhibition of 1851 to stimulate the growth of British commerce, industry and national pride. Although regarded by many Britons as a meddling foreigner, Albert succeeded in strengthening the monarchy and in encouraging social progress. Overburdened with work, he succumbed to typhoid fever at the age of 42.

   Children:

+ 2.　　i **Princess Royal Victoria Adelaide Mary** b. 21 Nov 1840.
+ 3.　　ii **King of England Edward VII** b. 9 Nov 1841.
+ 4.　　iii **Princess Alice Maud Mary** b. 25 Apr 1843.
+ 5.　　iv **Prince Alfred Ernest Albert** b. 6 Aug 1844.
+ 6.　　v **Princess Helena Augusta Victoria** b. 25 May 1846.
  7.　　vi **Princess Louise Caroline Alberta _____** b. 18 Mar 1848, Buckingham, Palace, London, England, m. 21 Mar 1871, in St. George Chap., Windsor, England, Duke of Argyll John Campbell, b. 1845, d. 1914. Princess died 3 Dec 1939, Kensington, Palace, London, England, buried: Frogmore, England. Titles: Princess Louise, Duchess of Argyll. Cremated at Golders Green Crematorium. Ashes buried in the Royal Burial Ground at Frogmore. Duke: John Campbell, 9th Duke of Argyll
+ 8.　　vii **Prince Arthur William Patrick** b. 1 May 1850.
+ 9.　　viii **Prince Leopold George Duncan** b. 7 Apr 1853.
+ 10.　　ix **Princess Beatrice Mary Victoria** b. 14 Apr 1857.

Second Generation

2. **Princess Royal Victoria Adelaide Mary __** b. 21 Nov 1840, Buckingham, Palace, London, England, m. 25 Jan 1858, in London, England, German Emperor Frederick III _____, b. 18 Oct 1831, Neues Palais, Potsdam, Germany, (son of Emperor William I of Germany _____ and Augusta of Saxe-Weimar _____) d. 15 Jun 1888, Neues Palais, Potsdam, Germany, buried: Friedenskirche, Potsdam, Germany. Princess died 5 Aug 1901, Friedrichshof, Near, Kronberg, Taunus, buried: Friedenskirche, Potsdam. Victoria Adelaide Mary Louise German: Frederick III, Emperor of Germany; German Emperor and King of Prussia Liberal in his political views, he opposed Prince Otto von Bismark throughout the ministry of the latter. A man of learning and culture, Frederick patronized art and literature and encouraged the work of the royal museums. As Crown Prince Frederick William, he was genially called "Our Fritz" by the German people, most of whom anticipated with pleasure his accession to the throne. Frederick became ill, however, in 1887 and lived only three months after succeeding to the throne on his father's death. Reign: March 9-June 15,

Cumberland Family Tree for Windows
Version 2.21x

Basic Information

Cumberland Family Software
385 Idaho Springs Road
Clarksville, TN 37043
Voice: 931-647-4012 (limited hours)
e-mail: ira.lund@cf-software.com
http://www.cf-software.com/
Shareware fee: $50.00–74.00 (depending on which version you purchase, and whether or not you wish a printed manual)
Demo available for download
Orders accepted online

System requirements: IBM or compatible, Windows 3.1 or later
RAM: minimum 4MB (8MB or more recommended)
Hard drive: required
Printer: optional
CD-ROM: not required

Program Information

Individuals per database: 1 million; unlimited number of databases
Spouses per individual: 12
Children per relationship: 30
Children and spouses reordered: yes, in chronological order
Multiple parents allowed: yes
Name options: surnames must be entered with slash marks to be located by the search function, father's surname automatically added to children's name, surname can appear in any part of the name field, global name-case change supported
Field sizes: name field (80 characters), place names (200 characters)
Event options: 250 events per individual allowed, user-definable event fields, event editor modifies events (edit, add, and delete)

Multimedia options: 250 photos per individual allowed, can add scanned images of documents or transcriptions and miscellaneous notes
Program options: spell-check dictionary (can add, delete and edit words), import ASCII text to notes or documents, export text to disk
Ditto-entry key: place names (names accessed by pop-up screen or place name identifying number)
Date options: date format in either DD/MM/YYYY or MM/DD/YYYY, free-form dates supported, can specify default date format
Search options: search for words and phrases in any field
Merge options: duplicate individuals
User flags: indicates if an individual is living; also 9 other user-definable flags
Database maintenance and options: data saved upon exit, database merge and split supported

Reports

View reports before printing: yes
Ancestral Story (a narrative book report style)
Pedigree Box Chart (cascading reports are supported)
Photo Pedigree Chart
Ahnentafel
Family Group Sheet
Individual Story (narrative report)
Photo Album (prints all photos for specific individuals)
Descendants Box Chart (cascading reports are supported)
Descendants List Chart
Descendants Story (narrative report)
Photo Descendants Chart
Lists
- Events
- Place Name

- Source Note
- Individual Summary

Indexed Book (function to create a book from
  your database using any of the reports)

- Pages automatically numbered
- All individuals are added to an index
- Title page
- Table of contents
- List of sources

Sources

Creation: notes allowed for each event
Types: regular source, and a document used
  as a source
Field size: 5,000 characters
Source note editor: access a list of sources,
  edit, add, delete, and merge notes
Sources printed on certain reports: yes

Bells and Whistles

- Tiny tafel export
- Can set bookmarks for up to 10 individuals
- CTREE 3.x and CFT-Pro 4.x files can be
  imported

Comments

The version reviewed was Cumberland
Family Tree for Windows 95. There is also a
separate Windows 3.x version available that
is (according to the author) similar to the
Windows 95 version. There is also an older
DOS version available which has fewer
functions, capabilities, reports, etc.

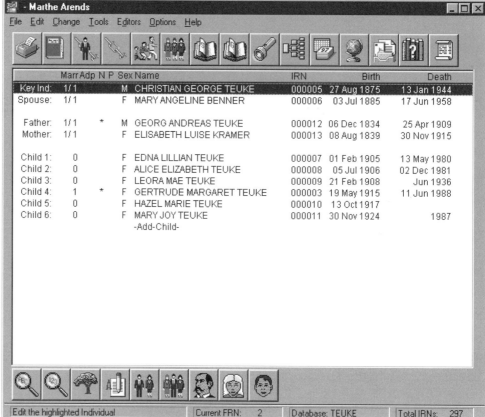

Figure 4.11
Cumberland Family
Tree Main Edit

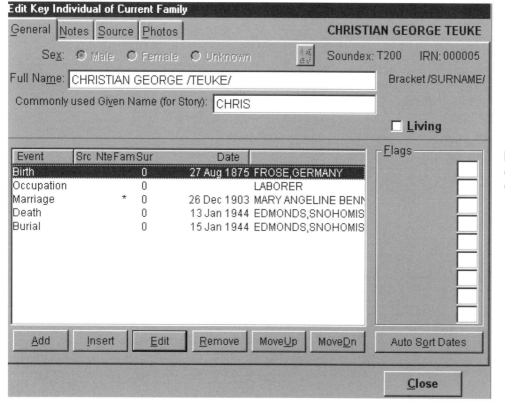

Figure 4.12
Cumberland Family
Tree Individual Edit

Ahnentafel	IRN	Sex	Name	Birth/Chr	Death/Burial
1	000001	F	Hanover, Victoria, Queen of England	24 May 1819	22 Jan 1901
			PARENTS		
2	000133	M	Hanover, Edward Augustus, Duke of Kent	02 Nov 1767	23 Jan 1820
3	000138	F	, Victoria Mary Louisa	17 Aug 1786	16 Mar 1861
			GRANDPARENTS		
4	000130	M	Hanover, George_III, King of England	04 Jun 1738	29 Jan 1820
5	000131	F	, (Sophia) Charlotte	19 May 1744	17 Nov 1818
6	000205	M	, Francis Frederick Anthony		
7	000206	F	, Augusta Reuss-Ebersdorf		
			GREAT GRANDPARENTS		
8	000323	M	Hanover, Frederick Louis, Prince of Wales	31 Jan 1701	31 Mar 1751
9	000332	F	, Augusta of_Saxe-Gotha	30 Nov 1719	08 Feb 1772
10	002147	M	, Charles Louis Frederick, Duke		
11	002148	F	Albertin, Elizabeth of_Saxe- Hildburghausen		
			5th GENERATION		
16	000321	M	Hanover, George_II, King of England	30 Oct 1683	25 Oct 1760
17	000322	F	, Caroline of_Ansbach	1683	1737
18	002142	M	, Frederick_II of_Saxe-Gotha, Duke		
19	002143	F	, Magdalena Augusta of_Anhalt-Zerbst		
			6th GENERATION		
32	000341	M	Hanover, George_I, King of England	28 May 1660	11 Jun 1727
33	000342	F	, Sophia Dorothea of_Celle	10 Sep 1666	13 Nov 1726
34	001694	M	, John Frederick of_Brandenburg-, Margrave		
			7th GENERATION		
64	000758	M	, Ernest Augustus of_Brunswick, Duke	1629	1698
65	000736	F	Hanover, Sophia	1630	1714
66	002140	M	, George William of_Brunswick, Duke		1726
67	002141	F	, Celle		
			8th GENERATION		
130	000735	M	, Frederick_V of_Palatinate, King of Bohemia	1596	1632
131	000728	F	Stuart, Elizabeth	19 Aug 1596	13 Feb 1662
			9th GENERATION		
262	000725	M	Stuart, James_I, King of England	19 Jun 1566	27 Mar 1625
263	000726	F	, Anne of_Denmark	14 Oct 1574	04 Mar 1619

GENERATION 1

1   Victoria Hanover Queen of England-000001

The parents of Victoria Hanover Queen of England-000001 are:

2+   Edward Augustus Hanover Duke of Kent-000133 was born 02 Nov 1767 at Buckingham House,,London,England; died 23 Jan 1820 at Sidmouth,Devon,,England.

3+   Victoria Mary Louisa-000138 was born 17 Aug 1786 at Coburg; died 16 Mar 1861 at Frogmore House,Windsor,,England.

Victoria was born 24 May 1819 at Kensington,Palace,London,England.
Victoria has a user reference number of 1.
Victoria and Albert Augustus Charles Prince-000002 {FRN-000001} (the son of Ernest_I of_Saxe-Coburg- Saalfeld Duke-000139 and Louise of_Saxe-Coburg-Altenburg-000140) were married 10 Feb 1840 at Chapel Royal,St. James Palace,England.
They had the following children:

4   i   Victoria Adelaide Mary Princess Royal-000003 was born 21 Nov 1840 at Buckingham,Palace,London,England; was christened 10 Feb 1841 at Throne Room,Buckingham Palac,England;Victoria and Frederick_III German Emperor-000020 {FRN-000003} were married 25 Jan 1858 at London,England; died 05 Aug 1901 at Friedrichshof,Near,Kronberg,Taunus; was buried at Friedenskirche,Potsdam.

5   ii Edward_VII Wettin King of England-000004 was born 09 Nov 1841 at Buckingham,Palace,London,England;Edward_VII and Alexandra of_Denmark "Alix" Princess-000012 {FRN-000002} were married 10 Mar 1863 at St. George Chap.,Windsor,,England; died 06 May 1910 at Buckingham,Palace,London,England.

6   iii Alice Maud Mary Princess-000005 was born 25 Apr 1843 at Buckingham,Palace,London,England;Alice and Louis_IV of_Hesse Grand Duke-000022 {FRN-000008} were married 01 Jul 1862 at Osborne House,Isle of Wight; died 14 Dec 1878 at Darmstadt,,,Germany.

7   iv Alfred Ernest Albert Prince-000006 was born 06 Aug 1844 at Windsor Castle,Berkshire,England;Alfred and Marie Alexandrovna Grand Duchess-000094 {FRN-000026} were married 23 Jan 1874 at Winter Palace,St. Petersburg,Russia; died 30 Jul 1900 at Schloss Rosenau,Near Coburg.

8   v   Helena Augusta Victoria Princess-000007 was born 25 May 1846 at Buckingham,Palace,London,England;Helena and (Frederick) Christian Charles Prince-000117 {FRN-000032} were married 05 Jul 1866 at Windsor Castle,,,England; died 09 Jun 1923 at Schomberg House,Pall Mall,London,England.

HUSBAND : Albert Augustus Charles Prince

Birth	:	26 Aug 1819	Schloss Rosenau,Near Coburg,Germany
Marriage	:	10 Feb 1840	Victoria Hanover Queen of England
			Chapel Royal,St. James Palace,England
Death	:	14 Dec 1861	Windsor Castle,Berkshire,England
Burial	:		Royal Masoleum,Frogmore,Windsor,England

Prince Albert of Saxe-Coburg and Gotha, aka: The Prince Consort of Queen Victoria; Christened: (Francis) Albert Augustus Charles Emmanuel; He was an active and effective patron of the arts and sciences, organizing such enterprises as the epochal Great Exhibition of 1851 to stimulate the growth of British commerce, industry and national pride. Although regarded by many Britons as a meddling foreigner, Albert succeeded in strengthening the monarchy and in encouraging social progress. Overburdened with work, he succumbed to typhoid fever at the age of 42.

Father : Ernest_I of_Saxe-Coburg- Saalfeld Duke
Mother : Louise of_Saxe-Coburg- Altenburg

WIFE : Victoria Hanover Queen of England

Birth	:	24 May 1819	Kensington,Palace,London,England
User Reference Num	:		1
Marriage	:	10 Feb 1840	Albert Augustus Charles Prince
			Chapel Royal,St. James Palace,England
Death	:	22 Jan 1901	Osborne House,Isle of Wight,England
Burial	:		Royal Mausoleum,Frogmore,Berkshire,England

Victoria, Queen of England, Empress of India; aka: Alexandrina Victoria Reign: 20 Jun 1837 - 22 Jan 1901; Crowned: Westminster Abbey 28 Jun 1838; She became queen at age 18. Her 63 year reign was the longest in the history of England. Her descendants, including 40 grandchildren, married into almost every royal family of Europe. With her personal example of honesty, patriotism and devotion to family life, Victoria became a living symbol of the solidity of the British Empire. The many years of her reign, often referred to as the Victorian age, witnessed the rise of middle class and were marked by a deeply conservative morality and intense nationalism. She was obsessed with the collecting of memorabilia of her family. She mourned her late husband, Albert, for more than 40 years.

Father : Edward Augustus Hanover Duke of Kent
Mother : Victoria Mary Louisa

CHILDREN

1	F	**Victoria Adelaide Mary Princess Royal**		
		Birth	:	21 Nov 1840	Buckingham,Palace,London,England
		Christening (Infan	:	10 Feb 1841	Throne Room,Buckingham Palac,England
		Marriage	:	25 Jan 1858	Frederick_III German Emperor
				London,England
		Death	:	05 Aug 1901	Friedrichshof,Near,Kronberg,Taunus
		Burial	:		Friedenskirche,Potsdam
				Victoria Adelaide Mary Louise

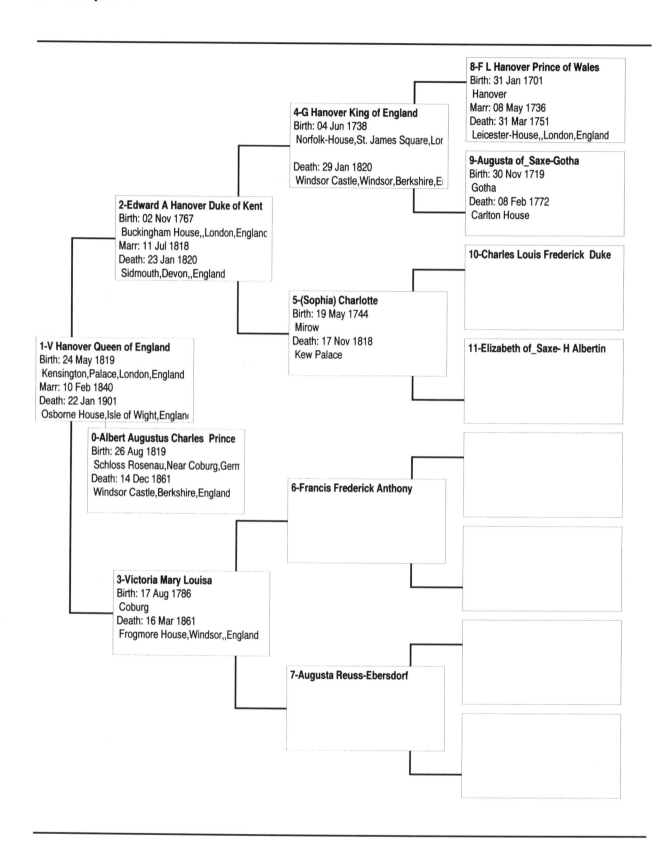

8-F L Hanover Prince of Wales
Birth: 31 Jan 1701
 Hanover
Marr: 08 May 1736
Death: 31 Mar 1751
 Leicester-House,,London,England

4-G Hanover King of England
Birth: 04 Jun 1738
 Norfolk-House,St. James Square,Lor

Death: 29 Jan 1820
 Windsor Castle,Windsor,Berkshire,E

9-Augusta of_Saxe-Gotha
Birth: 30 Nov 1719
 Gotha
Death: 08 Feb 1772
 Carlton House

2-Edward A Hanover Duke of Kent
Birth: 02 Nov 1767
 Buckingham House,,London,Englanc
Marr: 11 Jul 1818
Death: 23 Jan 1820
 Sidmouth,Devon,,England

10-Charles Louis Frederick Duke

5-(Sophia) Charlotte
Birth: 19 May 1744
 Mirow
Death: 17 Nov 1818
 Kew Palace

11-Elizabeth of_Saxe- H Albertin

1-V Hanover Queen of England
Birth: 24 May 1819
 Kensington,Palace,London,England
Marr: 10 Feb 1840
Death: 22 Jan 1901
 Osborne House,Isle of Wight,Englan

0-Albert Augustus Charles Prince
Birth: 26 Aug 1819
 Schloss Rosenau,Near Coburg,Gern
Death: 14 Dec 1861
 Windsor Castle,Berkshire,England

6-Francis Frederick Anthony

3-Victoria Mary Louisa
Birth: 17 Aug 1786
 Coburg
Death: 16 Mar 1861
 Frogmore House,Windsor,,England

7-Augusta Reuss-Ebersdorf

EZ-Tree

Version 2.3 for DOS

Basic Information

MicroFox Company
PO Box 447
Richfield, OH 44286-0447
Voice: 216-659-9489
Fax: 216-659-9489
e-mail: microfox@compuserve.com
http://ourworld.compuserve.com/homepages/
microfox
Shareware fee: $30.00
Shareware version available for download

System requirements: IBM compatible,
minimum 8086/8088, MS-DOS 1.0 or
higher
RAM: 256K RAM
Hard drive: 256K space
CD-ROM: not required

Program Information

Individuals per database: depends on the
amount of data included (the average
number of individuals allowed is
estimated at 587); 90 different databases
(per directory) may be linked together for
larger families
Spouses per individual: 16
Children per relationship: 32
Name options: first, last, middle, and maiden
Field sizes: name (16 characters), birth (58
characters), death (58 characters),
marriage (58 characters), divorce (58
characters), personal comments (144
characters)
Date options: U.S. or European formats
supported
Program options: screen saver supported
Database maintenance and options:
backup and restore function supported

Reports

View reports before printing: yes
Pedigree Statistics
◆ Prints only to the screen
All Persons Report
◆ Reference numbers in front of each
individual
Descendants Chart
Pedigree Chart
Print Inquiry
◆ Gives information about a specific
individual

Sources

Creation: no sourcing abilities separate from
the comments section

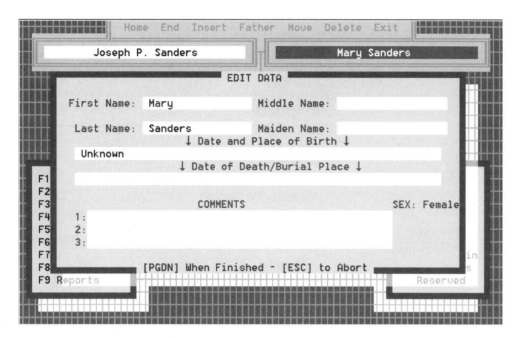

Figure 4.13
EZ-Tree
Main Edit

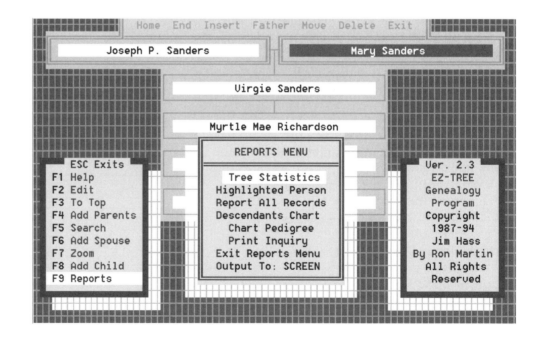

Figure 4.14
EZ-Tree
Reports Menu

FamilyBase for Windows
Version 2.10

Basic Information

Supplier:
S & N Genealogy Supplies
Greenacres, Salisbury Road
Chilmark, Salisbury
SP3 5AH England
Voice: 011-441-722-716121
Fax: 011-441-722-716121
e-mail: 100064.737@compuserve.com
Author: Mike Parsons
e-mail: 100570.2221@compuserve.com
http://ourworld.compuserve.com/homepages/
mikeparsons
Shareware fee: £15.00 plus 2.00

System requirements: Windows 3.1 or later
(works with Windows 95 and Windows NT)
RAM: at least 4MB
CD-ROM: not required
Mouse: required

Program Information

Individuals per database: 1,000
Field sizes: notes (40 lines)
Event options: 3,000 events per database
Program options: data can be viewed via a
  persons or events list, ancestor chart,
  descendant chart, relative list, index; can
  print from any of the view screens
Date options: standard date formats are
  supported, default century may be
  selected, incomplete dates are acceptable
Database maintenance and options: create
  a new database from all individuals in a
  file, or relatives of a selected individual,
  database integrity check supported,
  backup function supported

Reports

Customized reports
* Options: specify individuals to include in
  some reports
Persons List Report (full or summary list of
  individuals sorted by a specified field)
Descendants Chart
* Can customize appearance
Ancestors Chart
* Can customize appearance
Index (from any of the views)
Lists
* Events
* Individual's Relatives (sorted by 1 of 3
  fields)

Sources

Creation: sources can be entered using the
  related-notes field

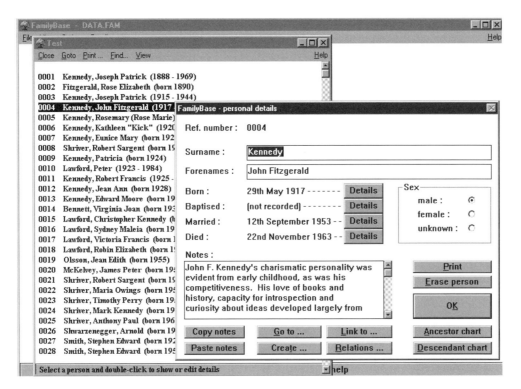

Figure 4.15
FamilyBase
Personal Details

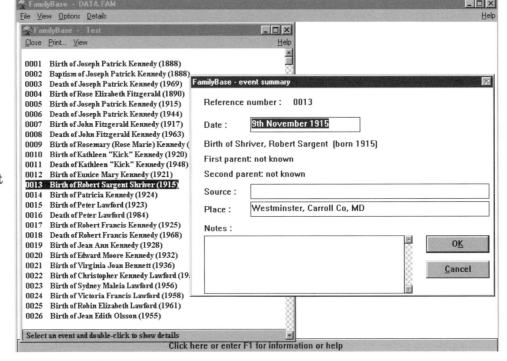

Figure 4.16
FamilyBase Event
Database

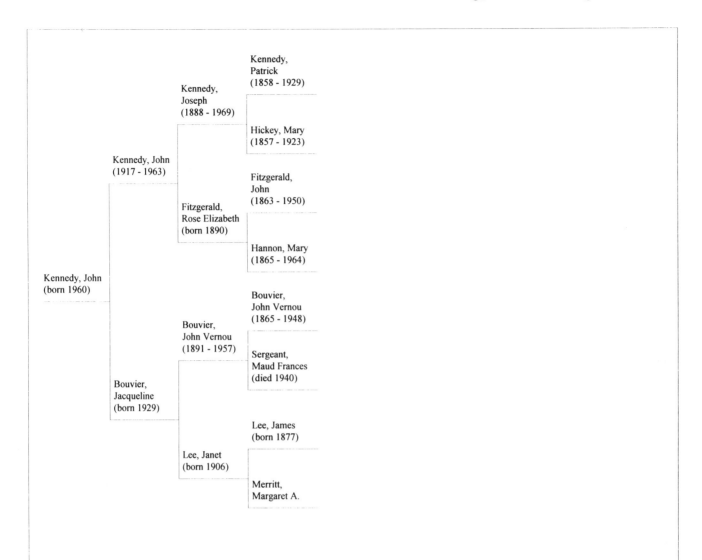

The information on this chart may not be correct and is for demonstration purposes only.

FamilyBase Ancestor Chart (4-19)

Ancestors of - Kennedy, Joseph Patrick

Name	*Parents*
0001) Kennedy, Joseph Patrick (1888 - 1969)	Kennedy, Patrick Joseph Hickey, Mary Augusta
0075) Kennedy, Patrick Joseph (1858 - 1929)	Kennedy, Patrick Murphy, Bridget
0115) Hickey, Mary Augusta (1857 - 1923)	Hickey, James Field, Margaret M.
0067) Kennedy, Patrick (1823 - 1858)	Kennedy, Patrick (-----), Mary Johanna
0070) Murphy, Bridget (1821 - 1888)	Murphy, Richard (-----), Mary
0114) Hickey, James (1836 - 1900)	Hickey, Michael Hassett, Catherine
0111) Field, Margaret M. (1836 - 1911)	Field, Patrick Sheehy, Mary
0065) Kennedy, Patrick	
0066) (-----), Mary Johanna	
0068) Murphy, Richard	
0069) (-----), Mary	
0112) Hickey, Michael	
0113) Hassett, Catherine	
0109) Field, Patrick	
0110) Sheehy, Mary	

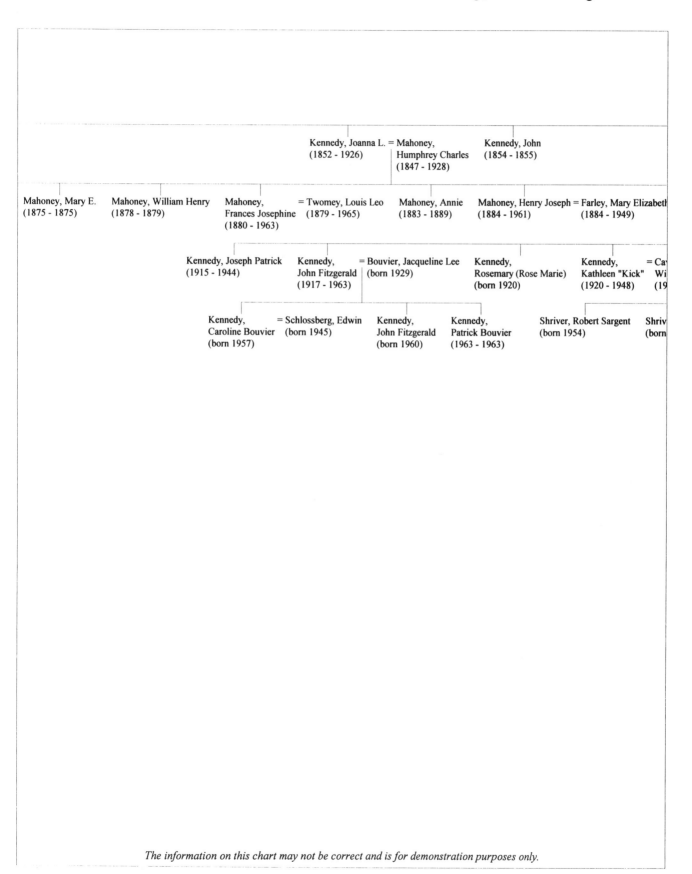

Kennedy, Joanna L. = Mahoney,   Kennedy, John
(1852 - 1926)   Humphrey Charles   (1854 - 1855)
                    (1847 - 1928)

Mahoney, Mary E.   Mahoney, William Henry   Mahoney,   = Twomey, Louis Leo   Mahoney, Annie   Mahoney, Henry Joseph = Farley, Mary Elizabeth
(1875 - 1875)   (1878 - 1879)   Frances Josephine   (1879 - 1965)   (1883 - 1889)   (1884 - 1961)   (1884 - 1949)
                                              (1880 - 1963)

                    Kennedy, Joseph Patrick   Kennedy,   = Bouvier, Jacqueline Lee   Kennedy,   Kennedy,   = Ca
                    (1915 - 1944)   John Fitzgerald   (born 1929)   Rosemary (Rose Marie)   Kathleen "Kick"   Wi
                                               (1917 - 1963)   (born 1920)   (1920 - 1948)   (19

                    Kennedy,   = Schlossberg, Edwin   Kennedy,   Kennedy,   Shriver, Robert Sargent   Shriv
                    Caroline Bouvier   (born 1945)   John Fitzgerald   Patrick Bouvier   (born 1954)   (born
                    (born 1957)   (born 1960)   (1963 - 1963)

The information on this chart may not be correct and is for demonstration purposes only.

FamilyBase Descendant Chart (4-21)

Family Heritage Deluxe
Version 2.0 for Windows

Basic Information

IMSI
1895 Francisco Blvd East
San Rafael, CA 94901-5506
Voice: 415-257-3000
Fax: 415-257-3565
e-mail: support@imsisoft.com
http://www.imsisoft.com/familyheritage/
Price: $49.95

System requirements: 486 DX 66Mhz or
    higher, Windows 95 or higher
RAM: minimum 8MB (12MB recommended)
Hard drive: minimum 40MB space
Monitor: VGA monitor with 256 colors
CD-ROM: 2x speed
Mouse: required

Program Information

Individuals per database: unlimited
Spouses per individual: unlimited
Children per relationship: unlimited
Multiple parents: supported
Non-traditional marriage: supported
Name options: nicknames, aliases, and
    honorific prefixes supported
Field sizes: name (32,000 characters),
    location (32,000 characters)
Event options: unlimited events per
    individual, 7 event fields supported, events
    can be selected from a pull-down menu,
    event types can be added; sources and
    notes can be included for each event
Multimedia options: unlimited graphics per
    individual, individual family album
    options (images, sound, and video clips
    can be included; albums may be created for
    specific events, albums may be saved
    separately and shared with others), 3
    preferred images may be specified, image
    captions are supported
Program options: variety of record types
    (individual, spouse, children, events,

medical, address, album, and notes), view
data in individual or tree view, PAF file
import, Smart Library function allows
you to add members to a family tree by
drag-and-drop
Ditto-key entry: via Smart Field function
Date options: dates can be displayed in a
    variety of formats, several date prefixes
    and qualifiers are available
Search options: search using operators and
    criteria; search for age, dates, and places
    of birth, death, marriage, names, and sex
    fields (Deluxe version adds additional
    fields you may search)
Merge options: duplicate individuals,
    databases cannot be merged
Database maintenance and options: date
    and relationship calculators supported,
    data integrity check, backup function
    supported; auto-save option

Reports

View reports before printing: yes
Customized reports
- Options: font, boxes, margins, borders,
  lines, backgrounds, items to include,
  number of generations, layout, title,
  footer
Blank reports: supported for some reports
Format wizard: supported (Auto Format
    feature guides you through report style
    selection)
Descendants Chart
- Show direct descendants
- Show siblings of direct descendants
- Show duplicates
- Layout
Ancestors Chart
- Show siblings for all individuals
- Show siblings of primary individual
- Show duplicates
- Show empty branches
- Blank report
- Layout

Family Group Sheet
◆ Report style (blank, standard, or worksheet)
◆ Number of additional blank rows for children and spouses
◆ Specify information to include (basic, spouse and children, medical, detailed events, address, notes, and sources)
◆ Event types (birth, death, marriage information only)
◆ Photos included

Fan Chart
◆ Cascading chart
◆ Chart style and layout
◆ Font smoothing
◆ Blank chart
◆ Specify information to include

Custom List
◆ Specify individuals
◆ Specify information to include
◆ Title and footer

Outline Descendant Report
◆ Show direct descendants only
◆ Show siblings of direct descendant
◆ Show spouses
◆ Show duplicates
◆ Report layout
◆ Show generation numbers
◆ Specify information to include

Register Report (Deluxe version only)
◆ Specify word processor
◆ Style (standard or Modified Register)
◆ Events (birth, marriage, death, or all events in the database)
◆ Include female lines
◆ Sources
◆ Biographical notes (information recorded on notes and details pages)

Sources

Creation: enter, edit, and delete sources via source manager
Source reliability levels: supported
Source options: can source a marriage as well as an individual; a list of sources can be printed to show how many times a source has been used as a reference

Bells and Whistles

◆ 200,000 surname histories included
◆ Masterclips backgrounds, fonts, borders, etc. which can be added to reports
◆ Creates Web pages
◆ High-quality printed reports
◆ Bookmark function supported in the Deluxe version
◆ Family Publisher feature allows you to share information with non-Family Heritage users

Comments

There are 2 versions of the program available, Standard and Deluxe. The Deluxe version includes: Family Publisher and Corel Photo House software, Ancestry software (*Red Book* and *The Source on CD*), *American Genealogical Gazetteer*, SSDI, and a variety of extra functions. The Family Heritage Web site includes FAQs, How-To information, links to genealogy sites, and a forum for discussion of the Family Heritage and Corel Family Tree Suite products.

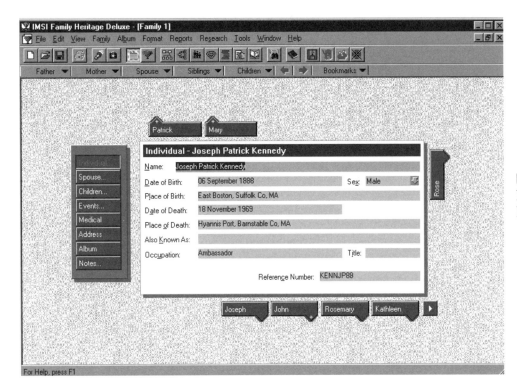

Figure 4.17
Family Heritage
Edit Screen

Figure 4.18
Family Heritage
Event Screen

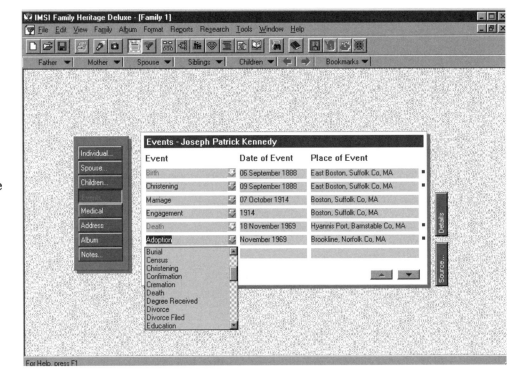

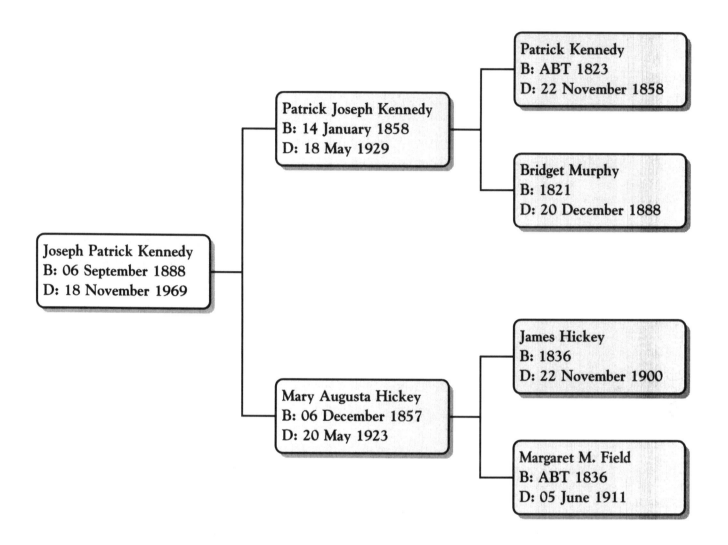

Patrick Joseph Kennedy

Sex: Male

Events	Dates	Places
Birth[1]	14 January 1858	East Boston, Suffolk Co, MA
Marriage	23 November 1887	Boston, Suffolk Co, MA
Death[2]	18 May 1929	Boston, Suffolk Co, MA
Marriage		

Father: Patrick Kennedy (Natural)
Mother: Bridget Murphy (Natural)

1st Spouse: **Mary Augusta Hickey**

> 1st Child: Joseph Patrick Kennedy
> 2nd Child: Francis Benedict Kennedy
> 3rd Child: Mary Loretta Kennedy
> 4th Child: Margaret Louise Kennedy

1st Spouse and Children for Patrick Joseph Kennedy

Spouse: Mary Augusta Hickey

Events	Dates	Places
Birth	06 December 1857	Winthrop, Suffolk Co, MA
Marriage	23 November 1887	Boston, Suffolk Co, MA
Death	20 May 1923	Boston, Suffolk Co, MA
Marriage		

Mother: Margaret M. Field (Natural)
Father: James Hickey (Natural)

1st Child: Joseph Patrick Kennedy

Events	Dates	Places
Birth	06 September 1888	East Boston, Suffolk Co, MA
Marriage	07 October 1914	Boston, Suffolk Co, MA
Death	18 November 1969	Hyannis Port, Barnstable Co, MA
Marriage		

1st Spouse: Rose Elizabeth Fitzgerald

2nd Child: Francis Benedict Kennedy

Events	Dates	Places
Birth	11 March 1891	East Boston, Suffolk Co, MA
Death	14 June 1892	East Boston, Suffolk Co, MA

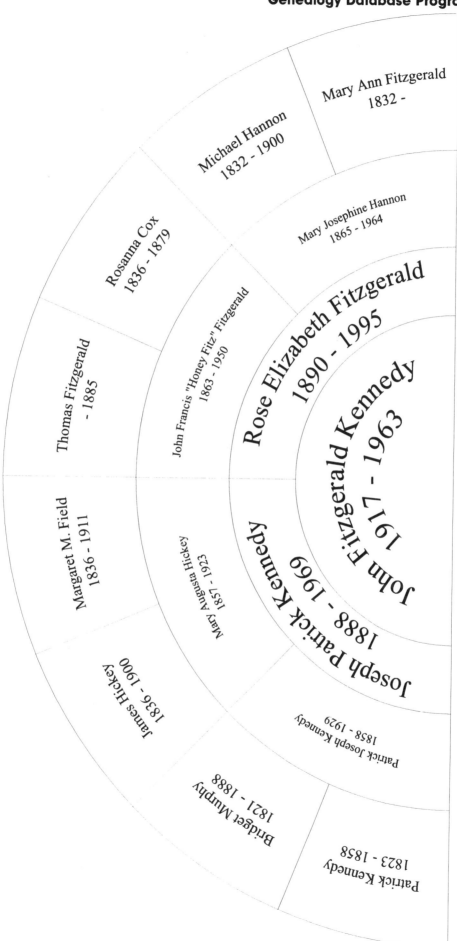

Family Heritage Fan Chart (4-24)

1 Patrick Kennedy, Male, B: ABT 1823, Dunganstown, Wexford Co, Ireland
+ Bridget Murphy, Female, B: 1821, Dunganstown, Wexford Co, Ireland
   2 Mary L. Kennedy, Female, B: 09 August 1851, East Boston, Suffolk Co, MA
   + Lawrence M. Kane, Male, B: 29 November 1858, Wexford Co, Ireland
      3 Joseph Lawrence Kane, Male, B: 29 November 1883, East Boston, Suffolk Co, MA
      3 Mary Margaret Kane, Female, B: 25 August 1885, East Boston, Suffolk Co, MA
      3 George Philip Kane, Male, B: 08 September 1888, East Boston, Suffolk Co, MA
      3 Gertrude Margaret Kane, Female, B: 26 May 1890, East Boston, Suffolk Co, MA
      + Charles Everett Metcalf, Male, B: 01 November 1891, Chelsea, Suffolk Co, MA
      3 Frederick Kane, Male, B: 1892, East Boston, Suffolk Co, MA
   2 Joanna L. Kennedy, Female, B: 27 November 1852, East Boston, Suffolk Co, MA
   + Humphrey Charles Mahoney, Male, B: 12 December 1847, Boston, Suffolk Co, MA
      3 Daniel Mahoney, Male, B: 14 October 1873, East Boston, Suffolk Co, MA
      3 Mary E. Mahoney, Female, B: 18 October 1875, East Boston, Suffolk Co, MA
      3 William Henry Mahoney, Male, B: 17 May 1878, East Boston, Suffolk Co, MA
      3 Frances Josephine Mahoney, Female, B: 02 March 1880, East Boston, Suffolk Co, MA
      + Louis Leo Twomey, Male, B: 12 December 1879, East Boston, Suffolk Co, MA
      3 Annie Mahoney, Female, B: 13 February 1883, East Boston, Suffolk Co, MA
      3 Henry Joseph Mahoney, Male, B: 15 October 1884, East Boston, Suffolk Co, MA
      + Mary Elizabeth Farley, Female, B: 15 October 1884, McKeesport, Allegheny Co, PA
      3 Gertrude Mahoney, Female, B: 07 October 1886, East Boston, Suffolk Co, MA
      3 Frederick Louis Mahoney, Male, B: 21 August 1890, East Boston, Suffolk Co, MA
   2 John Kennedy, Male, B: 04 January 1854, East Boston, Suffolk Co, MA
   2 Margaret M. Kennedy, Female, B: July 1855, East Boston, Suffolk Co, MA
   + John Thomas Caulfield, Male, B: January 1861, Weymouth, Norfolk Co, MA
      3 Mary Frances Caulfield, Female, B: 08 February 1884, East Boston, Suffolk Co, MA
      + Alexander G. Crawford, Male, B: ABT 1882, Liverpool, England
      3 Frederick Caulfield, Male, B: 20 June 1886, New York City, NY
      3 Edith M. Caulfield, Female, B: 08 April 1888, New York City, NY
      + Julius Baker, Male, B: February 1891, Boston, Suffolk Co, MA
      3 Henry R. Caulfield, Male, B: May 1889, New York City, NY
      3 Florence J. Caulfield, Female, B: 19 November 1891, New York City, NY
      3 Elsie G. Caulfield, Female, B: October 1894, Bayonne, Hudson Co, NJ
      3 Jeanette Dorothea Caulfield, Female, B: February 1896, Bayonne, Hudson Co, NJ
      + Frank William Finkfelt, Male, B: 16 November 1894, Boston, Suffolk Co, MA
      3 John Theodore Caulfield, Male, B: 03 June 1899, Winthrop, Suffolk Co, MA
      + Hazel Elizabeth Baker, Female, B: 29 November 1902, Lynn, Essex Co, MA
   2 Patrick Joseph Kennedy, Male, B: 14 January 1858, East Boston, Suffolk Co, MA
   + Mary Augusta Hickey, Female, B: 06 December 1857, Winthrop, Suffolk Co, MA
      3 Joseph Patrick Kennedy, Male, B: 06 September 1888, East Boston, Suffolk Co, MA
      + Rose Elizabeth Fitzgerald, Female, B: 22 July 1890, Boston, Suffolk Co, MA
         4 Joseph Patrick Kennedy Jr., Male, B: 25 July 1915, Hull, Plymouth Co, MA
         4 John Fitzgerald Kennedy, Male, B: 29 May 1917, Brookline, Norfolk Co, MA
         + Jacqueline Lee Bouvier, Female, B: 28 July 1929, Southampton, Long Island, NY

Family Heritage Outline Descendant Report (4-25)

Family Matters

Version for Windows

Basic Information

MatterWare
PO Box 2221
Valrico, FL 33495-2221
e-mail: matterware@aol.com
http://members.aol.com/matterware
Shareware fee: $25.00

System requirements: Windows 3.1 or higher
   (works with Windows 95)
CD-ROM: not required

Program Information

Individuals per database: unlimited
Children per relationship: unlimited
Children reordered: birth order of children
   can be specified
Name options: father's surname
   automatically added to children
Field sizes: surname (50 characters), given
   name (100 characters), free-form text field
   (65,000 characters)
Event options: unlimited events per
   individual and family, events may be
   chosen from a scrollable separate
   sub-menu, event view allows you to access
   events for each individual or family, can
   sort events by a variety of criteria, can
   add and edit events to event dictionary
Note options: individual, family, source, and
   repository notes supported
Multimedia options: photos can be attached
   to individuals, 3 photos allowed per family
   (associated with primary individual,
   spouse, and family)
Program options: family, individual, or
   event view; can use on a network
Date options: standard date qualifiers are
   supported, double dates are supported
Search options: any string in all fields, or a
   search limited to 1 field, wildcard searches
   allowed; can specify a match for any part of
   a field, an entire field, or the start of a field

Sort options: sort database by surname, given
   name, birth date, formation of family
   date, or record entry date; Quick-Sort
   function (sort any displayed form by any field)
Chronicles options: Chronicles feature allows
   you to store information on a place, time,
   or way of life; Chronicle Quick-Finder will
   search all chronicles in the database
Find and replace options: default behavior
   may be specified; replace function allows
   you replace a text string in all fields
Database maintenance and options:
   backup and restore supported

Reports

View reports before printing: yes
Print displayed records: yes (Quick-Print
   features allows you to print the currently
   displayed record)
Pedigree Form
   ◆ 2 title text fields
   ◆ Cascading charts
Descendancy Form
   ◆ Specify individuals to include
   ◆ Specify information to include
Family Group Sheet
   ◆ Can be customized
Individual Report
Lists
   ◆ Family
   ◆ Individual
   ◆ Chronicles
   ◆ Events
   ◆ Repositories
   ◆ Sources

Sources

Creation: via a source database
Repository database: supported (information
   such as addresses, and URLs are linked
   to the source database)

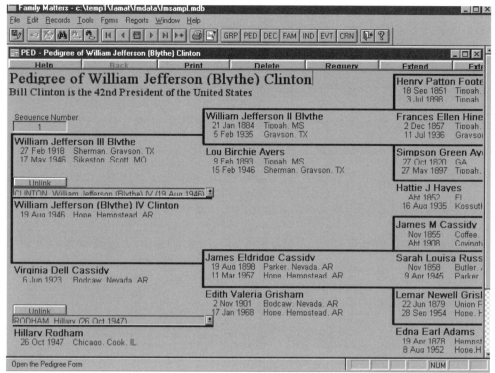

Figure 4.19
Family Matters
Pedigree Chart View

Figure 4.20
Family Matters
Family Group View

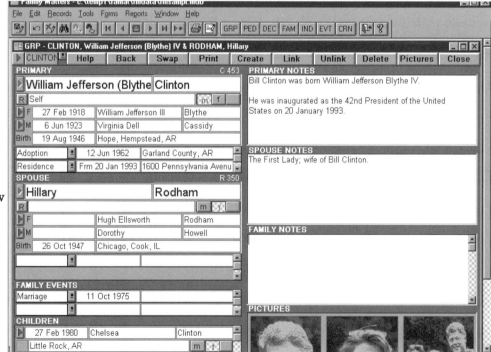

Family Origins
Version 7.0 for Windows

Basic Information

Parsons Technology
One Parsons Drive
PO Box 100
Hiawatha, IA 52233-0100
Voice: 319-395-9626
e-mail: info@parsonstech.com
http://www.parsonstech.com/genealogy/
index.html
Price: $29.00
Demo available for download
Orders accepted online

System requirements: IBM or compatible, Microsoft Windows 3.1 or later (works well with Windows 95)
RAM: 4MB (8MB recommended)
Hard drive: 4MB space
CD-ROM: 2x speed (for the CD version)
Mouse: required

Program Information

Individuals per database: unlimited
Spouses per individual: 200
Children per relationship: 200
Children and spouses reordered: yes
Multiple parents: supported
Field sizes: notes (30,000 characters)
Event options: unlimited facts (events) per individual, 50 pre-defined fact types (birth, marriage, death, occupation, religion, etc.), can add as many fact fields as you like
Multimedia options: images allowed for individual or family, scrapbook allows you to add multiple photos, sounds, and video clips for each person, can edit images within program
Program options: pedigree or family group sheet view, repository manager keeps track of the locations of records and other information (can add, delete, edit, and print a list of repositories)

Ditto-key entry: locations via place list function (automatically enter recognized location names by keying a few letters)
Date options: double dates are supported, can specify the default, partial dates allowed, date modifiers (before, after, about, circa, or, between, and from)
Search options: search for individual by name or by criteria; search box will list all of the fields you can search, find next and find prior supported, search by marriage (including wife's maiden name), global search and replace supported
Merge options: individuals, sources; can save position in a merge session, return to prior unmerged match in merge session
Database maintenance and options: backup and restore supported

Reports

View reports before printing: yes
Customized reports
- Options: fonts, boxes, colors, researcher name and address, chart frame styles
Blank reports: Pedigree Chart (4, 5, or 6 generations), Cemetery Records Form, Correspondence Log, Family Group Sheet, and Research Log
Data export in RTF: yes, for some reports
Photos included in reports: yes, for some reports
Pedigree Report
- Number of generations to print: 4, 5, or 6
- Cascading report: 30 generations
- Prints blank reports
Family Group Sheet
- Can add comments directly to the report
Descendants Report
- Number of generations: 30
- Includes photos
- Indented report available

Scrapbook Report (scrapbook page with all the photos entered for each individual)

Visual Tree Report (plot a photo pedigree/ancestor report with a tree as a background)

Lists

- Address
- Ahnentafel
- Birthday and Anniversary
- Descendants
- Duplicate records
- Facts
- Facts without sources
- Family Timeline
- Forests (how many trees per database)
- Individual
- Individuals with no parents
- Kinship
- LDS incomplete ordinances
- Marriage
- Multimedia
- Multiple Parents
- Places (with events)
- Problems
- Repository
- Source
- Statistics
- To-Do
- Unlinked individuals

Book (ancestor or descendants format for a selected individual)

- Include or exclude children
- Title allowed
- Specify number of generations to print
- Notes supported
- Sources supported
- Photos allowed
- Index
- Export book in ASCII or RTF file formats

Wall charts (ancestor and descendant format)

Organization forms

- Cemetery Records Form
- Correspondence Log
- Research Log
- Place List (with events)
- Repository List
- Research Log (To-Do List)

Sources

Creation: source manager is used to view a list of all sources; adding a source allows you to enter information on the name of the source (for Family Origins use only), description of the item, author, publisher, source text, and comments

Source options: can edit, merge, and delete sources, family notes and sources supported, unlimited number of sources, facts, and notes allowed per event; can add and edit source citations with detailed information about the specific location (volume, page number, sheet, dwelling, etc.) within the source referenced

Print options: all the source citations can be printed on 1 report

Source quality specified: yes

Bells and Whistles

- Web site creator lets you easily create a Web page from database information.
- Address features include the ability to print a complete address list, or export the information to a mail-merge file
- To-Do list (can attach a list to each individual)
- Spell check notes
- Forest command counts the number of separate "trees" in the database

Comments

The Family Origins Web site has a surname registry, users groups, and upload area for your Family Origins-created Web page.

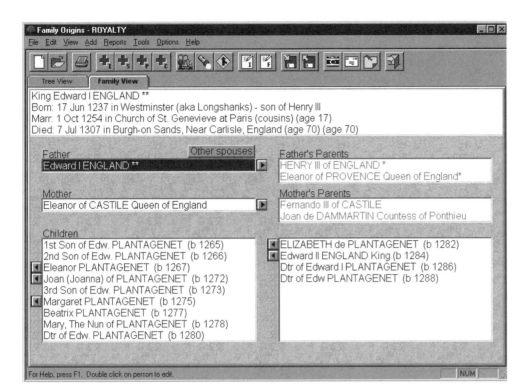

Figure 4.21
Family Origins
Family View

Figure 4.22
Family Origins
Source Library

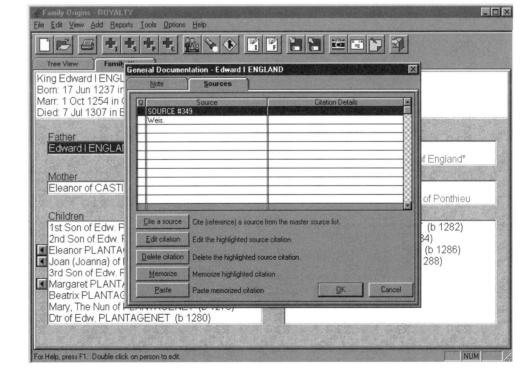

16 HANOVER King of Great Britain
cont. ___
B: 30 Oct 1683
D: 25 Oct 1760

8 F ENGLAND Prince of Wales
B: 1707
P: England? - son of George II
M: 27 Apr 1736
P: London?
D: 20 Mar 1751
P: England - age 44

17 ANSPACH Queen of England
cont. ___
B: 1683
D: 20 Nov 1737

4 GEORGE III of ENGLAND
B: May 1738
P: London (King 1760-1820) - son of Prince Frederick
M: 1761
P:
D: 29 Jan 1820
P: Windsor Castle (blind and mentally deranged)

9 Augusta of SAXE-GOTHA
B: 1719
P: Saxe-Gotha -
D: 1772
P:

18 Duke of SAXE-GOTHA
cont. ___
B: abt 1690
D:

19 Duchess of SAXE-GOTHA
cont. ___
B:
D:

2 Edward Duke of KENT
B: 1767
P: England - son of George III
M: 1818
P:
D: 1820
P:

10 MECKLENBURG-STRELITZ
B: abt 1725
P:
M:
D: aft 1755
P:

20 MECKLENBURG-STRELITZ
cont. ___
B: abt 1700
D:

21
cont. ___
B:
D:

5 MECKLENBURG-STRELITZ Queen of England
B: 1744
P: Mecklenburg, Germany
D: Nov 1818
P: Windsor Castle, England

11
B:
P:
D:

22
cont. ___
B:
D:

23
cont. ___
B:
D:

1 ENGLAND HM Queen England Empress of India
B: 1819
P: England - Alexandrina Victoria - dtr Edward Duke of Kent
M: 10 Feb 1840
P: St.James Palace, London (first cousins)
D: 1901
P: London? England (age 82)

12 Albert of SAXE-COBURG
B: abt 1630
P: Saxe-Gotha - son of Ernest I
M:
P:
D: 1699
P: Saxe-Coburg -

24 SAXE-GOTHA Duke of Saxe-Weimar
cont. ___
B: 1601
D: 1675

25 Duchess of SAXE-GOTHA
cont. ___
B: abt 1605
D:

6 Francis Frederick of COBURG
B: 1750
P: Saxe-Coburg (of Saafield)
M:
P:
D: 1806
P: Coburg (Duke 1800-1806)

13
B:
P:
D:
P:

26
cont. ___
B:
D:

27
cont. ___
B:
D:

3 V SAXE-SAALFED-COBURG
B: 1786
P: Germany - dtr of Francis Frederick
D: 1861
P: England - wife of Edward Duke of Kent

14
B:
P:
M:
P:
D:
P:

28
cont. ___
B:
D:

29
cont. ___
B:
D:

7
B:
P:
D:
P:

15
B:
P:
D:
P:

30
cont. ___
B:
D:

31
cont. ___
B:
D:

Family Origins Pedigree Chart (4-26)

Husband	Prince Albert of ENGLAND Prince Consort	
Chr	1819	Germany (Albert Francis Charles Augustus Emmanuel)
Birth	26 Aug 1819	Coburg, Bavaria (of Saxe-Coburg-Gotha)
Achievements	1851	Great Exhibition of England
Death	14 Dec 1869	England (of typhoid fever) (age 50)
Burial	14 Dec 1869	Royal Mausoleum, Frogmore, Windsor Castle
Marriage	10 Feb 1840	Chapel Royal, St.James Palace, London (first cousins)
Father	Ernest I of SAXE-SAALFELD-COBURG Duke (b 1784)	
Mother	Marie of WURTTEMBERG Princess (b 1799)	

Wife	Queen VICTORIA Regina of ENGLAND HM Queen England Empress of India	
Birth	1819	London, England - Alexandrina Victoria - dtr Edward Duke of Kent
Chr	1819	Germany (House of Hanover)
Ruled	bet 1837-1901	England
Coronation	bet 1877-1901	as Empress of India
Death	1901	London? England (age 82)
Burial	22 Jan 1901	Royal Mausoleum, Frogmore, Windsor Castle
Father	Edward Duke of KENT (b 1767)	
Mother	Victoria Mary Louisa SAXE-SAALFED-COBURG (b 1786)	

Children

1 F	Victoria of ENGLAND Princess	
Birth	Dec 1840	England - dtr of Queen Victoria
Death	1901	Prussia - wife of Frederick III
Chr		England - aka Princess Vicky
Burial		
Spouse	Kaiser Frederick III of PRUSSIA German Emperor, King of Prussia (m abt 1858)	

2 M	Edward VII of ENGLAND King of Great Britain	
Chr	1841	England - Albert Edward Prince of Wales
Birth	9 Nov 1841	England (Prince Albert Edward) son of Victoria
Ruled	bet 1901-1910	England
Death	6 May 1910	England
Burial	6 May 1910	St.George's Chapel, Windsor
Spouse	Alexandra of DENMARK Queen of England (m 10 Mar 1863)	

3 F	Alice Maud Mary of ENGLAND Duchess of Saxony	
Birth	1843	England
Death	1878	Hesse (Grand Duchess of Hesse-Darmstadt)
Chr		England (Princess of Great Britain & Ireland)
Burial		
Spouse	Louis IV of HESSE (m 1862)	

4 M	Prince Alfred Duke of EDINBURGH Duke of Saxe-Coburg-Gotha	
Birth	1844	England - son of Queen Victoria
Death	1900	Germany? Duke of Saxe-Coburg-Gotha
Chr		England - aka Affie
Burial		
Spouse	Grand Duchess Marie of RUSSIA (m 1874)	

5 F	Princess Helena of ENGLAND	
Birth	1846	England - dtr of Queen Victoria
Death	1923	Schleswig-Holstein - wife of Christian
Chr		England - aka Lenchen
Burial		
Spouse	Christian of SCHLESWIG-HOLSTEIN Prince (m abt 1866)	

6 F	Louise Alberta of ENGLAND HRH Princess	
Birth	1848	England - dtr of Queen Victoria
Namesake of	1882	Alberta, Canada
Death	3 Dec 1939	Scotland? - wife of the Duke of Argyll
Chr		England - Duchess of Argyl
Burial		Frogmore, Windsor Castle (cremation)
Spouse	John Douglas SUTHERLAND 9th Duke of Argyll (m 1871)	

7 M	PrincE Arthur Duke of CONNAUGHT	
Birth	1850	England - 3rd son of Victoria & Albert
Death	1942	England?
Burial		
Spouse	Louise Marguerite of PRUSSIA Duchess of Connaught (m 1879)	

Family Origins Family Group Record (4-27)

Descendants of Patrick Kennedy

FIRST GENERATION

1. **Patrick Kennedy** was born in Ireland. He died in Ireland. He was a farmer. He has reference number KENNPA.

He was married to Mary Johanna (-----) in Ireland.[1] **Mary Johanna (-----)** was born in Ireland. She died in Ireland. She has reference number KENNMJ. Patrick Kennedy and Mary Johanna (-----) had the following children:

+2   i.   **Patrick Kennedy.**

SECOND GENERATION

2. **Patrick Kennedy** was born about 1823 in Dunganstown, Wexford Co, Ireland. He immigrated about 1847 to Boston, Suffolk Co, MA. He died on 22 Nov 1858 in Boston, Suffolk Co, MA. He was buried on 23 Nov 1858 in Cambridge, Middlesex Co, MA. He had an estate probated on 13 Dec 1858 in Boston, Suffolk Co, MA. He was a cooper. He has reference number KENNPA23. Patrick Kennedy was the son of a prosperous farmer from County Wexford, Ireland. He emmigrated to America at the age of 26 to improve his fortunes. He left a country in the middle of a devastating famine and arrived in an immigrant ghetto where thousands of his countrymen had fled to escape near certain death. On board he had met Bridget Murphy, also from County Wexford and soon married her. He worked as a cooper and died of consumption in 1858. He only survived 9 years in this country.

He was married to Bridget Murphy (daughter of Richard Murphy and Mary (-----)) on 26 Sep 1849 in Boston, Suffolk Co, MA.[1] **Bridget Murphy** was born in 1821 in Dunganstown, Wexford Co, Ireland. She immigrated about 1847 to Boston, Suffolk Co, MA. She died on 20 Dec 1888 in Boston, Suffolk Co, MA. She was buried in Malden, Middlesex Co, MA. She has reference number MURPBR21. Patrick Kennedy and Bridget Murphy had the following children:

+3   i.   **Mary L. Kennedy.**
+4   ii. **Joanna L. Kennedy.**
 5   iii. **John Kennedy** was born on 4 Jan 1854 in East Boston, Suffolk Co, MA. He was christened on 5 Jan 1854 in East Boston, Suffolk Co, MA. He died on 24 Sep 1855 in Boston, Suffolk Co, MA. He was buried in Cambridge, Middlesex Co, MA. He has reference number KENNJO54.
+6   iv. **Margaret M. Kennedy.**
+7   v.   **Patrick Joseph Kennedy.**

THIRD GENERATION

3. **Mary L. Kennedy** was born on 9 Aug 1851 in East Boston, Suffolk Co, MA. She was christened on 10 Aug 1851 in East Boston, Suffolk Co, MA. She was buried in Mar 1926 in Malden, Middlesex Co, MA. She died on 7 Mar 1926 in Boston, Suffolk Co, MA. She was a skirtmaker. She has reference number KENNML51.

She was married to Lawrence M. Kane (son of Philip Kane and Margaret Murphy) on 1 Jan 1883 in Boston, Suffolk Co, MA.[1] **Lawrence M. Kane** was born on 29 Nov 1858 in Wexford Co, Ireland. He immigrated on 15 May 1876 to New York City, NY. He died on 19 Jul 1905 in East Boston, Suffolk Co, MA. He was buried in Malden, Middlesex Co, MA. He was a laborer. He has reference number KANELM58. Mary L. Kennedy and Lawrence M. Kane had the following children:

 8   i.   **Joseph Lawrence Kane** was born on 29 Nov 1883 in East Boston, Suffolk Co, MA. He was christened on 2 Dec 1883 in East Boston, Suffolk Co, MA. He died on 19 Mar 1967 in Brookline, Norfolk Co, MA. He was a politician. He has reference number KANEJL83.
 9   ii. **Mary Margaret Kane** was born on 25 Aug 1885 in East Boston, Suffolk Co, MA. She was christened on 30 Aug 1885 in East Boston, Suffolk Co, MA. She died on 14 Sep 1885 in East Boston, Suffolk Co, MA. She has reference number KANEMM85.
10   iii. **George Philip Kane** was born on 8 Sep 1888 in East Boston, Suffolk Co, MA. He was christened on

FIRST GENERATION

1. **Queen VICTORIA Regina of ENGLAND HM Queen England Empress of India**: born in 1819 in London, England - Alexandrina Victoria - dtr Edward Duke of Kent; died in 1901 in London? England (age 82)

SECOND GENERATION

2. **Edward Duke of KENT**: born in 1767 in England - son of George III; married in 1818; died in 1820

3. **Victoria Mary Louisa SAXE-SAALFED-COBURG**: born in 1786 in Germany - dtr of Francis Frederick; died in 1861 in England - wife of Edward Duke of Kent

THIRD GENERATION

4. **King GEORGE III of ENGLAND**: born in May 1738 in London (King 1760-1820) - son of Prince Frederich; married in 1761; died on 29 Jan 1820 in Windsor Castle (blind and mentally deranged)

5. **Sophia Charlotte of MECKLENBURG-STRELITZ Queen of England**: born in 1744 in Mecklenburg, Germany; died in Nov 1818 in Windsor Castle, England

6. **Duke Francis Frederick of COBURG**: born in 1750 in Saxe-Coburg (of Saafield); died in 1806 in Coburg (Duke 1800-1806)

FOURTH GENERATION

8. **Frederick Louis of ENGLAND Prince of Wales**: born in 1707 in England? - son of George II; married on 27 Apr 1736 in London?; died on 20 Mar 1751 in Kew Gardens, London, England - age 44

9. **Augusta of SAXE-GOTHA**: born in 1719 in Saxe-Gotha -; died in 1772

10. **Duke of MECKLENBURG-STRELITZ**: born about 1725; died after 1755

12. **Albert of SAXE-COBURG**: born about 1630 in Saxe-Gotha - son of Ernest I; died in 1699 in Saxe-Coburg -

FIFTH GENERATION

16. **GEORGE II of HANOVER King of Great Britain**: born on 30 Oct 1683 in Hanover; married in 1705; died on 25 Oct 1760 in England- King of England 1727-1760

17. **Caroline of ANSPACH Queen of England**: born in 1683 in Anspach (Bavarian Germany) dtr John Frederick; died on 20 Nov 1737 in Hampton Court, London, England

18. **Duke of SAXE-GOTHA**: born about 1690 in Germany

19. **Duchess of SAXE-GOTHA**

Family Scrapbook
Version 3.1 for DOS

Basic Information

Visionary Endeavors Software Development
PO Box 330439
Atlantic Beach, FL 32233-0439
Voice: 904-247-0062
Fax: 904-247-2762
e-mail: vesd@southeast.net
http://users.southeast.net/~vesd/index.html
Price: $50.00

System requirements: DOS 3.2 or higher, or
    Windows 95
RAM: 384K
Hard drive: 3MB space
CD-ROM: not required

Program Information

Individuals per database: 999,999
Spouses per individual: 9
Children per relationship: 32
Spouses reordered: yes
Non-traditional marriages: supported
Field sizes: surname (26 characters), other
    name fields (18 characters), notes (1,000
    lines of 75 column text)
Name options: honorific prefixes and suffixes
    are supported
Field options: surname, given, middle1, and
    middle2
Event options: can add, delete, and edit events
    from a large list; using the View Sentence
    function, you can edit the event sentence
    style used in narrative reports
Notes options: can be entered for each
    individual, private notes allow you to
    enter information which will be printed
    only if specified
Date options: standard modifiers supported
Search options: by personal record number,
    surnames (can specify which gender), given
    name, date of birth or death, family
    record number, name, place, and other
    fields

Reports

View reports before printing: yes (most
    reports)
Customized reports
*   Options: varies with report (specify the
    number of generations, a verbose report,
    headers, page numbers, record numbers,
    date format, notes included, sources);
    modified reports can be generated using
    the Custom Reports function
Blank reports: several reports can be printed
    blank, including all U.S. Census forms
Ahnentafel
Book (Ancestors or Descendants)
*   Register format
*   Modified Register format
Chronological Report
Drop Box Tree Descendancy Chart
Indented List Descendancy Chart
End of Line Persons Report
Family Group Sheet
List of Families, Sources, and Repositories
Missing Information Report
Narrative Report
Pedigree Chart
Record Problems
Relationship Report
Timeline

Sources

Creation: entered for almost every field,
    citation screen includes fields for name,
    fidelity (type of information), surety,
    repository, what the source proves, and
    call number; Document Filer feature
    keeps track of records, documents, and
    scanned images
Source options: a database of sources can
    be accessed for any source, can view a
    full bibliographic entry from the
    source citation screen

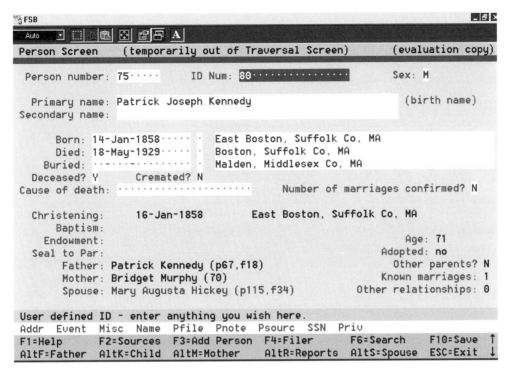

Figure 4.23
Family Scrapbook
Person Edit

Figure 4.24
Family Scrapbook
Source Citations

FAMILY GROUP SHEET for the Kennedy family (1)

==

Husband: **Joseph Patrick Kennedy** (1)
    Born: 6-Sep-1888   in: Boston, MA
    Died: 18-Nov-1969   in: Hyannis Port, MA
  Buried: in: Holyhood Cemetery, Brookline, MA
  Father: Patrick Joseph Kennedy (44)
G Father: Patrick Kennedy (46)
G Mother: Bridget Murphy (47)
  Mother: Mary Augusta Hickey (45)
G Father:
G Mother:

    Wife: **Rose Fitzgerald** (2)
    Born: 22-Jul-1890   in: North End, Boston, MA
    Died: 22-Jan-1995   in: Hyannis Port, MA
  Buried: 25-Jan-1995   in: Holyhood Cemetery, Brookline, MA
  Father: John F. Fitzgerald (50)
G Father:
G Mother:
  Mother: Josephine Mary Hannon (51)
G Father:
G Mother:

Married: 7-Oct-1914   in: Boston, MA
Not divorced
9 known children

Child 1: **Joseph Patrick Kennedy** (3)
Gender: Male
    Born: Jul-1915   in: Boston, MA
    Died: 2-Aug-1944   in: Suffolk, England
  Buried: in:
No known marriage

Child 2: **John Fitzgerald Kennedy** (52)
Gender: Male
    Born: 29-May-1917   in: Brookline, MA
    Died: 22-Nov-1963   in: Dallas, TX
  Buried: 25-Nov-1963   in: Arlington National, VA
Married: Jacqueline Bouvier (53) 12-Sep-1953
  Child: Caroline Bouvier Kennedy (54), b. 27-Nov-1957
  Child: John Fitzgerald Kennedy (55), b. 25-Nov-1960
  Child: Patrick Bouvier Kennedy (56), b. 7-Aug-1963, d. 9-Aug-1963

Child 3: **Rosemary Kennedy** (4)
Gender: Female
    Born: Sep-1918   in: Boston, MA
    Died: in:
  Buried: in:
No known marriage

Child 4: **Kathleen Kennedy** (6)
Gender: Female
    Born: 1920   in: Boston, MA

The Ancestors of Patrick Joseph Kennedy

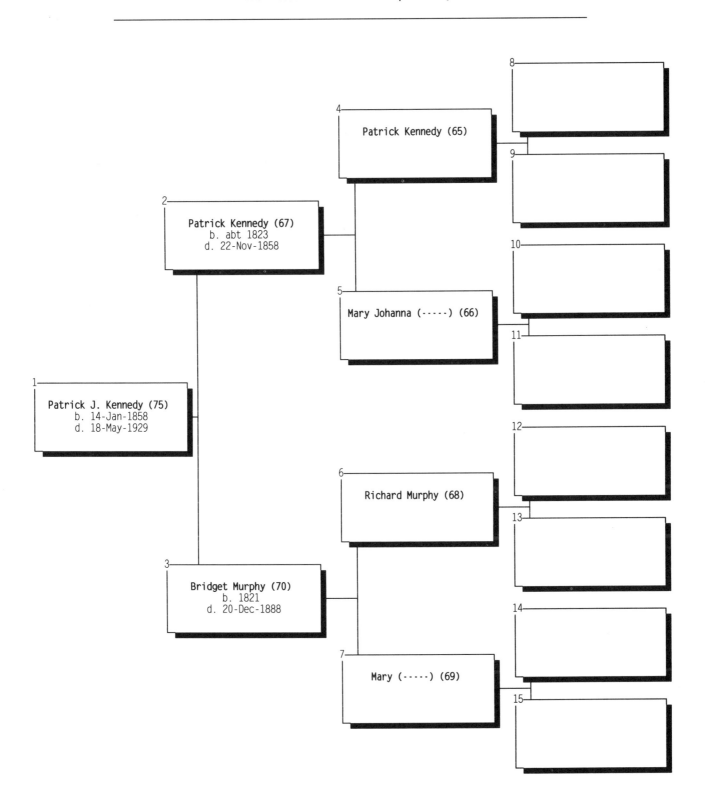

Family Scrapbook Pedigree Chart (4-31)

Generation 1 ───

1. Patrick Kennedy (46) was born in 1823 in Dunganstown, Ireland. He married Bridget Murphy (47) on September 28, 1849 in Holy Cross Cathedral, Boston, MA, and they have five known children. Patrick died on November 22, 1858 in Boston, MA.

@NI46@

          Children
2.   i. Mary Kennedy (60) was born on August 9, 1851 in Boston, MA. She married Laurence Kane (66) in 1883 in Boston, MA, and they have no known children.
3.   ii. Johanna Kennedy (61) was born on December 4, 1852. She married Humphrey Mahoney (64) on September 22, 1872 in Boston, MA, and they have no known children.
4. iii. John Kennedy (62) was born on January 4, 1854 in Boston, MA. John died on September 24, 1855.
5.   iv. Margaret Kennedy (63) was born on July 18, 1855 in Boston, MA. She married John T. Caulfield (65) in 1882 in Boston, MA, and they have no known children.
+ 6.   v. Patrick Joseph Kennedy (44) was born on January 14, 1858.

Generation 2 ───

6. Patrick Joseph Kennedy (44), the son of Patrick Kennedy (46) and Bridget Murphy (47), was born on January 14, 1858 in Boston, MA. He married Mary Augusta Hickey (45) in 1887, and they have three known children. Patrick died in May of 1929.

@NI44@

          Children
+ 7.   i. Joseph Patrick Kennedy (1) was born on September 6, 1888.
8.   ii. Loretta Kennedy (67) was born in 1892 in Boston, MA.
9. iii. Margaret Kennedy (57) was born in 1898. She married Charles Burke (58), and they have no known children.

Generation 3 ───

7. Joseph Patrick Kennedy (1), the son of Patrick Joseph Kennedy (44) and Mary Augusta Hickey (45), was born on September 6, 1888 in Boston, MA. He married Rose Fitzgerald (2) on October 7, 1914 in Boston, MA, and they have nine known children. Joseph died on November 18, 1969 in Hyannis Port, MA. He was buried in Holyhood Cemetery, Brookline, MA.

@NI1@ @MI1@

          Children
   i. Joseph Patrick Kennedy (3) was born in July of 1915 in Boston, MA. Joseph died on August 2, 1944 in Suffolk, England. @NI3@
  ii. John Fitzgerald Kennedy (52) was born on May 29, 1917 in Brookline, MA. He married Jacqueline Bouvier (53) on September 12, 1953 in Newport, RI, and they have three known children. John died on November 22, 1963 in Dallas, TX. He was buried on November 25, 1963 in Arlington National, VA. @NI52@ @MI52@
 iii. Rosemary Kennedy (4) was born in September of 1918 in Boston, MA. @NI4@
  iv. Kathleen Kennedy (6) was born in 1920 in Boston, MA. She married William John Robert Cavendish (5) on May 6, 1944 in London, and they have no known children. Kathleen died on May 13, 1948 in France. @NI6@
  v. Eunice Mary Kennedy (8) was born in July of 1921 in Boston, MA. She married Robert Sargent Shriver (7) on May 23, 1953, and they have five known children. @NI8@
  vi. Patricia Kennedy (16) was born on May 6, 1924 in Boston, MA. She married Peter Lawford (15), and they have four known children. @NI16@
 vii. Robert Francis Kennedy (21) was born on November 20, 1925 in Boston, MA. He married Ethel Skakel (22) on June 17, 1950 in Greenwich, Connecticut, and they have eleven known children. Robert died on June 6, 1968 in

Family Tree in a Window

Version 1.08 for Windows

Basic Information

C. A. Hartley
PO Box 251752
West Bloomfield, MI 48325
Shareware Fee: $29.95

System requirements: IBM compatible,
running Windows 3.1 or Windows 95
CD-ROM: not required

Program Information

Individual edit: individuals can be added via
list boxes
Name options: given and last name are
expected for each individual, name
modifiers are allowed, no duplicate names
are allowed, the first letter of all
surnames is automatically capitalized
Multimedia options: photos can be linked to
an individual
Date options: can specify U.S. or European-
style dates
Search options: search by by any portion of a
name

Reports

View reports before printing: yes
Customized reports
+ Options: specify individuals to be
included, font, by what field the individuals
are sorted, whether to include photos,
how many generations to include, headers
and footers, borders, margins, whether to
include biography, birth, and death years,
name format, and chart orientation
Detail Report (photos and information for
each individual)
Individual Report (information on selected
individuals)
Tree Chart (ancestors and descendants)
+ Photos can be included

Descendants Report (spouses and
descendants of individuals)
Mosiac Report (selected photos)
Lifeline Chart
Birthday Report

Sources

Creation: no sourcing of events is available;
biography field can be used to enter notes
and biographical details

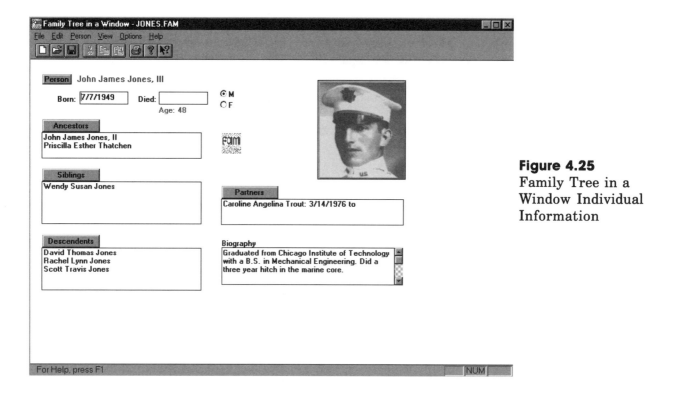

Figure 4.25
Family Tree in a
Window Individual
Information

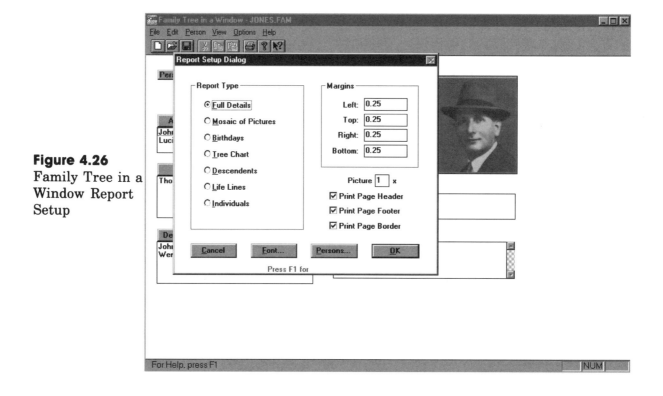

Figure 4.26
Family Tree in a
Window Report
Setup

Detailed Report

Clara Nehl Albert
Partner(s): Fitzgerald Everly Trout: to
*Descendent:*Caroline Angelina Trout

Lucinda Bell Horner   Age: 95 (d)   Born: 3/1880   Died: 17/6/1975
Partner(s): John James Jones: to
*Descendent:*Thomas Lee Jones   John James Jones, II

David Thomas Jones   Age: 12   Born: 3/11/1985
Ancestors: John James Jones, III   Caroline Angelina Trout
Siblings: Rachel Lynn Jones   Scott Travis Jones
Biography: Born at Beaumont General Hospital, Ridgeport, Illinois.

John James Jones, II   Age: 66 (d)   Born: 13/9/1917   Died: 25/1/1984
Ancestors: John James Jones   Lucinda Bell Horner
Partner(s): Priscilla Esther Thatchen: to
Siblings: Thomas Lee Jones
*Descendent:*Wendy Susan Jones   John James Jones, III

John James Jones, III   Age: 48   Born: 7/7/1949
Ancestors: John James Jones, II   Priscilla Esther Thatchen
Partner(s): Caroline Angelina Trout: 14/3/1976 to
Siblings: Wendy Susan Jones
*Descendent:*David Thomas Jones   Rachel Lynn Jones   Scott Travis Jones
Biography: Graduated from Chicago Institute of Technology with a B.S. in Mechanical Engineering. Did a three year hitch in the marine core.

John James Jones   Age: 64 (d)   Born: 1875   Died: 15/4/1939
Partner(s): Lucinda Bell Horner: to
*Descendent:*Thomas Lee Jones   John James Jones, II

Rachel Lynn Jones   Age: 10   Born: 21/8/1987
Ancestors: John James Jones, III   Caroline Angelina Trout
Siblings: David Thomas Jones   Scott Travis Jones
Biography: Born in Brown County, Illinois at 8:10 a.m.

Scott Travis Jones   Age: 11   Born: 7/7/1986
Ancestors: John James Jones, III   Caroline Angelina Trout
Siblings: David Thomas Jones   Rachel Lynn Jones

Thomas Lee Jones   Age: 1 (d)   Born: 15/12/1914   Died: 1/4/1916
Ancestors: John James Jones   Lucinda Bell Horner
Siblings: John James Jones, II
Biography: Died as infant from polio.

Wendy Susan Jones   Age: 46   Born: 27/3/1951
Ancestors: John James Jones, II   Priscilla Esther Thatchen
Siblings: John James Jones, III

Priscilla Esther Thatchen   Age: 57 (d)   Born: 1918   Died: 1975
Partner(s): John James Jones, II: to
*Descendent:*Wendy Susan Jones   John James Jones, III

Caroline Angelina Trout   Age: 43   Born: 12/8/1954
Ancestors: Clara Nehl Albert   Fitzgerald Everly Trout
Partner(s): John James Jones, III: 14/3/1976 to
Siblings:
*Descendent:*David Thomas Jones   Rachel Lynn Jones   Scott Travis Jones
Biography: Elementary school teacher.

Fitzgerald Everly Trout
Partner(s): Clara Nehl Albert: to
*Descendent:*Caroline Angelina Trout

Family Tree in a Window Detailed Report (4-33)

John James Jones, II

Born: 13/9/1917   Died: 25/1/1984

⦿M ◯F

Age: 66 (d)

Ancestors:
John James Jones
Lucinda Bell Horner

Siblings:
Thomas Lee Jones

Partners:
Priscilla Esther Thatchen: to

Descendents:
Wendy Susan Jones
John James Jones, III

Biography:

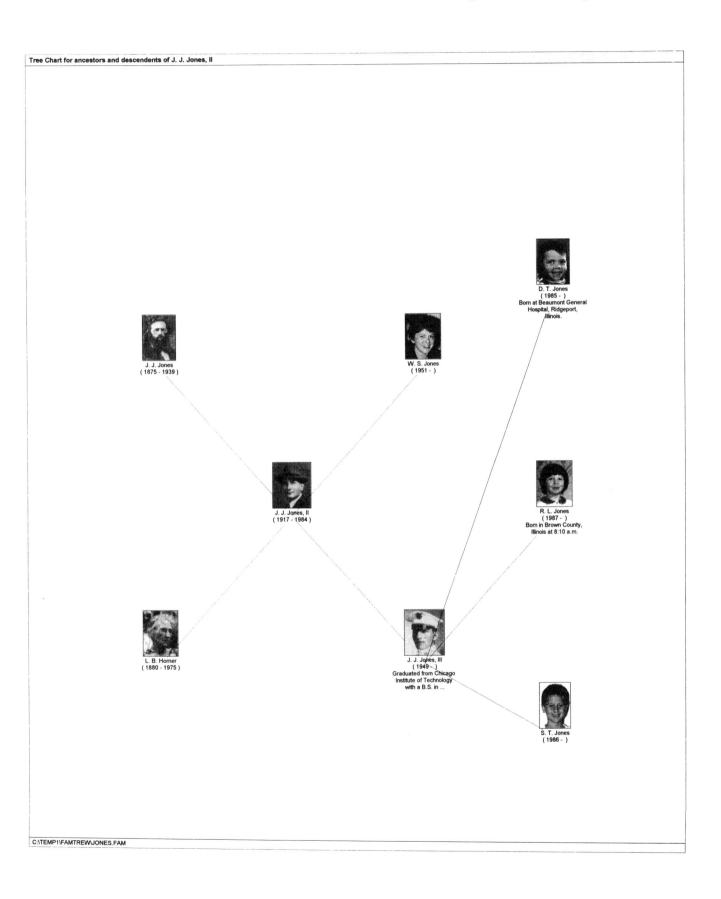

Tree Chart for ancestors and descendents of J. J. Jones, II

D. T. Jones
(1985 -)
Born at Beaumont General
Hospital, Ridgeport,
Illinois.

J. J. Jones
(1875 - 1939)

W. S. Jones
(1951 -)

J. J. Jones, II
(1917 - 1984)

R. L. Jones
(1987 -)
Born in Brown County,
Illinois at 8:10 a.m.

L. B. Horner
(1880 - 1975)

J. J. Jones, III
(1949 -)
Graduated from Chicago
Institute of Technology
with a B.S. in ...

S. T. Jones
(1986 -)

C:\TEMP1\FAMTREW\JONES.FAM

Family Tree in a Window Tree Chart (4-35)

Family Tree Maker
Version 5.0 (CD)

Basic Information

Broderbund Software, Inc.
Banner Blue Division
39500 Stevenson Place, Suite 204
Fremont, CA 94539-3103
Voice: 510-494-2754
Voice Response System: 510-794-6850
Fax: 510-794-9152
e-mail: info@familytreemaker.com
http://www.familytreemaker.com
Price: $89.99 Family Tree Maker Deluxe 10-CD Set, $59.99 Deluxe 4-CD Set, $29.99 Basic Edition (updated v. 4.4)
Demo available for download
Orders accepted online

System requirements: For v. 5.0: 486 or higher IBM or compatible, Windows 95 or Windows 98; for v. 4.4: Windows 3.1 or Windows 95
RAM: 8MB (16MB recommended)
Hard drive: 16MB space (v. 4.4); 20MB (v. 5.0)
Monitor: VGA (at least 16 colors)
CD-ROM: required
Mouse: required
Optional hardware: scanner, video capture, sound board, and modem

Program Information

Individuals per database: unlimited; unlimited number of databases allowed
Children per relationship: 99
Children reordered: yes
Multiple parents: supported
Specify relationship between parent and child: supported (natural, step, adopted)
Specify preferred parent and spouse: supported
Non-traditional relationships: supported (adopted, step, and foster children allowed)
Name options: father's last name automatically entered for children (function can be disabled); nicknames, aliases, honorific prefixes, and suffixes are supported
Field sizes: comment (80 characters), location (80 characters), notes (32,000 characters)
Field options: individuals have 13 fact fields consisting of date (optional), comment, and location field; can change field labels
Notes options: additional notes can be entered using the Book word processor function, notes can be entered for each marriage, can import and export text into notes
Multimedia options: 2,000 multimedia items allowed per person, pictures, sound, video, and OLE objects can be stored in scrapbooks for each individual and marriage, photos in scrapbook can be manipulated by rotating, cropping, mirroring, and flipping; caption and description can be included for each item, specify preferred photo to be used when printing, can import graphics from Kodak Photo CD or scanned images, items can be searched within the scrapbook, can sort and edit scrapbook items, specify resolution and compression of scrapbook graphics; specify preferred item for trees, labels, cards, and Family Group Sheet, can format and customize printed scrapbooks
Program options: can enter your own reference numbers, More About function includes fields for recording facts, address, medical, and lineage information; long notes can also be entered
Ditto-key entry: locations (last 50 locations entered only), name; feature can be disabled
Date options: double dates, specify date formats, standard date modifiers supported (About, Before, After, Est, Circa), can exclude individuals from calendars
Search options: Quick-Search function will search a list of individuals, Find Name command will search partial names (can

use wildcards); can sort individuals list by last or given name, or birth date (oldest first or youngest first); can search for dates, locations, and sources

Merge options: individuals

Database maintenance and options: backup function (automatic backup can be disabled), error-check function supported

Reports

View reports before printing: yes

Customized reports
- Options: select individuals to include, number of generations, information to include, title, footnote, display options, text formatting, column width, sorting, box, border, line style, and font

Photos included: yes, in some reports

Sources included: yes, in most reports

Blank reports: Family Group Sheet and Ancestor Tree only

Ancestor Tree (pedigree chart)
- Variety of layouts available

Descendant Tree
- Information presented in boxes
- 3 choices of layouts

Outline Descendant Tree
- Information in outline format

Family Group Sheet
- Register format
- NGS Quarterly format
- Ahnentafel format

Kinship Report
- Canon and civil formats

Book (feature allows you to create an outline of items you want included in a book)
- Narrative style supported
- Title page
- Preface
- Dedication
- Table of contents
- Introduction
- Variety of reports (custom reports as well)
- Index
- Calendar
- Text

Hourglass Trees
- Ancestors and descendants on one tree

Historical Timelines

Relationship Only Report

Data Errors Report
Medical Information Report
Address List
Birthdays of Living Individuals List
Marriage Report
Parentage Report
Documented Events Report
Bibliography
PAF: Incomplete Individual Ordinances
PAF: Incomplete Marriage Sealings

Sources

Creation: master list of sources is supported; can source name, birth, marriage, death dates (and locations), marriage fact, each of the 13 fact fields, cause of death, marriage ending date and location, medical information

Source options: universal change in master sources is supported, bibliography of sources can be printed, documented events report listing events which have been sourced

Footnote options: include citation information in footnote, can edit footnote information

Bells and Whistles

- Deluxe versions come with extra CDs (SSDI and others)
- CD contains Genealogy How-To Guide which can be printed (not available in Basic version)
- Can create Web page from the database and upload it to the FTM site; Web page creation includes InterneTree to display your family info on the Internet
- Internet FamilyFinder feature allows you to search online for sites with individuals in whom you are interested
- Can use FTM to view/search Broderbund's line of genealogy CDs
- Alternate Facts can record conflicting evidence
- Foreign language form letters can be generated to request records from foreign countries

Comments

There are 3 versions of Family Tree Maker
for IBM compatibles: Basic (1 CD), Deluxe 4-
CD Set, and Deluxe 10-CD Set; the basic
program for all 3 versions is the same.
Broderbund sells a German language version
of Family Tree Maker called
Familienstammbaum. Lots of
information is available on the Family Tree
Maker Web site at no cost:

- Genealogy How-To Guide
- FamilyFinder index of more than 130
  million names on Broderbund CDs
- Internet FamilyFinder (genealogy
  search engine)
- Genealogy articles
- Genealogy lessons
- Vendor mall

Items for FTM purchasers *only* include
message boards and user home pages (home
pages are available for all to view).

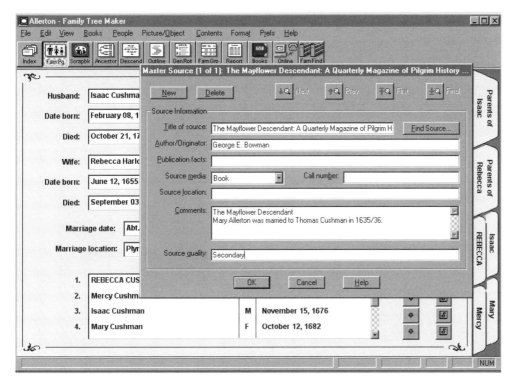

Figure 4.27
Family Tree Maker
Master Source
Edit Screen

Figure 4.28
Family Tree
Maker Book
Outline Screen

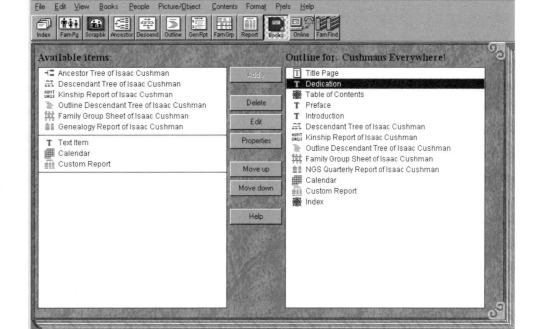

Ancestors of John Fitzgerald Kennedy

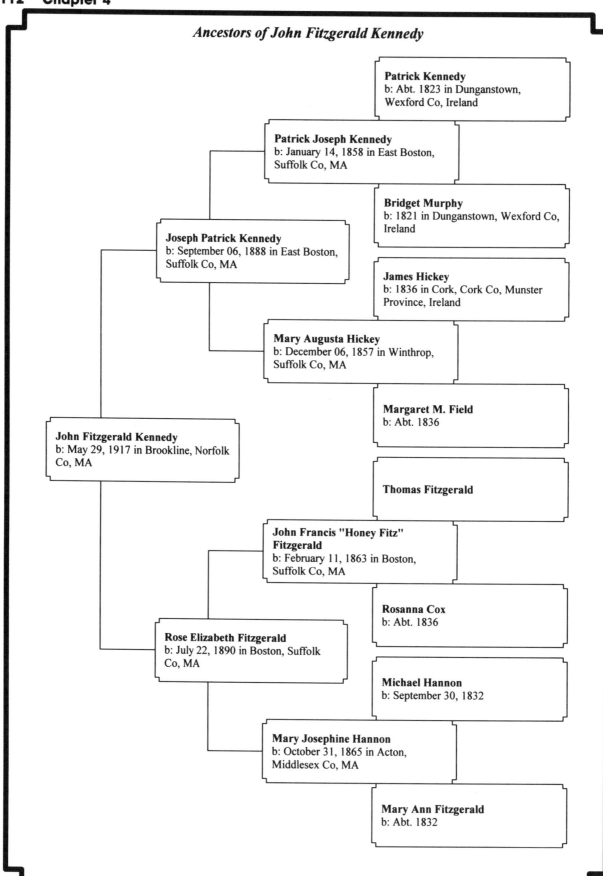

Patrick Kennedy
b: Abt. 1823 in Dunganstown, Wexford Co, Ireland

Patrick Joseph Kennedy
b: January 14, 1858 in East Boston, Suffolk Co, MA

Bridget Murphy
b: 1821 in Dunganstown, Wexford Co, Ireland

Joseph Patrick Kennedy
b: September 06, 1888 in East Boston, Suffolk Co, MA

James Hickey
b: 1836 in Cork, Cork Co, Munster Province, Ireland

Mary Augusta Hickey
b: December 06, 1857 in Winthrop, Suffolk Co, MA

Margaret M. Field
b: Abt. 1836

John Fitzgerald Kennedy
b: May 29, 1917 in Brookline, Norfolk Co, MA

Thomas Fitzgerald

John Francis "Honey Fitz" Fitzgerald
b: February 11, 1863 in Boston, Suffolk Co, MA

Rosanna Cox
b: Abt. 1836

Rose Elizabeth Fitzgerald
b: July 22, 1890 in Boston, Suffolk Co, MA

Michael Hannon
b: September 30, 1832

Mary Josephine Hannon
b: October 31, 1865 in Acton, Middlesex Co, MA

Mary Ann Fitzgerald
b: Abt. 1832

Family Tree Maker Ancestor Tree (4-36)

Descendants of Patrick Joseph Kennedy

Generation No. 1

1. PATRICK JOSEPH[2] KENNEDY *(PATRICK[1])* was born January 14, 1858 in Boston, MA, and died May 1929. He married MARY AUGUSTA HICKEY 1887.

    Children of PATRICK KENNEDY and MARY HICKEY are:

2.   i.   JOSEPH PATRICK[3] KENNEDY, b. September 06, 1888, Boston, MA; d. November 18, 1969, Hyannis Port, MA.
       ii. LORETTA KENNEDY, b. 1892, Boston, MA.
      iii. MARGARET KENNEDY, b. 1898; m. CHARLES BURKE.

Generation No. 2

2. JOSEPH PATRICK[3] KENNEDY *(PATRICK JOSEPH[2], PATRICK[1])* was born September 06, 1888 in Boston, MA, and died November 18, 1969 in Hyannis Port, MA. He married ROSE FITZGERALD October 07, 1914 in Boston, MA, daughter of JOHN FITZGERALD and JOSEPHINE HANNON.

More About ROSE FITZGERALD:
Cause of Death: Died of complications due to pneumonia.

    Children of JOSEPH KENNEDY and ROSE FITZGERALD are:
       i.   JOSEPH PATRICK[4] KENNEDY, b. July 1915, Boston, MA; d. August 02, 1944, Suffolk, England.
3.   ii. JOHN FITZGERALD KENNEDY, b. May 29, 1917, Brookline, MA; d. November 22, 1963, Dallas, TX.
      iii. ROSEMARY KENNEDY, b. September 1918, Boston, MA.
      iv. KATHLEEN KENNEDY, b. 1920, Boston, MA; d. May 13, 1948, France; m. WILLIAM JOHN ROBERT CAVENDISH, May 06, 1944, London.
4.   v.   EUNICE MARY KENNEDY, b. July 1921, Boston, MA.
5.   vi. PATRICIA KENNEDY, b. May 06, 1924, Boston, MA.
6.   vii. ROBERT FRANCIS KENNEDY, b. November 20, 1925, Boston, MA; d. June 06, 1968, Los Angeles, CA.
7.   viii. JEAN ANN KENNEDY, b. February 1928, Boston, MA.
8.   ix. EDWARD MOORE KENNEDY, b. February 22, 1932, Brookline, MA.

Generation No. 3

3. JOHN FITZGERALD[4] KENNEDY *(JOSEPH PATRICK[3], PATRICK JOSEPH[2], PATRICK[1])* was born May 29, 1917 in Brookline, MA, and died November 22, 1963 in Dallas, TX. He married JACQUELINE BOUVIER September 12, 1953 in Newport, RI, daughter of JOHN BOUVIER and JANET LEE.

More About JOHN FITZGERALD KENNEDY:
Cause of Death: Assassination in Dallas, TX

    Children of JOHN KENNEDY and JACQUELINE BOUVIER are:
       i.   CAROLINE BOUVIER[5] KENNEDY, b. November 27, 1957, New York; m. EDWIN SCHLOSSBERG.
      ii. JOHN FITZGERALD KENNEDY, b. November 25, 1960, Washington, DC; m. CAROLYNE.
      iii. PATRICK BOUVIER KENNEDY, b. August 07, 1963, Otis Air Force B, Mass; d. August 09, 1963, Boston, Mass.

4. EUNICE MARY[4] KENNEDY *(JOSEPH PATRICK[3], PATRICK JOSEPH[2], PATRICK[1])* was born July 1921 in Boston, MA. She married ROBERT SARGENT SHRIVER May 23, 1953.

    Children of EUNICE KENNEDY and ROBERT SHRIVER are:

Family Group Sheet

Husband: Joseph Patrick Kennedy	

Born: September 06, 1888	in: Boston, MA
Married: October 07, 1914	in: Boston, MA
Died: November 18, 1969	in: Hyannis Port, MA
Father: Patrick Joseph Kennedy	
Mother: Mary Augusta Hickey	

Wife: Rose Fitzgerald	

Born: July 22, 1890	in: North End, Boston, MA
Died: January 22, 1995	in: Hyannis Port, MA
Father: John F. Fitzgerald	
Mother: Josephine Mary Hannon	

CHILDREN

1 M
Name: Joseph Patrick Kennedy
Born: July 1915 — in: Boston, MA
Died: August 02, 1944 — in: Suffolk, England

2 M
Name: John Fitzgerald Kennedy
Born: May 29, 1917 — in: Brookline, MA
Married: September 12, 1953 — in: Newport, RI
Died: November 22, 1963 — in: Dallas, TX
Spouse: Jacqueline Bouvier

3 F
Name: Rosemary Kennedy
Born: September 1918 — in: Boston, MA

4 F
Name: Kathleen Kennedy
Born: 1920 — in: Boston, MA
Married: May 06, 1944 — in: London
Died: May 13, 1948 — in: France
Spouse: William John Robert Cavendish

5 F
Name: Eunice Mary Kennedy
Born: July 1921 — in: Boston, MA
Married: May 23, 1953
Spouse: Robert Sargent Shriver

6 F
Name: Patricia Kennedy
Born: May 06, 1924 — in: Boston, MA
Spouse: Peter Lawford

7 M
Name: Robert Francis Kennedy
Born: November 20, 1925 — in: Boston, MA
Married: June 17, 1950 — in: Greenwich, Connecticut
Died: June 06, 1968 — in: Los Angeles, CA
Spouse: Ethel Skakel

8 F
Name: Jean Ann Kennedy
Born: February 1928 — in: Boston, MA
Married: 1956
Spouse: Stephen Edward Smith

9 M
Name: Edward Moore Kennedy
Born: February 22, 1932 — in: Brookline, MA
Married: November 29, 1958
Spouse: Virginia Joan Bennett

The information on this chart may not be correct and is for demonstration purposes only.

Family Tree Maker Family Group Sheet (4-38)

Generations Grande Suite
Version 5.2 for Windows 3.1 and Windows 95

Basic Information

Sierra On-Line, Inc.
3380 146th Place SE, Suite 300
Bellevue, WA 98007
Voice: 425-649-9800
Voice: 800-757-7707
http://www.sierra.com
Price: $69.95 for the Grande Suite Edition
Demo available for download

System requirements: IBM compatible
   486DX 66MHz or higher, running
   Windows 3.1 or higher
RAM: 12MB
Hard Drive: 10MB space
Monitor: SVGA 480x640 with 256 colors
CD-ROM: 2x speed

Program Information

Individuals per database: unlimited; only 1
   family file can be open at a given time
Spouses per individual: 50
Children per relationship: 50
Children and spouses reordered: yes
**Specify relationship between parent and
   child:** supported (from a list of 15 items
   such as adopted, twin, stillborn, etc.); a
   child also may be specified as a direct line
   ancestor or descendant
Multiple parents allowed: yes
Name options supported: nicknames,
   honorific prefixes, aliases, and suffixes
Field sizes: name (75 characters first and last
   name), notes (64,000 characters), memo
   (1,000 characters), logs (64,000 characters)
Event options: unlimited events per individual,
   can choose events from list, or define your
   own; family events are supported
Note options: each individual is allowed 1
   miscellaneous note, and 2 custom-note
   fields; you may specify the title of the
   custom note from a list, free-form and
   structured notes supported, color text allowed
Ditto-key entries: locations (user can pick a

place name from a list of the 50 previously
entered locations), surnames (users can
select a name from the last 50 surnames
entered), Ditto Shortcut feature allows a
simple keystroke to repeat the last entry
in the same field
Multimedia options: graphics can be linked
   to each family card, description for each
   graphic (up to 45 characters), specify up
   to 3 picture directories; graphics can
   be cropped, inverted, or scaled
Program options: specify colors for child
   status type, change the titles and
   abbreviations for the custom fields,
   specify a word processor for use with the
   report feature, what family card you wish
   to begin with when you open the program,
   fonts and colors, export data in a spread
   sheet or database format file (tab- and
   return-delimited), also Macintosh
   Reunion format
Date options: preferred date format can be
   specified, standard modifiers are
   supported (as well as expressions such as
   yesterday, from now, ago), a reference
   note is allowed for each date, date ranges
   are supported, feature to display a list of
   people who have a birthday, death, or
   anniversary for that day, can generate a
   calendar for several dates; a function will
   indicate on what day of the week a birth
   or marriage date fell, as well as calculate
   the age of an individual, or how long a
   couple was married
Search options: search for an individual by
   name, or use the AutoMark feature to
   search by conditions, Quick-List feature
   enables a list of the last 10–150
   individuals added or edited, can mark
   family cards for search, sorting, and
   inclusion in reports, find and replace
   function available
Research and correspondence tracking:
   supported via Family File Log feature
   that allows you to keep track of research
   and correspondence

Database maintenance and options: can merge and separate family files (merge is accomplished via GEDCOM import), repair and compact functions supported, backup and restore functions supported

Reports

View reports before printing: most reports
Customized reports
- Options: can specify font, color, individuals to include, items to include, and whether a report is printed in standard, questionnaire, or blank style, 99 generations and unlimited size allowed

Person Sheet
- Can be automatically generated for marked individuals

Family Group Sheet
- Can be automatically generated for marked individuals
- LDS ordinances are supported

Pedigree Chart
- EasyChart feature allows you to create fully-customized, high-quality graphic Pedigree Charts
- Enhanced Pedigree Chart shows siblings, aunts, and uncles

Family Card
Descendant Chart
- Indented and graphic format
- EasyChart feature allows you to create fully-customized, high-quality graphic Descendant Charts

Hourglass Chart
- Shows both ancestors and descendants on one chart

Timeline
Exported reports (printed by use of a word processor or text editor; data is exported via text or RTF format)
- Person Report
- Family Group Report
- Descendant Report
- Family History Report with index (lists all information about a couple and their descendants)
- Register Report (with index)
- Ahnentafel
- Mailing List Report

Lists
- Ages
- Direct Lines
- Index of the database
- Relationships

Sources

Creation: a library of reference notes (sources) contains source citations which may be used for any event field; unlimited sources available
Citation template: supported (you may create your own citation templates)
Source options: general and automatic sources, reference notes can have hypertext links to the actual citation, can search the entire library of citations for a text string; unlimited sources supported
Sources included on reports: supported

Bells and Whistles

- Internet Detective feature accesses Cyndi's List (hosted by Sierra) online
- Professional-quality charts can be printed using the EasyChart feature; options allow user to include captions with lines and arrows, colored text in chart boxes, and colored shadows

Comments

The Grande Suite version includes SnapShot SE (photo manipulation software), MasterCook Heritage Edition (family recipes), the World Name Index, and the book *Netting Your Ancestors* by Cyndi Howells (Baltimore: Genealogical Publishing Co., 1997). The Deluxe version includes the Social Security Death Index (SSDI) on CD, and a CD containing Historic Records (8 databases, including Union and Confederate Generals, U.S. Immigrants, and Medal of Honor Recipients), and *Netting Your Ancestors*; the price for the Deluxe version is $49.95. A basic version of the software, *Easy Family Tree 4.2*, is available for $10.00–15.00 depending on the place of purchase. Note: at the time of my review, Generations 5.2 was in beta testing; there may be slight differences between the reviewed version and later releases.

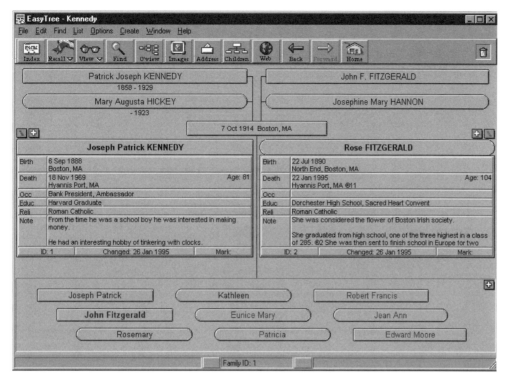

Figure 4.29
Generations
Grande Suite
Family Card

Figure 4.30
Generations
Grande Suite
Individual Facts

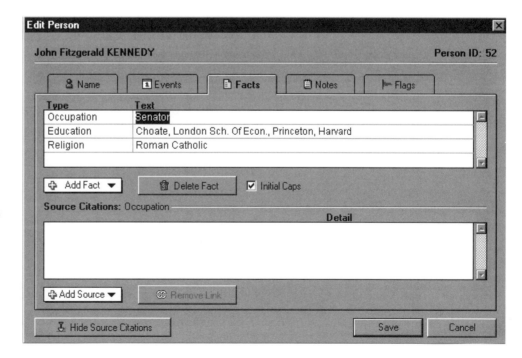

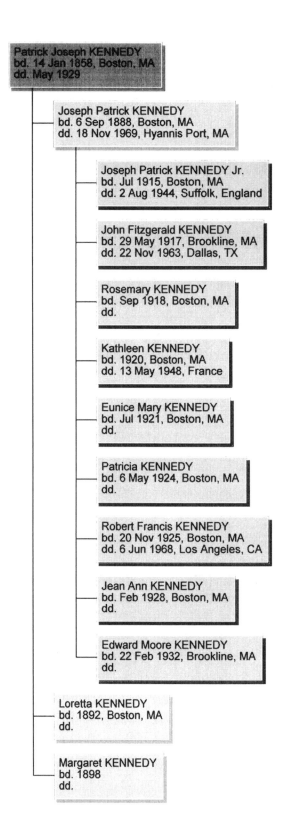

Patrick Joseph KENNEDY
bd. 14 Jan 1858, Boston, MA
dd. May 1929

Joseph Patrick KENNEDY
bd. 6 Sep 1888, Boston, MA
dd. 18 Nov 1969, Hyannis Port, MA

Joseph Patrick KENNEDY Jr.
bd. Jul 1915, Boston, MA
dd. 2 Aug 1944, Suffolk, England

John Fitzgerald KENNEDY
bd. 29 May 1917, Brookline, MA
dd. 22 Nov 1963, Dallas, TX

Rosemary KENNEDY
bd. Sep 1918, Boston, MA
dd.

Kathleen KENNEDY
bd. 1920, Boston, MA
dd. 13 May 1948, France

Eunice Mary KENNEDY
bd. Jul 1921, Boston, MA
dd.

Patricia KENNEDY
bd. 6 May 1924, Boston, MA
dd.

Robert Francis KENNEDY
bd. 20 Nov 1925, Boston, MA
dd. 6 Jun 1968, Los Angeles, CA

Jean Ann KENNEDY
bd. Feb 1928, Boston, MA
dd.

Edward Moore KENNEDY
bd. 22 Feb 1932, Brookline, MA
dd.

Loretta KENNEDY
bd. 1892, Boston, MA
dd.

Margaret KENNEDY
bd. 1898
dd.

Generations Grande Suite Descendant Chart (4-39)

Family Group Sheet - 1

Husband	**Joseph Patrick KENNEDY - 1**	
Born	6 Sep 1888	Boston, MA
Christen		
Died	18 Nov 1969	Hyannis Port, MA
Buried		Holyhood Cemetery, Brookline, MA[11]
Occupation	Bank President, Ambassador	
Education	Harvard Graduate	
Religion	Roman Catholic	
Father	Patrick Joseph KENNEDY - 44 (1858-19	**Mother**	Mary Augusta HICKEY - 45 (-1923)
Other Spouses:		
Married	7 Oct 1914	Boston, MA
Status		

Wife	**Rose FITZGERALD - 2**	
Born	22 Jul 1890	North End, Boston, MA
Christen		
Died	22 Jan 1995	Hyannis Port, MA[11]
Buried	25 Jan 1995	Holyhood Cemetery, Brookline, MA[11]
Occupation		
Education	Dorchester High School, Sacred Heart Convent	
Religion	Roman Catholic	
Father	John F. FITZGERALD - 50	**Mother**	Josephine Mary HANNON - 51
Other Spouses:		

Children		
1	**M**	**Joseph Patrick KENNEDY Jr. - 3**
Born	Jul 1915	Boston, MA
Christen		
Died	2 Aug 1944	Suffolk, England
Buried		
Occupation		
Education	Harvard University, Harvard Law School	
Religion	Roman Catholic	
2	**M**	**John Fitzgerald KENNEDY - 52**
Born	29 May 1917	Brookline, MA
Christen		
Died	22 Nov 1963[8]	Dallas, TX
Buried	25 Nov 1963	Arlington National, VA
Occupation	Senator	
Education	Choate, London Sch. Of Econ., Princeton, Harvard	
Religion	Roman Catholic	
Spouse	Jacqueline BOUVIER - 53	
Married	12 Sep 1953	Newport, RI
Status		
3	**F**	**Rosemary KENNEDY - 4**
Born	Sep 1918	Boston, MA
Christen		
Died		
Buried		
Occupation		
Education		
Religion		
Spouse		
Married		
Status		

Name	**Joseph Patrick KENNEDY - 1**	
Born	6 Sep 1888	Boston, MA
Died	18 Nov 1969	Hyannis Port, MA
Buried		Holyhood Cemetery, Brookline, MA[11]
Occupation	Bank President, Ambassador	
Education	Harvard Graduate	
Religion	Roman Catholic	
Father	Patrick Joseph KENNEDY - 44 (1858-19	Mother	Mary Augusta HICKEY - 45 (-1923)

Spouses		
1	**Rose FITZGERALD - 2**	
Married	7 Oct 1914	Boston, MA

Children: Joseph Patrick - 3, John Fitzgerald - 52, Rosemary - 4, Kathleen - 6, Eunice Mary - 8, Patricia - 16, Robert Francis - 21, Jean Ann - 35, Edward Moore - 39

Notes

From the time he was a school boy he was interested in making money.

He had an interesting hobby of tinkering with clocks.

Joe was a poor student, but good at athletics and had an attractive personality. He was able to overcome many ethnic barriers during his school years at Boston Latin, a protestant and primarily Yankee school.[1]

Was one of the youngest Bank Presidents in US history.[1]

He was fiercely proud of his family. He was quoted as having said his family was the finest thing in his life.[5]

Medical

Joe Kennedy was a very hard worker, which often deteriorated his health. At times he was hospitalized for his run down condition.

Residences

Bronxville, MA
Hyannis, MA
Palm Beach, FL
Brookline, MA

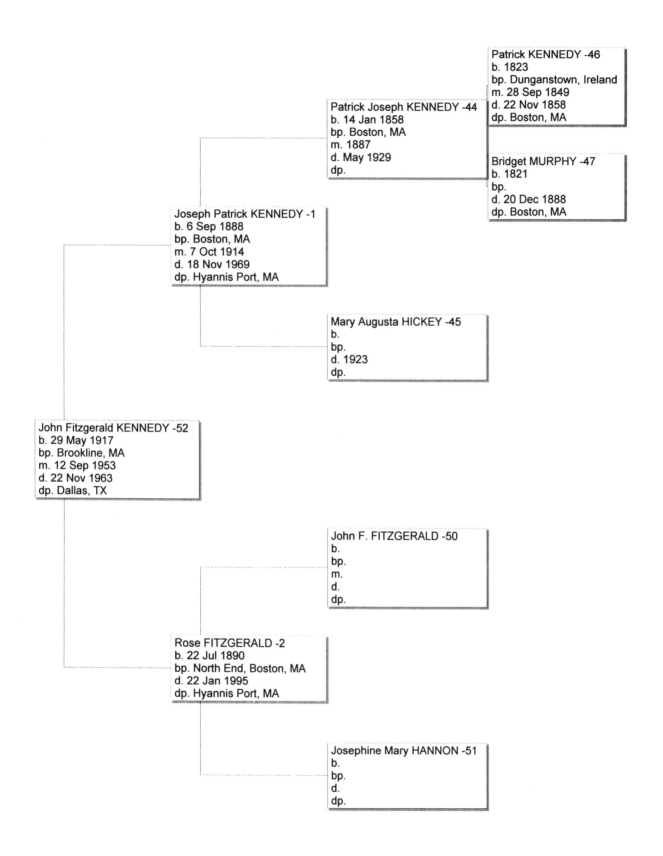

Patrick KENNEDY -46
b. 1823
bp. Dunganstown, Ireland
m. 28 Sep 1849
d. 22 Nov 1858
dp. Boston, MA

Patrick Joseph KENNEDY -44
b. 14 Jan 1858
bp. Boston, MA
m. 1887
d. May 1929
dp.

Bridget MURPHY -47
b. 1821
bp.
d. 20 Dec 1888
dp. Boston, MA

Joseph Patrick KENNEDY -1
b. 6 Sep 1888
bp. Boston, MA
m. 7 Oct 1914
d. 18 Nov 1969
dp. Hyannis Port, MA

Mary Augusta HICKEY -45
b.
bp.
d. 1923
dp.

John Fitzgerald KENNEDY -52
b. 29 May 1917
bp. Brookline, MA
m. 12 Sep 1953
d. 22 Nov 1963
dp. Dallas, TX

John F. FITZGERALD -50
b.
bp.
m.
d.
dp.

Rose FITZGERALD -2
b. 22 Jul 1890
bp. North End, Boston, MA
d. 22 Jan 1995
dp. Hyannis Port, MA

Josephine Mary HANNON -51
b.
bp.
d.
dp.

Genius Family Tree

Version 1.5 for Windows

Basic Information

Peter Resch
PO Box 720
Woodridge QLD 4114
Australia
Voice: 011-61-7-3208-5657
e-mail: genius@gensol.com.au
http://www.gensol.com.au/genius.htm
Shareware fee: With Manual and Disk copy,
U.S. $48.00, AU $55.00 (Australian dollars)
With no Manual or Disk copy, U.S. $39.00,
AU $48.00
Demo available for download

System requirements: 386 or higher IBM
compatible, running Windows version 3.1,
or higher
RAM: at least 4MB
Hard drive: at least 1MB space
CD-ROM: not required

Program Information

Individuals per database: 5,000
Spouses per individual: 20
Children per relationship: 34 children
Spouses and children reordered: yes
Multiple parents: not supported
Field sizes: family name (20 characters),
given name (30 characters), location
(50 characters), individual notes (32,000
characters)
Note options: 1 note file per individual is
allowed, 1 note file for each family is
allowed (limited to 200 characters)
Program options: on-screen prompts, Tight
Date Checking, automatic uppercase
surnames, password protection, and
F-keys (hot keys)
Date options: can enter date in numerous
formats, but all will be converted
automatically to DDMMYYYY format,
partial dates are supported, Tight Date
Checking option allows to you make sure

all dates entered are valid, Date Checking
allows the use of the standard date
modifiers; can specify MDY or DMY
format by configuring Windows
International Short Date format
Search options: search for individuals by a
full or partial name, by the first and/or
last name field; precise search function
allows you to display only results which
match exactly names entered in the
search fields
Database maintenance and options:
backup and restore supported

Reports

View reports before printing: yes
Customized reports
♦   Options: can specify font, items to be
included
Data Sheets for Individuals
Descendant Chart
Pedigree Chart
List of All Individuals in the Database
List of Individuals with the Same Surname

Sources

Creation: sources can be entered in the notes
fields for each individual; a smaller
source field is available from the
individual edit screen

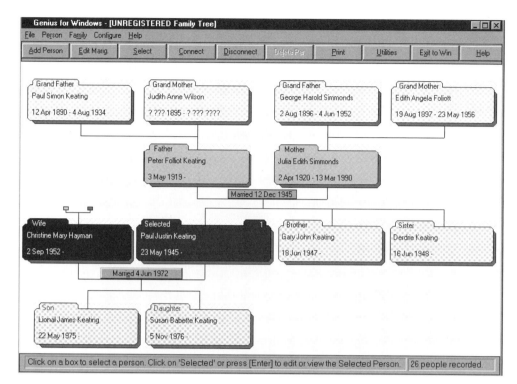

Figure 4.31
Genius Family
Tree: Tree View

Figure 4.32
Genius Family
Tree Individual
Edit

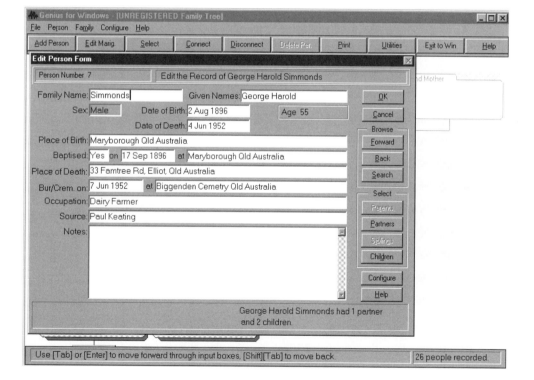

Pedigree Chart for Suzanne Deborah Keating
Person Number: 14

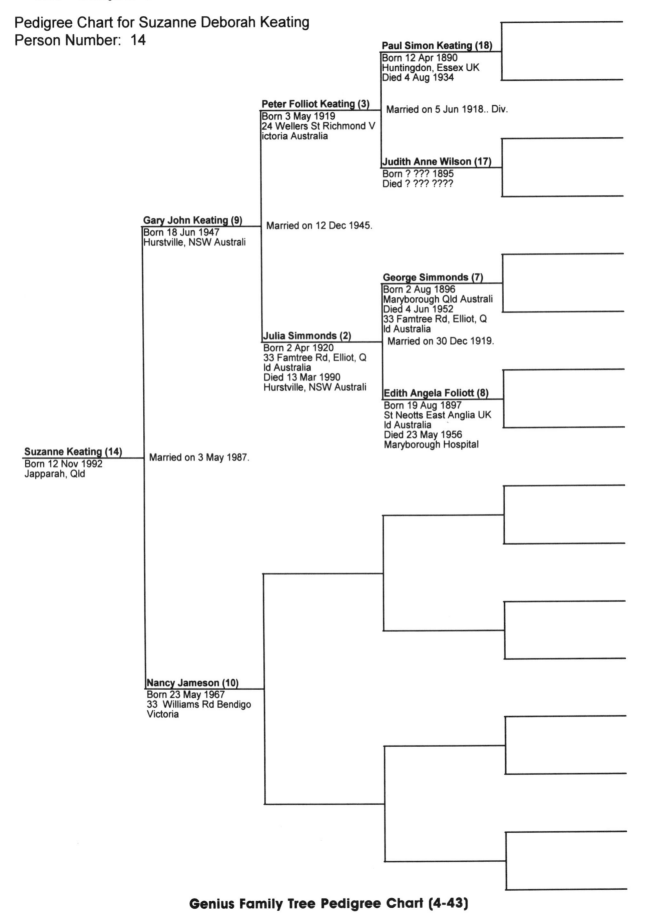

Paul Simon Keating (18)
Born 12 Apr 1890
Huntingdon, Essex UK
Died 4 Aug 1934

Peter Folliot Keating (3)
Born 3 May 1919
24 Wellers St Richmond Victoria Australia

Married on 5 Jun 1918.. Div.

Judith Anne Wilson (17)
Born ? ??? 1895
Died ? ??? ????

Gary John Keating (9)
Born 18 Jun 1947
Hurstville, NSW Australi

Married on 12 Dec 1945.

George Simmonds (7)
Born 2 Aug 1896
Maryborough Qld Australi
Died 4 Jun 1952
33 Famtree Rd, Elliot, Qld Australia

Married on 30 Dec 1919.

Julia Simmonds (2)
Born 2 Apr 1920
33 Famtree Rd, Elliot, Qld Australia
Died 13 Mar 1990
Hurstville, NSW Australi

Edith Angela Foliott (8)
Born 19 Aug 1897
St Neotts East Anglia UK
ld Australia
Died 23 May 1956
Maryborough Hospital

Suzanne Keating (14)
Born 12 Nov 1992
Japparah, Qld

Married on 3 May 1987.

Nancy Jameson (10)
Born 23 May 1967
33 Williams Rd Bendigo
Victoria

Genius Family Tree Pedigree Chart (4-43)

Descendants Chart for Edith Angela Foliott

1   2   3 <- Generation
Edith Angela Foliott (8)
Born 19 Aug 1897 at St Neotts East Anglia UK
Died 23 May 1956 at Maryborough Hospital
Married on 30 Dec 1919
George Harold Simmonds (7)
Born 2 Aug 1896 at Maryborough Qld Australia
Died 4 Jun 1952 at 33 Famtree Rd, Elliot, Qld Australia
    Julia Edith Simmonds (2)
    Born 2 Apr 1920 at 33 Famtree Rd, Elliot, Qld Australia
    Died 13 Mar 1990 at Hurstville, NSW Australia
    Married on 12 Dec 1945
    Peter Folliot Keating (3)
    Born 3 May 1919 at 24 Wellers St Richmond Victoria Australia
        Paul Justin Keating (1)
        Born 23 May 1945 at Hurstville, NSW Australia
        Married on 4 Jun 1972
        Christine Mary Hayman (4)
        Born 2 Sep 1952 at Biggenden Qld
        Gary John Keating (9)
        Born 18 Jun 1947 at Hurstville, NSW Australia
        Married on 3 May 1987
        Nancy Christine Jameson (10)
        Born 23 May 1967 at 33 Williams Rd Bendigo Victoria
        Derdrie Keating (20)
        Born 16 Jun 1948 at Hurstville, NSW Australia
         Not Married to
         Unknown (21)
         Born ? ??? ????
    Sally Simmonds (19)
    Born 9 Sep 1923 at Elliot, Qld Australia
    Died 26 Jul 1934 at Maryborough Hospital Qld.

Date:

Person Number: 8

Name: Foliott, Edith Angela   Female

Born 19 Aug 1897, Died 23 May 1956, Age   58

Born at St Neotts East Anglia UK

Baptised on ? ??? ???? at St Agnes Church, St Neotts East Anglia UK

Died at Maryborough Hospital

Interred at ? on ? ??? ????

Occupation: Farmers Wife

CHILDREN:
2.   Julia Edith Simmonds   2 Apr 1920 - 13 Mar 1990
19.   Sally Simmonds   9 Sep 1923 - 26 Jul 1934

PARTNER(s):
7.   George Harold Simmonds   2 Aug 1896 - 4 Jun 1952
      Married on 30 Dec 1919.
      St Andrews Church Biggenden Qld

Genus Senior

Version 2.13 for Windows

Basic Information

Business Computer of Finland, Inc.
Lonnrotinkatu 12 A
87100 KAJAANI
Finland
Voice: 011-358-8-6130-988
Fax: 011-358-8-6121-825
e-mail: Helpdesk@sytk.fi
http://www.mediabase.fi/suku/genupgb.htm
Price: 617–790 FIM (Finnish Marks) or about
$115.00–147.00 U.S.
Demo available for download

System requirements: IBM compatible
computer, Windows 3.1 or higher
RAM: 2MB (4MB recommended)
Hard drive: 2MB space (4MB recommended)
CD-ROM: not required

Program Information

Individuals per database: unlimited
Field options: can customize 5 numerical
fields, and 5 logical fields for each
individual (logical fields can be used to
assign surety levels)
Note options: each individual has unlimited
free-form text
Multimedia options: 5 images may be
attached to each individual (4 graphics
and 1 sound file), can specify preferred
photo
Date options: 4 extra date fields may be
added, can specify which date to use as
the conversion date from the Julian to
Gregorian calendar, can show weekdays
with dates
Program options: check for duplicate
individuals when information is saved,
set age limits (minimum and maximum)
for spouses and parents, specify in which
language you want to view the program,
unspecified gender-supported, personal

filters can be set for many operations
including graphic preview, export of
data, and searching; can display the
closest common ancestors of 2 individuals,
descendant-ancestor path for 2 individuals
Search options: surname, given name,
birth date, and numerical fields, can add
search words; can specify gender, whether
parents, spouses, or children exist (also
search for close relatives)
Index: supported (can specify whether or not
to create an index when the database is
opened)
Script options: edit relations for only those
people you specify via a script (which is
not saved upon exit of the program)
Database maintenance and options:
password protection supported

Reports

Customized reports
♦ Options (supported on most reports):
specify font, information to be included,
and terminology
Photos included: yes, in Ancestor and
Descendant Reports
Export data to text file: some reports
Sources included: most reports
Print reports in different languages:
supported
Ancestor Diagram
Ancestor Report (Pedigree Chart)
Descendant Diagram
Descendant List
Descendant Tables
Family Table Form (Family Group Sheet)
Persons List

Sources

Creation: can source all events, including the
4 extra data fields, with the exception
of marriage events

Comments

An older, less-featured version of the Genus
software (Genus Junior) is also available.

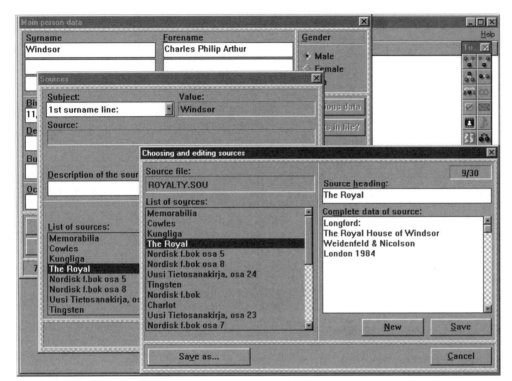

Figure 4.33
Genus Senior
Editing Sources

Figure 4.34
Genus Senior
Individual Edit

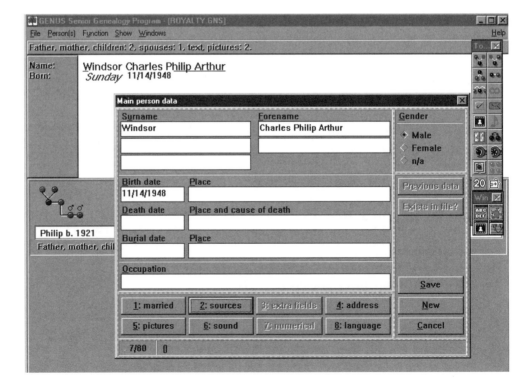

Name	Father	From table
Windsor, Charles Philip Arthur	, Philip	
	Mother	From table
	, Elizabeth II	1

Birth date and place	
11/14/1948.	
Death date and place	

Spouse	Table
Spencer, Diana Frances	
Wedding day and place	
Birth date and place	
07/01/1961.	
Death date and place	

Spouse's parents	Table
	Table

Spouse	Table
Wedding day and place	
Birth date and place	
Death date and place	

Spouse's parents	Table
	Table

Biographical data on main person and his/hers spouses

[ ] Continued on the other side of the page

Children	Table		Table
William b. 1982			
d.	Table		Table
Henry b. 1984			
d.	Table		Table
	Table		Table

Sources

The information on this chart may not be correct and is for demonstration purposes only.

Genus Senior Family Table (4-46)

```
    George VI (Albert) (1)
    b. 1895  d. 1952
    !
    +- Elizabeth II (2)
    !  b. 1926
    !  !
    !  +-Windsor Charles Philip Arthur (3)
    !  !  b. 11/14/1948
    !  !  !
    !  !  +- William (4)
    !  !  !  b. 1982
    !  !  !
    !  !  +- Henry (4)
    !  !     b. 1984
    !  !
    !  +- Anne (3)
    !  !  b. 1950
    !  !  !
    !  !  +- Peter (4)
    !  !     b. 1977
    !  !
    !  +- Andrew (3)
    !  !  b. 1960
    !  !  !
    !  !  +- Eunige Victoria Helena (4)
    !  !  !
    !  !  +- Beatrice (4)
    !  !     b. 1988
    !  !
    !  +- Edward (3)
    !     b. 1964
    !
    +- Margaret (Margaret Rose) (2)
       b. 1930
       !
       +- David - Viscount Linley (3)
       !  b. 1961
       !
       +- Lady Sarah Armstrong-Jones (3)
          b. 1964
```

There were 14 persons in the report.

Genus Senior Descendant List (4-47)

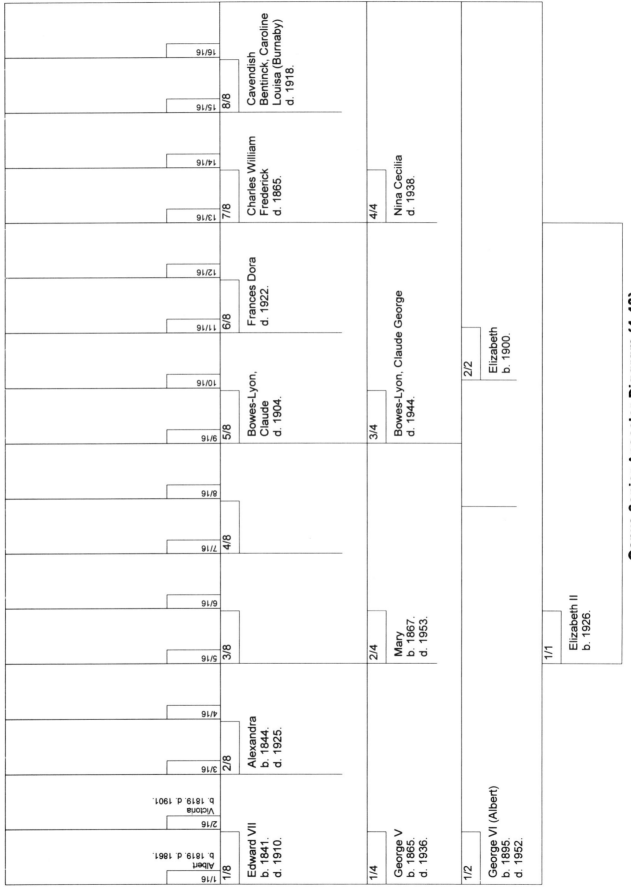

Genus Senior Ancestor Diagram (4-48)

16/16

8/8 Cavendish Bentinck, Caroline Louisa (Burnaby) d. 1918.

15/16

14/16

7/8 Charles William Frederick d. 1865.

13/16

4/4 Nina Cecilia d. 1938.

12/16

6/8 Frances Dora d. 1922.

11/16

10/16

5/8 Bowes-Lyon, Claude d. 1904.

9/16

3/4 Bowes-Lyon, Claude George d. 1944.

2/2 Elizabeth b. 1900.

8/16

4/8

7/16

6/16

3/8

5/16

2/4 Mary b. 1867. d. 1953.

1/1 Elizabeth II b. 1926.

4/16

2/8 Alexandra b. 1844. d. 1925.

3/16

Victoria b. 1819. d. 1901.

2/16

1/8 Edward VII b. 1841. d. 1910.

Albert b. 1819. d. 1861.

1/16

1/4 George V b. 1865. d. 1936.

1/2 George VI (Albert) b. 1895. d. 1952.

Kindred Konnections

For Windows

Basic Information

Kindred Konnections, Inc.
PO Box 1882
Orem, UT 84059
Voice: 801-229-7967
e-mail: feedback@kindredkonnections.com
http://www.kindredkonnections.com
Telephone support: $20.00 per year
Demo available for download

System requirements: IBM compatible,
    running Windows 3.1 or higher
CD-ROM: not required

Program Information

Individuals per database: 8 million
Children reordered: yes
Name options: titles supported
Field sizes: surname (60 characters), 3 given
    names (40 characters), 4 place fields (40
    characters)
Notes options: each individual is allowed a
    notes section, and a historical documents
    file accessed by means of a word processor
Program options: reminder exit message can
    be created, function to view Kindred
    Konnections CDs is available
Update options: update find lists and
    pedigree chart numbers supported
Database maintenance and options:
    Backup and restore function supported

Reports

Customized reports
- Options: can specify font and individuals
  to include

Family Pedigree Chart
- 4 generation
- Cascading charts

Descendancy Chart
- Specify the number of generations

Birthday Calendar
Family Group Sheets
Index

Sources

Creation: notes section linked to each event
    is available (general, name, birth,
    christening, death, burial, and ordinance)
    as well as notes for each marriage
    (marriage date, place, divorce, sealing
    date, and annulment)

Comments

This software is geared for customers of the
Kindred Konnections products (Crystal
Connections CD and a Web-based library of
GEDCOM submissions). As such, it is not a
"power" genealogy program.

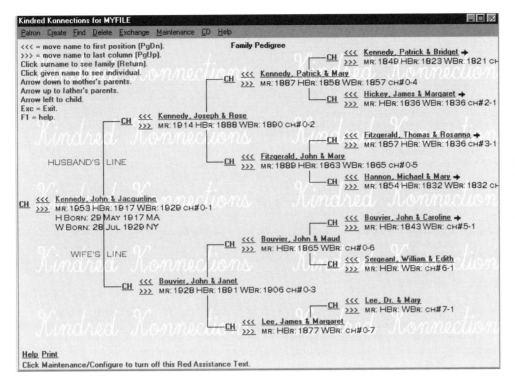

Figure 4.35
Kindred
Konnections
Pedigree View

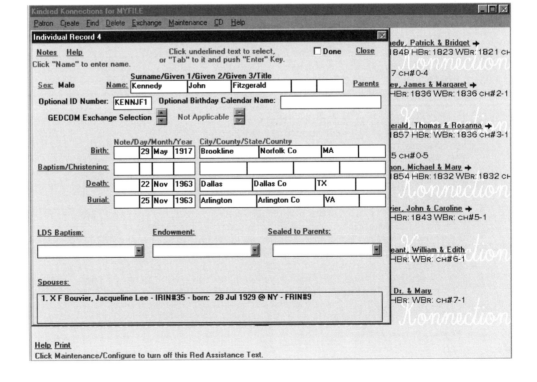

Figure 4.36
Kindred
Konnections
Individual Edit

DESCENDANCY CHART

```
1-- Kennedy, Joseph Patrick - IRIN#1 - Born:  6 Sep 1888 - Died:  18 Nov 1969
 sp-Fitzgerald, Rose - IRIN#2 - Born:  22 Jul 1890 - Died:  22 Jan 1995 - MRIN#1 - Marr:  7
    2-- Kennedy, Joseph Patrick - IRIN#3 - Born:   Jul 1915 - Died:  2 Aug 1944
    2-- Kennedy, John Fitzgerald - IRIN#52 - Born:  29 May 1917 - Died:  22 Nov 1963
       sp-Bouvier, Jacqueline - IRIN#53 - Born:  28 Jul 1929 - Died:  19 May 1994 - MRIN#13 -
          3-- Kennedy, Caroline Bouvier - IRIN#54 - Born:  27 Nov 1957 - Died:
          3-- Kennedy, John Fitzgerald - IRIN#55 - Born:  25 Nov 1960 - Died:
           sp-Carolyne - IRIN#71 - Born:        - Died:        - MRIN#21 - Marr:
          3-- Kennedy, Patrick Bouvier - IRIN#56 - Born:  7 Aug 1963 - Died:  9 Aug 1963
    2-- Kennedy, Rosemary - IRIN#4 - Born:     Sep 1918 - Died:
    2-- Kennedy, Kathleen - IRIN#6 - Born:       1920 - Died:  13 May 1948
     sp-Cavendish, William John Robert - IRIN#5 - Born:  10 Dec 1917 - Died:  10 Sep 1944 -
    2-- Kennedy, Eunice Mary - IRIN#8 - Born:    Jul 1921 - Died:
     sp-Shriver, Robert Sargent - IRIN#7 - Born:  9 Nov 1915 - Died:        - MRIN#3 - Marr:  2
        3-- Shriver, Robert Sargent - IRIN#9 - Born:       1954 - Died:
        3-- Shriver, Maria - IRIN#11 - Born:      - Died:
         sp-Schwarzenegger, Arnold - IRIN#10 - Born:        - Died:        - MRIN#4 - Marr:
        3-- Shriver, Timothy - IRIN#12 - Born:      - Died:
        3-- Shriver, Mark Kennedy - IRIN#13 - Born:    Feb 1964 - Died:
        3-- Shriver, Anthony Paul - IRIN#14 - Born:  20 Jul 1965 - Died:
    2-- Kennedy, Patricia - IRIN#16 - Born:  6 May 1924 - Died:
     sp-Lawford, Peter - IRIN#15 - Born:  7 Sep 1923 - Died:        - MRIN#5 - Marr:
        3-- Lawford, Christopher - IRIN#17 - Born:       - Died:
        3-- Lawford, Victoria - IRIN#18 - Born:        - Died:
        3-- Lawford, Sydney - IRIN#19 - Born:        - Died:
        3-- Lawford, Robin - IRIN#20 - Born:        - Died:
    2-- Kennedy, Robert Francis - IRIN#21 - Born:  20 Nov 1925 - Died:  6 Jun 1968
     sp-Skakel, Ethel - IRIN#22 - Born:       1928 - Died:        - MRIN#6 - Marr:  17 Jun 1950
        3-- Kennedy, Kathleen Hartington - IRIN#23 - Born:  4 Jul 1951 - Died:
        3-- Kennedy, Joseph Patrick - IRIN#24 - Born:       1952 - Died:
        3-- Kennedy, Robert Francis - IRIN#25 - Born:       1953 - Died:
        3-- Kennedy, David Anthony - IRIN#26 - Born:       1954 - Died:
        3-- Kennedy, Mary Courtney - IRIN#27 - Born:       1955 - Died:
        3-- Kennedy, Michael L. - IRIN#28 - Born:       1957 - Died:
        3-- Kennedy, Mary Kerry - IRIN#29 - Born:       1958 - Died:
        3-- Kennedy, Christopher George - IRIN#30 - Born:  4 Jun 1963 - Died:
        3-- Kennedy, Matthew Maxwell Taylor - IRIN#31 - Born:  9 Jan 1965 - Died:
        3-- Kennedy, Douglas Harriman - IRIN#32 - Born:  24 Mar 1967 - Died:
        3-- Kennedy, Rory Elizabeth - IRIN#33 - Born:  12 Dec 1968 - Died:
    2-- Kennedy, Jean Ann - IRIN#35 - Born:    Feb 1928 - Died:
     sp-Smith, Stephen Edward - IRIN#34 - Born:        - Died:        - MRIN#7 - Marr:    1956
        3-- Smith, Stephen - IRIN#36 - Born:        - Died:
        3-- Smith, William Kennedy - IRIN#37 - Born:    Sep 1960 - Died:
        3-- Smith, Amanda - IRIN#38 - Born:        - Died:
    2-- Kennedy, Edward Moore - IRIN#39 - Born:  22 Feb 1932 - Died:
     sp-Bennett, Virginia Joan - IRIN#40 - Born:        - Died:        - MRIN#8 - Marr:  29 Nov 19
        3-- Kennedy, Kara Ann - IRIN#41 - Born:    Mar 1960 - Died:
        3-- Kennedy, Edward More - IRIN#42 - Born:  26 Sep 1961 - Died:
        3-- Kennedy, Patrick Joseph - IRIN#43 - Born:    Aug 1963 - Died:
```

The information on this chart may not be correct and is for demonstration purposes only.

Kindred Konnections Descendancy Chart (4-49)

FAMILY GROUP RECORD (FRIN) - 1
Found on Pedigree Chart #0-1

HUSBAND - Kennedy, Joseph Patrick - IRIN#1

BORN: 6 Sep 1888   PLACE: Boston, MA
CHR.:   PLACE:
DIED: 18 Nov 1969   PLACE: Hyannis Port, MA
BUR: PLACE: Holyhood Cemetery, Brookline, MA
MARR: 7 Oct 1914   PLACE: Boston, MA
FATHER: Kennedy, Patrick Joseph - IRIN#44   PARENTS' FRIN: 9
MOTHER: Hickey, Mary Augusta - IRIN#45

WIFE - Fitzgerald, Rose - IRIN#2

BORN: 22 Jul 1890   PLACE: North End, Boston, MA
CHR.:   PLACE:
DIED: 22 Jan 1995   PLACE: Hyannis Port, MA
BUR: 25 Jan 1995   PLACE: Holyhood Cemetery, Brookline, MA
MARR: 7 Oct 1914   PLACE: Boston, MA
FATHER: Fitzgerald, John F. - IRIN#50   PARENTS' FRIN: 12
MOTHER: Hannon, Josephine Mary - IRIN#51

CHILDREN

---

1.   NAME: Kennedy, Joseph Patrick - IRIN#3
---   BORN: Jul 1915   PLACE: Boston, MA
M   CHR.:   PLACE:
      DIED: 2 Aug 1944   PLACE: Suffolk, England
      BUR: PLACE:
      SPOUSE:
      MARR: PLACE: SS:

---

2.   NAME: Kennedy, John Fitzgerald - IRIN#52
---   BORN: 29 May 1917   PLACE: Brookline, MA
M   CHR.:   PLACE:
      DIED: 22 Nov 1963   PLACE: Dallas, TX
      BUR: 25 Nov 1963   PLACE: Arlington National, VA
      SPOUSE: Bouvier, Jacqueline - IRIN#53 - FRIN#13
      MARR: 12 Sep 1953   PLACE: Newport, RI

---

3.   NAME: Kennedy, Rosemary - IRIN#4
---   BORN: Sep 1918   PLACE: Boston, MA
F   CHR.:   PLACE:
      DIED: PLACE:
      BUR: PLACE:
      SPOUSE:
      MARR: PLACE: SS:

---

4.   NAME: Kennedy, Kathleen - IRIN#6
---   BORN: 1920   PLACE: Boston, MA
F   CHR.:   PLACE:
      DIED: 13 May 1948   PLACE: France
      BUR: PLACE:
      SPOUSE: Cavendish, William John Robert - IRIN#5 - FRIN#2
      MARR: 6 May 1944   PLACE: London

Relationship to:

Husband:_____

Wife:_____

Kindred Konnections Family Group Record (4-50)

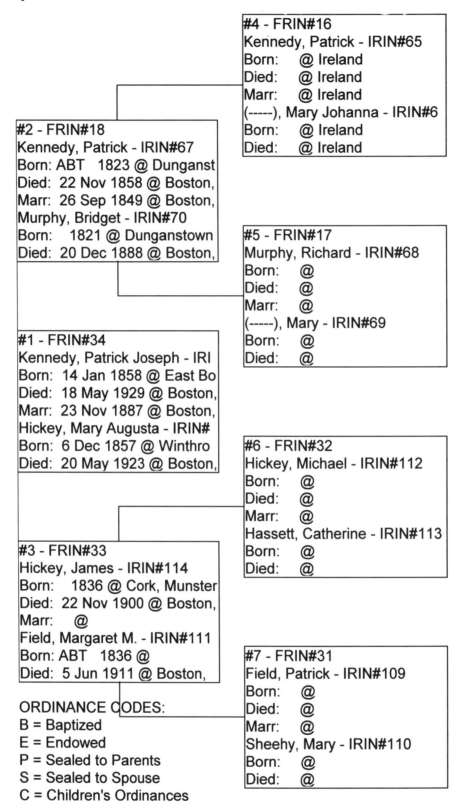

#4 - FRIN#16
Kennedy, Patrick - IRIN#65
Born: @ Ireland
Died: @ Ireland
Marr: @ Ireland
(-----), Mary Johanna - IRIN#6
Born: @ Ireland
Died: @ Ireland

#2 - FRIN#18
Kennedy, Patrick - IRIN#67
Born: ABT   1823 @ Dunganst
Died: 22 Nov 1858 @ Boston,
Marr: 26 Sep 1849 @ Boston,
Murphy, Bridget - IRIN#70
Born: 1821 @ Dunganstown
Died: 20 Dec 1888 @ Boston,

#5 - FRIN#17
Murphy, Richard - IRIN#68
Born: @
Died: @
Marr: @
(-----), Mary - IRIN#69
Born: @
Died: @

#1 - FRIN#34
Kennedy, Patrick Joseph - IRI
Born: 14 Jan 1858 @ East Bo
Died: 18 May 1929 @ Boston,
Marr: 23 Nov 1887 @ Boston,
Hickey, Mary Augusta - IRIN#
Born: 6 Dec 1857 @ Winthro
Died: 20 May 1923 @ Boston,

#6 - FRIN#32
Hickey, Michael - IRIN#112
Born: @
Died: @
Marr: @
Hassett, Catherine - IRIN#113
Born: @
Died: @

#3 - FRIN#33
Hickey, James - IRIN#114
Born: 1836 @ Cork, Munster
Died: 22 Nov 1900 @ Boston,
Marr: @
Field, Margaret M. - IRIN#111
Born: ABT   1836 @
Died: 5 Jun 1911 @ Boston,

ORDINANCE CODES:
B = Baptized
E = Endowed
P = Sealed to Parents
S = Sealed to Spouse
C = Children's Ordinances

#7 - FRIN#31
Field, Patrick - IRIN#109
Born: @
Died: @
Marr: @
Sheehy, Mary - IRIN#110
Born: @
Died: @

Kindred Konnections Family Pedigree Chart (4-51)

Kith and Kin
Version 3.11 for Windows

Basic Information

SpanSoft
11 Rowan Terrace
Cowdenbeath, Fife
KY4 9JZ Scotland
Voice/Fax: 011-441-383-510597
e-mail: SpanSoft@compuserve.com
http://ourworld.compuserve.com/homepages/
SpanSoft
Shareware fee: $48.00 U.S. (£28)
Demo available for download

System requirements: minimum 286,
    Windows 3.1 or higher
RAM: 4MB
Hard drive: 2MB space
CD-ROM: not required

Program Information

Individuals per database: 16,383 people and
    families (combined)
Spouses per individual: unlimited
Children per relationship: unlimited
Non-traditional marriages: supported
Name options: aliases supported
Field sizes: name (60 characters), location
    (200 characters), notes (9,500 characters)
Field options: 2 user-defined fields for
    individuals can be customized
Notes: individuals and families; can search
    and replace text in notes field, external
    notes are supported, can enter notes about
    image or other OLE object linked to
    individual or family
Multimedia options: unlimited graphics and
    OLE objects may be attached to individuals
Program options: a timeline of each family
    is available, the timeline database can be
    edited using the TimeGen utility (free to
    registered users), the right mouse button
    over a family graphic will display a
    summary of facts, Kithkin.ini file

allows you to change field names, date
names, etc. for translation into another
language, or your own customization
Date options: can specify date format,
    standard date modifiers are allowed,
    partial dates are allowed
Search options: text search function
    searches the entire database, specific
    fields can be selected for searching, date
    search is allowed; On This Day search
    displays all dates that match a specified day
Database maintenance and options: data
    integrity check is supported

Reports

View reports before printing: yes
Customize reports
◆   Options: can specify fonts for both
    screen and printed reports, individuals to
    include
Export data to text file: comma-delimited text
    file can be generated for some reports;
    some reports can be saved as text files
Notes printed: for families and individuals
Family Group Sheet
Index of Persons (or family)
Tree Layout
Indented Descendant Tree
Descendant Tree
Ancestral Tree
Timeline
Census Report
Missing Data Report

Sources

Creation: sources can be entered in the notes
    field for each individual and marriage

Comments

Kith and Kin is also known as *Of That Ilk* in
Australia and New Zealand.

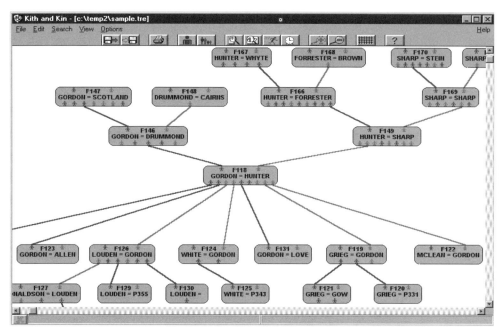

Figure 4.37
Kith and Kin
Pedigree/Tree View

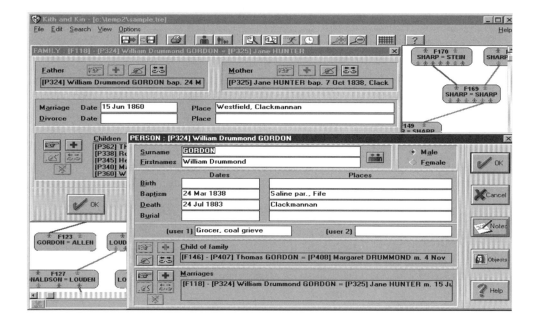

Figure 4.38
Kith and Kin
Individual Edit

Descendants of William Drummond GORDON [P324]

0   [P324] William Drummond GORDON bap. 24 March 1838 Saline par., Fife d. 24 July 1883 Clackmann
     m. [F118] 15 June 1860 Westfield, Clackmannan
     [P325] Jane HUNTER bap. 7 October 1838 Clackmannan d. 16 October 1916 Castle Street, Clackma

1   [P362] Thomas Drummond GORDON b. 7 May 1861 Saline, Fife d. 16 January 1919 Ladysmith,
         m. [F132] 9 October 1891 Vancouver, BC, Canada
         [P363] Elizabeth Charleston CALDERHEAD

2   [P364] Elizabeth Charleston Calderhead GORDON b. 27 May 1895 Wellington, BC, Canada

2   [P365] Jean Hunter GORDON b. 29 September 1898 Wellington, BC, Canada d. 22 Februar

2   [P366] Helen Mary GORDON b. 27 June 1900 Clackmannan d. 20 January 1935 Kamloops,

2   [P367] William Drummond GORDON b. 18 February 1902 Ladysmith, BC, Canada

2   [P369] Thomas Drummond GORDON b. EST 1907 Ladysmith, BC, Canada d. EST 1936 Ka

1   [P338] Robert Hunter GORDON b. 27 July 1863 Westfield, Clackmannan d. 17 April 1951 Stirling
         m. [F123] 13 June 1913 St. Giles, Edinburgh
         [P339] Jean ALLEN

1   [P345] Helen GORDON b. 19 July 1865 Hillend, Clackmannan
         m. [F126]
         [P346] James LOUDEN

2   [P347] Jean LOUDEN
             m. [F127]
             [P348] Stuart DONALDSON

3   [P349] Lorna DONALDSON

3   [P350] William DONALDSON

3   [P351] Stuart DONALDSON
                 m. [F128]
                 [P352] Sharon

Kith and Kin Descendant Tree (4-52)

Ancestors of William Drummond GORDON [P360]

[P486] Charles
FORRESTER
b. Kennet, Clackmannan

[P484] William   [P485] Jean
HUNTER   WHYTE

[P482] Peter   [P483] Mary
HUNTER   FORRESTER
b. 6 October 1766, Kennet, Clackmannan   b. 28 September 1766, Cl

[P413] Thomas
GORDON   [P414] Isabel
b. EST 20 May 1781   SCOTLAND

[P421] William   [P422] Williamina Eugenia
DRUMMOND   CAIRNS

[P407] Thomas
GORDON
b. 15 September 1810, Kinross
bap. 23 September 1810, Kinross
d. 6 August 1893, Kennet, Clackmannan

[P408] Margaret
DRUMMOND
b. EST 1813, Tillicoultry
d. 28 April 1888, Clackmannan Green

[P423] Robert
HUNTER
b. 10 December 1810, Clackmannan
d. 14 January 1880, Clackmannan

[P324] William Drummond
GORDON
bap. 24 March 1838, Saline par., Fife
d. 24 July 1883, Clackmannan

[P325] Jane
HUNTER
bap. 7 October 1838, Clackmannan
d. 16 October 1916, Castle Street, Clackmannan

[P360] William Drummond
GORDON
b. 26 January 1870, Clackmannan

Timeline

24 March 1838	[P324] William Drummond GORDON baptised at Saline par., Fife
7 October 1838	[P325] Jane HUNTER baptised at Clackmannan
15 June 1860	[F118] - [P324] William Drummond GORDON married at Westfield, Clackmannan
7 May 1861	[P362] Thomas Drummond GORDON born at Saline, Fife
27 July 1863	[P338] Robert Hunter GORDON born at Westfield, Clackmannan
19 July 1865	[P345] Helen GORDON born at Hillend, Clackmannan
6 November 1867	[P340] Margaret Hunter Drummond GORDON born at Clackmannan
26 January 1870	[P360] William Drummond GORDON born at Clackmannan
16 June 1872	[P337] James GORDON born at Clackmannan
7 July 1876	[P282] Mary Jane Hunter GORDON born at Clackmannan
2 June 1879	[P326] Catherine Hunter GORDON born
24 July 1883	[P324] William Drummond GORDON died at Clackmannan
October 1899	*Start of Boer War*
1900	*Invention of rigid airship by von Zeppelin*
23 January 1901	*Start of reign of Edward VII*
5 April 1902	*20 killed as terracing collapses at Ibrox Park*
1 June 1902	*End of Boer War*
4 October 1905	*Convicted Suffragettes choose to go to prison*
1906	*Wassermann test for syphilis developed*
6 May 1910	*End of reign of Edward VII*
7 May 1910	*Start of reign of George V*
31 July 1910	*Radio used to arrest Dr Crippen fleeing to Quebec*
31 August 1911	*Troops clash with strikers in north of England*
15 April 1912	*SS Titanic sinks with loss of 1513 lives*
10 February 1913	*Capt. Scott found dead in Antartica [sic]*
28 June 1914	*Austrian Archduke Ferdinand assassinated in Sarajevo*
28 July 1914	*Austria declares war on Serbia*
28 July 1914	*Start of World War I*
August 1914	*Battle of Tannenberg*
1 August 1914	*Germany declares war on Russia*
3 August 1914	*Germany declares war on France*
4 August 1914	*Britain declares war on Germany*
4 August 1914	*Germany invades Belgium*
September 1914	*First Battle of the Marne*
4 October 1914	*First bombs fall on London*
February 1915	*Start of German submarine blockade of Britain*
22 April 1915	*Germans first use of mustard gas at Ypres*

Legacy
Version 2.0 for Windows

Basic Information

Millennia Corporation
PO Box 1800
Duvall, WA 98019
Voice: 800-753-3453
Fax: 425-788-4493
e-mail: info@millenniacorp.com
http://www.legacyfamilytree.com
Price: $49.95
Demo available for download

System requirements: Intel 386, 486 or
   Pentium IBM compatible (Pentium
   recommended), running Windows 3.1 or
   Windows 95
RAM: 8MB (16MB recommended)
Hard drive: 10MB
CD-ROM: required for the CD version

Program Information

Individuals per database: unlimited,
   unknown genders allowed; database sizes
   up to 1GB are supported, 2 databases can
   be open simultaneously
Spouses per individual: unlimited
Children per relationship: 60
Children reordered: yes
Multiple parents allowed: yes
Name options: aliases, unlimited alternate
   names, titles (title fields are 50 characters)
Field sizes: name (120 characters), location
   (120 characters), notes (65,535 characters)
Event options: unlimited events per
   individual, unlimited sources per event,
   can add and remove events to the pre-
   defined master event list; can change the
   display order of events
Note options: general notes, research notes,
   and medical notes sections supported
Multimedia options: unlimited pictures and
   sounds may be linked to an individual,
   can change picture attributes in photo
   album (caption, date, picture description),

can print or create slide show from photo
album, can specify which picture is
preferred for use on family and pedigree
views, pictures may be manipulated by the
zoom, edit, and print picture functions
Program options: data can be viewed in
   either family view or pedigree view,
   reference numbers and Ancestral File
   numbers are supported, can open 8
   Family or Pedigree view windows at once;
   in Pedigree view, information box pops up
   when you hold the cursor over an
   individual with links to the edit screen,
   photo gallery, and the notes section
Ditto-key entries: calendar pop-up allows you
   to quickly fill in a date field
Date options: can specify date format,
   standard date qualifiers, and double dates
   are supported
Search options: query by example (fill in the
   info you want to search, and how you
   want to search for it: name, gender, exact
   search, starts with, anywhere in field),
   detailed search (use AND/OR modifiers to
   look for individuals in specific places),
   miscellaneous search (special purpose
   searches: find ancestors, descendants,
   youngest direct-line generation, records
   with bad dates, etc.)
Tag options: can tag and mark individuals
   and marriages, 3 tags (levels) available
Database maintenance and options:
   database and duplicate individual merge
   supported, backup and restore function
   supported, database compact supported

Reports

View reports before printing: yes
Customized reports
♦ Options: specify font, individuals to
   include, information to include, layout and
   format
Photos included: yes (most reports)

Family Group Sheet
- Cascading charts
- Photos

Descendant and Ancestor Reports
- Specify number of generations to include
- Layout (boxes, drop shadows)

Pedigree Charts
- 4, 5, or 6 generations
- Cascading charts
- Layout (boxes, drop shadows)
- Sorted index

Individual Report
- Photos
- Index

Timeline
- Specify number of years across page, and average life span

Lineage Report
- Photos

Ahnentafel
- Photos
- Specify number of generations
- Title page
- Table of contents
- Index in a variety of formats
- Customize layout

Modified Register Books
- Photos
- Specify number of generations
- Title page
- Table of contents
- Index in a variety of formats
- Customize layout

Ages Reports (shows ages of a couple for certain events)

Source Citation Report
- Sources and comments for each individual and marriage

Calendar Report

List Reports

Surname Summary

Potential Problems Report

Information Report

LDS Ordinance Report

Blank Reports
- Census Forms (1790–1920)
- Family Information Questionnaire
- Relationship Diagram
- Research Log

Sources

Creation: add, delete, or edit a source citation (editing a source allows you to globally change the citation), new source types can be added to the pre-defined list; source clipboard holds a copy of the current citation you are working with (allowing you to record the source quickly)

Source library: master source list allows source citation for multiple people

Surety levels: supported

Bells and Whistles

- Up to 160 bookmarks can be set (book marks allow you to return to a specific individual quickly)
- Can generate a Web page from database
- Data import (PAF) and export (PAF, Ancestral File, TempleReady formats)

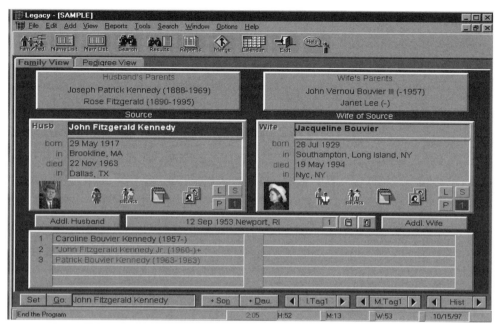

Figure 4.39
Legacy Family
View

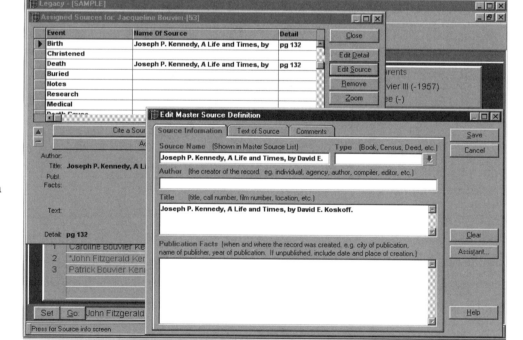

Figure 4.40
Legacy
Sourcing Screen

Family Group Sheet

Husband	Patrick Joseph Kennedy			
Born	14 Jan 1858	Boston, MA		
Christened				
Died	May 1929			
Buried				
Father	Patrick Kennedy (1823-1858)		Mother	Bridget Murphy (1821-1888)
Married	1887			

Wife	Mary Augusta Hickey	
Born		
Christened		
Died	1923	
Buried		

Children			
1	**M**	**Joseph Patrick Kennedy**	
Born		6 Sep 1888	Boston, MA
Christened			
Died		18 Nov 1969	Hyannis Port, MA
Buried			Holyhood Cemetery, Brookline, MA
Spouse		Rose Fitzgerald (1890-1995)	7 Oct 1914, Boston, MA
2	**F**	**Loretta Kennedy**	
Born		1892	Boston, MA
Christened			
Died			
Buried			
3	**F**	**Margaret Kennedy**	
Born		1898	
Christened			
Died			
Buried			
Spouse		Charles Burke (-)	

Husband's Notes

As a young man, Patrick dropped out of school to work on
the docks of Boston.

Patrick was able to work his way from being a SaloonKeeper
to becoming a Ward Boss, helping out other Irish
immigrants. His popularity rose and at the age of thirty
he had become a power in Boston politics. In 1892 and 1893
he was elected to the Massachusetts Senate.

Patrick later became a very successful businessman getting
into wholesale liquor sales, owning a coal company and
becoming the president of a bank.

His personality was mild-mannered, quiet and reserved, and
he was viewed as a man of moderate habits.

Meridian St., East Boston, MA

Pedigree Chart

No. 1 on this chart is the same as no. 1 on chart no. 1

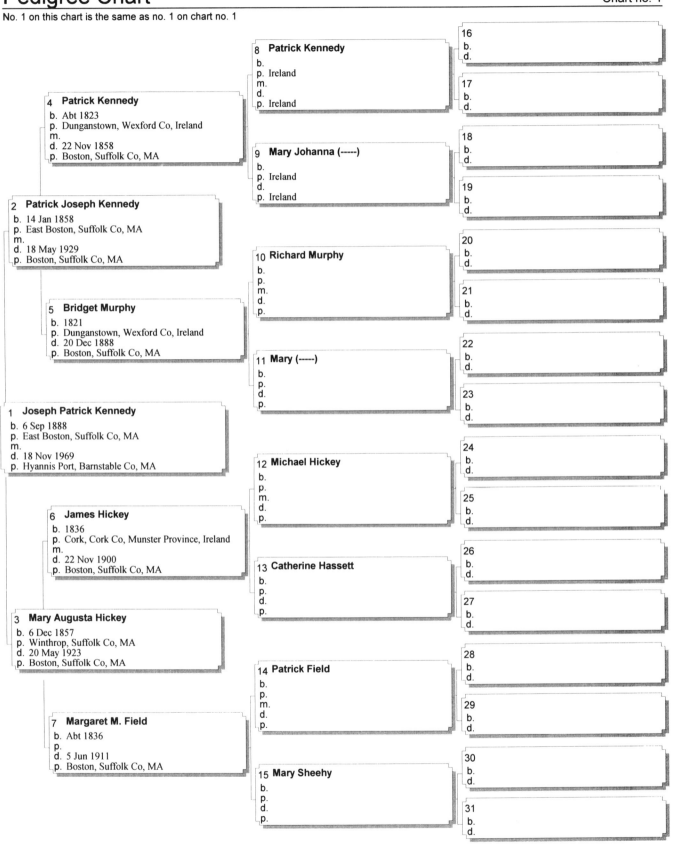

16
b.
d.

8 **Patrick Kennedy**
b.
p. Ireland
m.
d.
p. Ireland

17
b.
d.

4 **Patrick Kennedy**
b. Abt 1823
p. Dunganstown, Wexford Co, Ireland
m.
d. 22 Nov 1858
p. Boston, Suffolk Co, MA

18
b.
d.

9 **Mary Johanna (-----)**
b.
p. Ireland
d.
p. Ireland

19
b.
d.

2 **Patrick Joseph Kennedy**
b. 14 Jan 1858
p. East Boston, Suffolk Co, MA
m.
d. 18 May 1929
p. Boston, Suffolk Co, MA

20
b.
d.

10 **Richard Murphy**
b.
p.
m.
d.
p.

21
b.
d.

5 **Bridget Murphy**
b. 1821
p. Dunganstown, Wexford Co, Ireland
d. 20 Dec 1888
p. Boston, Suffolk Co, MA

22
b.
d.

11 **Mary (-----)**
b.
p.
d.
p.

23
b.
d.

1 **Joseph Patrick Kennedy**
b. 6 Sep 1888
p. East Boston, Suffolk Co, MA
m.
d. 18 Nov 1969
p. Hyannis Port, Barnstable Co, MA

24
b.
d.

12 **Michael Hickey**
b.
p.
m.
d.
p.

25
b.
d.

6 **James Hickey**
b. 1836
p. Cork, Cork Co, Munster Province, Ireland
m.
d. 22 Nov 1900
p. Boston, Suffolk Co, MA

26
b.
d.

13 **Catherine Hassett**
b.
p.
d.
p.

27
b.
d.

3 **Mary Augusta Hickey**
b. 6 Dec 1857
p. Winthrop, Suffolk Co, MA
d. 20 May 1923
p. Boston, Suffolk Co, MA

28
b.
d.

14 **Patrick Field**
b.
p.
m.
d.
p.

29
b.
d.

7 **Margaret M. Field**
b. Abt 1836
p.
d. 5 Jun 1911
p. Boston, Suffolk Co, MA

30
b.
d.

15 **Mary Sheehy**
b.
p.
d.
p.

31
b.
d.

Legacy Pedigree Chart (4-56)

Ancestors of Joseph Patrick Kennedy

First Generation

1. Joseph Patrick Kennedy (3) was born 6 Sep 1888 in East Boston, Suffolk Co, MA. He was christened 9 Sep 1888 in East Boston, Suffolk Co, MA. Joseph died 18 Nov 1969 in Hyannis Port, Barnstable Co, MA. He was buried Nov 1969 in Brookline, Norfolk Co, MA. User ID:KENNJP88.

Joseph married Rose Elizabeth Fitzgerald, daughter of John Francis "Honey Fitz" Fitzgerald and Mary Josephine Hannon, on 7 Oct 1914 in Boston, Suffolk Co, MA(3).

Second Generation (Parents)

2. Patrick Joseph Kennedy (3) was born 14 Jan 1858 in East Boston, Suffolk Co, MA. He was christened 16 Jan 1858 in East Boston, Suffolk Co, MA. Patrick died 18 May 1929 in Boston, Suffolk Co, MA. He was buried in Malden, Middlesex Co, MA. User ID:KENNPJ58.

Patrick married Mary Augusta Hickey, daughter of James Hickey and Margaret M. Field, on 23 Nov 1887 in Boston, Suffolk Co, MA(3).

3. Mary Augusta Hickey (3) was born 6 Dec 1857 in Winthrop, Suffolk Co, MA. She died 20 May 1923 in Boston, Suffolk Co, MA. Mary was buried in Malden, Middlesex Co, MA. User ID:HICKMA57.

Mary married Patrick Joseph Kennedy, son of Patrick Kennedy and Bridget Murphy, on 23 Nov 1887 in Boston, Suffolk Co, MA(3).

Third Generation (Grandparents)

4. Patrick Kennedy (3) was born Abt 1823 in Dunganstown, Wexford Co, Ireland. He died 22 Nov 1858 in Boston, Suffolk Co, MA. Patrick was buried 23 Nov 1858 in Cambridge, Middlesex Co, MA. User ID:KENNPA23.

Patrick married Bridget Murphy, daughter of Richard Murphy and Mary (-----), on 26 Sep 1849 in Boston, Suffolk Co, MA(3).

5. Bridget Murphy (3) was born 1821 in Dunganstown, Wexford Co, Ireland. She died 20 Dec 1888 in Boston, Suffolk Co, MA. Bridget was buried in Malden, Middlesex Co, MA. User ID:MURPBR21.

Bridget married Patrick Kennedy, son of Patrick Kennedy and Mary Johanna (-----), on 26 Sep 1849 in Boston, Suffolk Co, MA(3).

6. James Hickey (3) was born 1836 in Cork, Cork Co, Munster Province, Ireland. He died 22 Nov

The Master Genealogist

Version 3.5 for Windows

Basic Information

Wholly Genes, Inc.
5144 Flowertuft Court
Columbia, MD 21044
Voice: 410-796-2447
Fax: 410-379-5424
e-mail: tmg@whollygenes.com
http://www.whollygenes.com
Price: $99.00 (Gold edition), $59.00 (Silver edition), or $99.00 (DOS)
Demo (slide show only) available for download

System requirements: IBM compatible (386 required, 486 recommended) running Windows 3.x or higher, Windows NT, or OS/2
RAM: 8MB (16MB recommended)
Hard drive: at least 15MB (Gold Edition)
Monitor: VGA or higher
CD-ROM: required for CD version
Optional hardware: TWAIN-compatible scanner, and sound card

Program Information

Individuals per database: unlimited
Spouses per individual: unlimited
Children per relationship: unlimited
Children and spouses reordered: yes (can specify children's birth order)
Name options: can specify primary name; honorific titles, prefixes, and suffixes are supported
Field sizes: fields default to 100 characters, but you can change that number in the program's preferences
Event options: unlimited events (aka tags) per individual, can edit and create new tag types (100 pre-set tags available), can assign surety levels, can add citations for each tag, can specify if an individual was a witness to an event
Note options: private information can be specified not to be included on reports by

using 4 exclude features (exclusion marker, double exclusion marker, sensitivity brackets, hidden text); can create memos
Multimedia options: sound and image files supported, 4 ways to attach an object to an individual (internal, external, linked, embedded), OLE objects supported, can modify images, can scan directly into the program, several image formats supported
Program options: 3 data views (person, family, tree), tags (item of information about a person or persons such as events, names, etc.) record information about individuals, text macros and hot keys are supported, can set flags (which marks certain characteristics) to locate individuals, can view individual data in a timeline, master place list supported, global search and replace supported
Ditto-key entry: supported
Date options: calendar feature available, can specify date format (9 display formats available), regnal date converter supported (dates given in terms of the reign of an English monarch), standard modifiers supported, double dating supported, date field can be sorted
Search options: search by ID number, ahnentafel number, or Picklist (sorted names of individuals in the database); you can use a filter to search Picklist
Merge options: database files, individuals
Database options: backup and restore, repair, re-index, and optimize database supported

Reports

View reports before printing: yes
Customized reports
• Options: customized via Custom Report Writer function (can specify font, layout, format, items to include, individuals to

include), Report Definition function show specific characteristics for each report, filters, can copy report template and modify to your own specifications

Save file to text: yes

Ahnentafel
- Note missing people as unknown people
- Display information in columns
- Embedded memos

Audit (checks data for errors)

Bibliography (alphabetical list of sources)

Descendancy Chart
- Sort children
- Follow surname only

Descendancy Narrative
- Sort children
- Specify outline numbering style

Distribution of People report

Family Group Sheet
- Restrict to only birth, marriage, and death events
- Spouse and children options

Genealogy Report
- Sort children
- Specify sentence construction style
- Descendants or ancestors format
- Register, Modified Register, TAG (The American Genealogist), and custom formats available

Index

Individual Detail
- Timeline can be printed for an individual

Individual Narrative
- Bibliography available

Linear Ahnentafel
- Lineage from 1 person directly to another
- Display information in columns

Lists
- Citations
- Events
- Names
- People
- Repositories
- Sources
- Tasks

Memos/Sources (can be included in narrative reports and charts)

Pedigree Report
- 4 or 5 generations
- Compressed pedigree supported

Table of Contents

Sources

Creation: master source list manages sources, can search for sources, source definition has 4 parts (general information, supplemental, attachments, output form specification)

Options: source abbreviations limited to 30 characters, master repository list is supported, can cite a source globally

Bells and Whistles

- Highly customizable reports
- Can set bookmarks
- Spell checker available
- Import data from PAF or Roots III
- Useful research log allows you to assign research tasks to an individual, event, source, or repository
- Export to text, dBase, Lotus, and Excel file formats
- Built-in text editor
- Report Wizard guides you through creating reports from scratch
- National Geographic Names Database is included with the CD-ROM version
- Creates Web pages

Comments

There are 2 versions of The Master Genealogist (TMG) available: The Gold Edition (includes Ancestry Genealogy Library CD) and the Silver Edition (program and National Geographic Names Database only). TMG is also available for DOS. The Wholly Genes Web site contains information about the program, an interactive demo, an online newsletter, and information about user's groups.

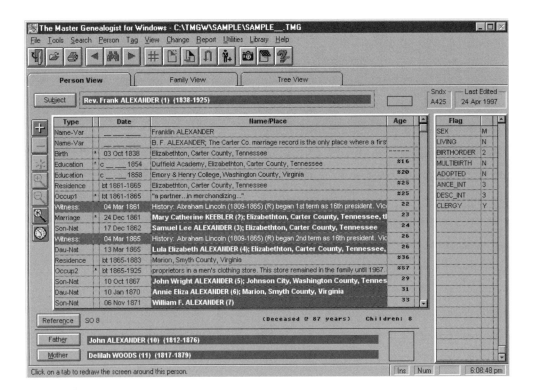

Figure 4.41
The Master
Genealogist Person
View

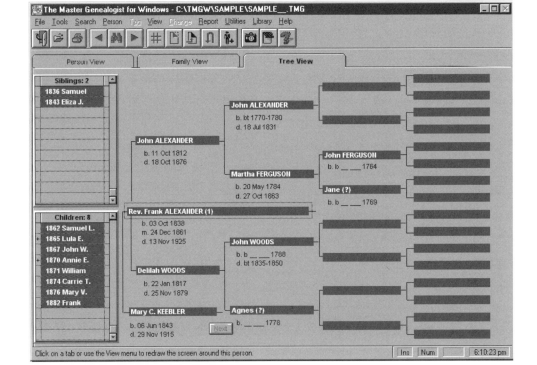

Figure 4.42
The Master
Genealogist
Pedigree View

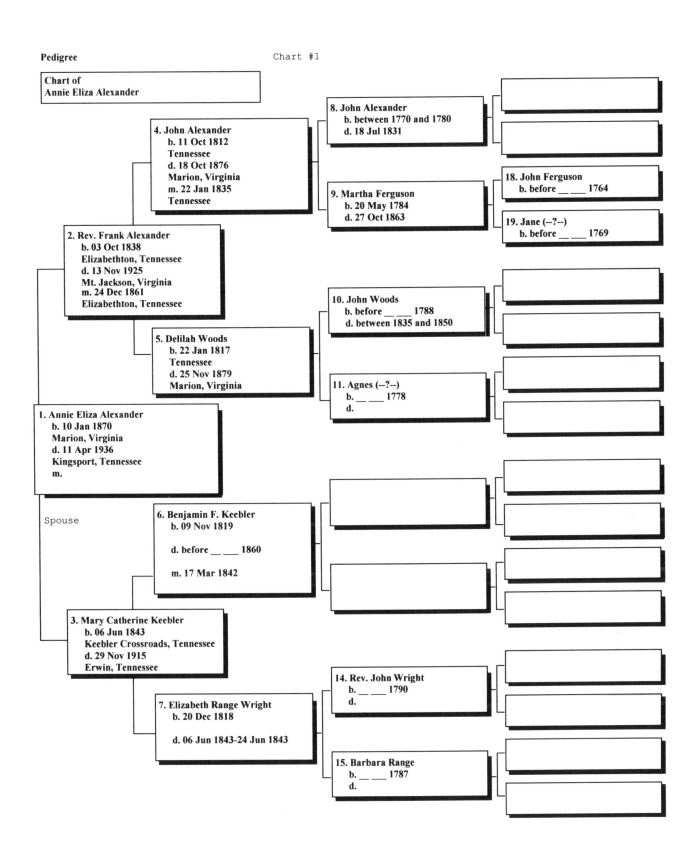

The Master Genealogist Pedigree Chart (4-58)

Family Group

Subject* Rev. Frank ALEXANDER
        Birth*   03 Oct 1838   Elizabethton, Tennessee.[1,2]
        Death*   13 Nov 1925   Mt. Jackson, Virginia.[3,4]
        Burial*   __ ___ ____   Marion, Virginia.[5]
Father* John ALEXANDER (1812-1876)
Mother* Delilah WOODS (1817-1879)

        Marriage*   24 Dec 1861   Elizabethton, Tennessee.[6,7,4]

Spouse* Mary Catherine KEEBLER
        Birth*   06 Jun 1843   Keebler Crossroads, Tennessee.[4,6]
        Death*   29 Nov 1915   Erwin, Tennessee.[6,8,9]
        Burial*   __ ___ ____   Marion, Virginia.[10]
Father* Benjamin Franklin KEEBLER (1819-1860)
Mother* Elizabeth Range WRIGHT (1818-1843)

Eight Children

1/M   Samuel Lee ALEXANDER
        Birth*   17 Dec 1862   Elizabethton, Tennessee.[6]
        Death*   29 Nov 1932   [8]
        Burial*   __ ___ ____   Marion, Virginia.[8]

2/F   Lula Elizabeth ALEXANDER
        Birth*   13 Mar 1865   Elizabethton, Tennessee.[6,11]
        Marriage*   22 Jul 1885   Robert Moore BALDWIN (1866-1946); Union, Virginia.[12]
        Daughter: 01 Oct 1893   Louise Kyle BALDWIN[12]
        Death*   18 Oct 1954   Richmond, Virginia.[12]

3/M   John Wright ALEXANDER
        Birth*   10 Oct 1867   Johnson City, Tennessee.[6,8]
        Death*   04 Jan 1891   Belfast Mills, Virginia.[6]
        Burial*   __ ___ ____   Marion, Virginia.[13]

4/F   Annie Eliza ALEXANDER
        Birth*   10 Jan 1870   Marion, Virginia.[6,4]
        Marriage*   08 Dec 1896   John Keys FUGATE (1859-1922); Dickensonville, Virginia.[14]
        Son: 11 Dec 1900   Joseph Alexander FUGATE[15]
        Daughter: 10 May 1903   Mary Virginia FUGATE[12]
        Daughter: 13 May 1906   Elizabeth Keys FUGATE; Castlewood, Virginia.[12]
        Death*   11 Apr 1936   Kingsport, Tennessee.[16]
        Burial*   __ ___ ____   Bristol, Tennessee.[12]

5/M   William Franklin ALEXANDER
        Birth*   06 Nov 1871   [6,4]

The Master Genealogist Family Group Sheet (4-59)

Ahnentafel of Mary Virginia Alexander

--- 1st Generation ---

1. Mary Virginia Alexander was born on 13 May 1876. She married Rev. Thomas Jefferson Houts on 11 Sep 1912 at New Blountville, Tennessee. She died on 12 Nov 1958 at Knoxville, Tennessee, at age 82. She was buried at Marion, Smyth County, Virginia.

--- 2nd Generation ---

2. Rev. Frank Alexander was born on 3 Oct 1838 at Elizabethton, Carter County, Tennessee, son of John Alexander and Delilah Woods. He married Mary Catherine Keebler, daughter of Benjamin Franklin Keebler and Elizabeth Range Wright, on 24 Dec 1861 at Elizabethton, Carter County, Tennessee. He died on 13 Nov 1925 at Mt. Jackson, Shenandoah County, Virginia, at age 87 while visiting at the home of his daughter, Carrie Alexander Barns. He was buried at Marion, Smyth County, Virginia.

3. Mary Catherine Keebler was born on 6 Jun 1843 at Keebler Crossroads, Washington County, Tennessee. She married Rev. Frank Alexander, son of John Alexander and Delilah Woods, on 24 Dec 1861 at Elizabethton, Carter County, Tennessee. She died on 29 Nov 1915 at Erwin, Unicoi County, Tennessee, at age 72. She was buried at Marion, Smyth County, Virginia.

--- 3rd Generation ---

4. John Alexander was born on 11 Oct 1812 at Washington County, Tennessee. He was born on 12 Oct 1812 at Washington County, Tennessee. He married Delilah Woods, daughter of John Woods and Agnes (--?--), on 22 Jan 1835 at Sullivan County, Tennessee. He died on 18 Oct 1876 at Marion, Smyth County, Virginia, at age 64. He was buried at Marion, Smyth County, Virginia.

5. Delilah Woods was born on 22 Jan 1817 at Sullivan County, Tennessee. She married John Alexander, son of John Alexander and Martha Ferguson, on 22 Jan 1835 at Sullivan County, Tennessee. She died on 25 Nov 1879 at Marion, Smyth County, Virginia, at age 62. She was buried at Marion, Smyth County, Virginia.

6. Benjamin Franklin Keebler was born on 9 Nov 1819. He married Elizabeth Range Wright, daughter of Rev. John Wright and Barbara Range, on 17 Mar 1842. He married Barshaba Kelly, daughter of Elizabeth Kelly, on 20 Jan 1844 at Carter County, Tennessee. He died before 1860.

7. Elizabeth Range Wright was born on 20 Dec 1818. She married Benjamin Franklin Keebler on 17 Mar 1842. She died between 6 Jun 1843 and 24 Jun 1843. She died in Jun 1845 at age 26.

Ancestors of John Alexander

Generation One

1. JOHN[1] ALEXANDER (*John*, #2);[1] b. 11 Oct 1812 at Washington County, Tennessee;[2,3] m. Delilah Woods, daughter of John Woods and Agnes (--?--), 22 Jan 1835 at Sullivan County, Tennessee;[4,5] d. 18 Oct 1876 at Marion, Smyth County, Virginia, at age 64;[6,7,8] bur. at Round Hill Cemetery, Marion, Smyth County, Virginia.[9,10]

Between 20 Mar 1865 and 1925 John Alexander and Rev. Frank Alexander were proprietors in a men's clothing store. This store remained in the family until 1967.[11]

Generation Two

2. JOHN[2] ALEXANDER;[12,13] b. between 1770 and 1780;[14] m. Martha Ferguson (see #3), daughter of John Ferguson and Jane (--?--), circa 1800;[15] d. 18 Jul 1831 at Washington County, Tennessee;[16] bur. at Fairview Cemetery, Jonesborough, Washington County, Tennessee.[17,18]

He lived between 1790 and 1831 at Leesburg, Washington County, Tennessee.[19,20] He served in the War of 1812 in the East Tennessee Militia, from 5 January 1814 to 14 January 1814 under Col. Allison and Capt. McCray, and from 13 September 1814 to 3 May 1815, as a substitute for Daniel Bowman, under Col. Johnson and Capt. Tunnell.

Children of John[2] Alexander and Martha Ferguson (see #3) were as follows:

       i.   JANE[1];[21] b. 4 Dec 1802;[22] m. David Woods, son of John Woods and Agnes (--?--), after 1828;[23,24] d. before 1850.[25,26]

       ii.   MARY;[27] b. 11 Jan 1805;[28] m. (--?--) Myers after 1820.[29,30]

       iii.   ELIZABETH;[31] b. 10 Jun 1807;[32] d. 27 Mar 1866 at age 58.[33]

       iv.   SUSANNA;[34] b. 6 Sep 1810;[35] bur. at Fairview Cemetery, Jonesborough, Washington County, Tennessee.[36,37]

  1.   v.   JOHN.

       vi.   MARGARET;[38] b. 22 Oct 1814;[39] m. (--?--) Wilson 1838.[40]

       vii.   JULIAN;[41] b. 12 Feb 1817;[42] d. 4 Jul 1828 at age 11.[43]

       viii.   REV. JOSIAH;[44] b. 8 Aug 1819 at Jonesborough, Washington County, Tennessee;[45,46,47] m. Sarah Martha Buchanan after 1839;[48,49] m. Susan Hutchinson after 1839;[50] d. 12 Apr 1883 at New Wilmington, Lawrence County, Pennsylvania, at age 63.[51,52,53]

       ix.   REV. SAMUEL;[54] b. 21 Jul 1822 at Jonesborough, Washington County, Tennessee;[55,56,57] m. Mary Ann Buchanan after 1842;[58,59] m. Serapta Duira Silliman 17 Jan 1861;[60] d. 11 May 1895 at Lyndon, Osage County, Kansas, at age 72.[61,62,63]

3. MARTHA[2] FERGUSON (*John*, #6);[64,65] b. 20 May 1784;[66,67] m. John Alexander (see #2) circa 1800;[68] d. 27 Oct 1863 at age 79;[69,70] bur. at Fairview Cemetery, Jonesborough, Washington County, Tennessee.[71]

My Family History
Version 1.02 for Windows

Basic Information

Black Fire Technology
PO Box 817
Capalaba QLD 4157
Australia
Voice: 011-61-7-3823-1993
Fax: 011-61-7-3390-3526
e-mail: info@blackfire.com.au
http://www.blackfire.com.au
http://www.ozemail.com.au/~pkortge
Price: AU $59.00

System requirements: Intel 386, 486, or
   Pentium IBM PC or compatible computer,
   running Windows 3.1 or higher
RAM: 2MB
Monitor: VGA display or better
CD-ROM: not required
Mouse: required

Program Information

Individuals per database: 3,000 individuals
   and 3,000 families; only 1 family file
   can be open at a time
Spouses per individual: 26
Children per relationship: 20
Spouses and children reordered: yes
Multiple parents allowed: yes
Name options: titles, father's surname
   automatically added to children, can
   convert surnames to uppercase letters
Field sizes: surname (25 characters), given
   name (40 characters), location (60
   characters), occupation (60 characters),
   custom fact fields (60 characters), notes
   field (32,000 characters)
Field options: 5 custom fields, 1 custom
   event, 2 custom facts, 2 custom notes
Note options: 3 notes fields supported, 1
   miscellaneous, 2 custom notes (the
   default custom notes are medical and
   sources), SeeNotes command references
   an individual's notes for date information

Multimedia options: unlimited graphics per
   individual, can describe attached graphics
Program options: the last 50 family cards are
   remembered via the Previous Family
   function, right clicking on an individual
   brings up a spouse or sibling pop-up
   menu; fonts for the program, printed
   reports, and dialog boxes can be specified
Date options: dates entered in a variety of
   formats can be automatically converted
   to specified default date style, standard
   date and non-standard qualifiers (yesterday,
   2 weeks after birth, 5 days before burial)
   are supported, a function will indicate on
   what day of the week a birth or marriage
   date fell, as well as calculate the age of
   an individual, or how long a couple was
   married
Search options: can search individuals by an
   index; the Find command will search
   using partial names

Reports

View reports before printing: most reports
Customized reports
♦   Options: can specify font, color,
    information to be included, individuals to
    include, boxes, lines, shadow, border, and
    captions
Notes included: most reports
Blank reports: some reports (includes blank
   fields which can be used as a worksheet)
Person Sheet (individual information)
Family Group Sheet
Family Cards
Descendant Chart
Pedigree Chart
Wall Chart

Sources

Creation: can enter source notes for each individual using 1 of the custom fields (sources are a default field), can also enter miscellaneous notes (no master source library)

Bells and Whistles

◆ A Macintosh and Windows Player is included so you may share your information with others not using My Family History

◆ Separate (included) program, My Family Chart, creates reports

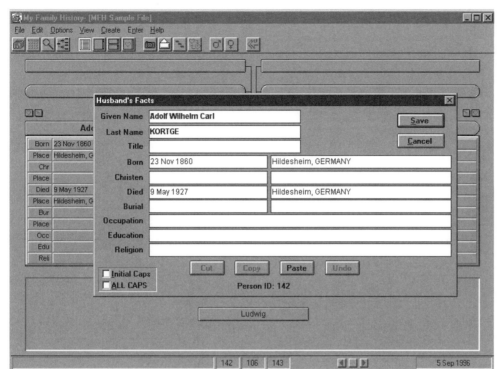

Figure 4.43
My Family History
Individual Edit

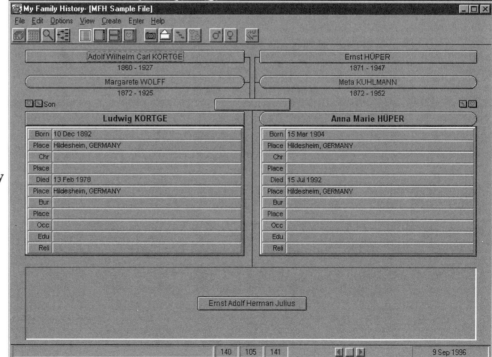

Figure 4.44
My Family History
Family View

William PINCHAM (1785 - 18 Jan 1836)

William PINCHAM (21 Apr 1828 - 1915)

George PATFIELD (- 1809)

Ann PATFIELD (28 Mar 1796 - 21 Sep 1855)

Mary BRIEN (1768 - 28 Apr 1853)

William PINCHAM (1852 - 1944)

Jane MASHAM (- 1904)

Amelia May (Millie) PINCHAM (12 Jul 1891 - 24 Mar 1990)

David MARTIN

Bridget MARTIN (1856 - 1942)

Mary KEATING (About 1829 - 1902)

My Family History Pedigree Chart (4-62)

George PATFIELD (- 1809)

Ann PATFIELD (28 Mar 1796 - 21 Sep 1855)

William PINCHAM (21 Apr 1828 - 1915)

William PINCHAM (1852 - 1944)

Florence Catherine (Kitty) PINCHAM (31 Mar 1889 - 21 Dec 1983)

Amelia May (Millie) PINCHAM (12 Jul 1891 - 24 Mar 1990)

Malcolm TORRANCE (22 Jul 1926 -)

Margaret TORRANCE (6 Sep 1928 -)

Peter Ernst KORTGE (6 Sep 1956 -)

Xian Talia KORTGE (1 Feb 1995 -)

Christopher William KORTGE (3 Nov 1957 -)

John Ludwig KORTGE (27 Nov 1959 -)

Margaret KORTGE (10 Feb 1964 -)

My Family History Descendants Chart (4-63)

Husband	**William PINCHAM**		
Born	1852		
Died	1944		
Buried		Presbyterian Section, Mona Vale Cemetery NSW 2103	
Father	William PINCHAM (1828-1915)	Mother	Jane MASHAM (-1904)
Married	19 Dec 1877	Hawthorn Hill, Coonabarabran NSW 2357	

Wife	**Bridget MARTIN**		
Born	1856	Golden Abbey, Tipperary, IRELAND	
Died	1942		
Buried		Presbyterian Section, Mona Vale Cemetery NSW 2103	
Father	David MARTIN	Mother	Mary KEATING (1829-1902)
Other Spouses: Patrick KING			

Children			
1	F	**Florence Catherine (Kitty) PINCHAM**	
Born	31 Mar 1889	Fancy Ground, Registered At Coonabarabran NSW 2357	
Died	21 Dec 1983	Tarro NSW 2322	
Buried		Beresfield NSW 2322 Crematoriam	
Occupation	Teacher/Headmistress		
2	F	**Amelia May (Millie) PINCHAM**	
Born	12 Jul 1891	Coonabarabran NSW 2357	
Died	24 Mar 1990	Tarro NSW 2322	
Buried		Beresfield NSW 2322 Crematoriam	
Occupation	Nurse		
Religion	Presbyterian		
Spouse	William TORRANCE		
Married	18 Jun 1920	Cashel12 , Carlton NSW 2218	

Wife's Notes
Bridget arrived (with her mother) in Sydney aboard the Peerless on 23rd September, 1863.
She left IRELAND as a 6 weeks old baby.
She married Patrick KING (a 36 year old widower) when she was 15 years old.
The family home at Coonabarabran was named "Cashel".

Parents

Version 4.5 for Windows

Basic Information

NickleWare
PO Box 393
Orem, UT 84059
e-mail: 72730.1002@compuserve.com
http://ourworld.compuserve.com/homepages/
nickleware/
Price: Parents 4.0 is for Windows 3.1
(shareware) is $25.00; Parents 4.6 for
Windows 95 (commercial version) is $44.95
Demo available for download

System requirements: IBM compatible 386
 or higher, running Windows 3.1 or higher
CD-ROM: not required

Program Information

Individuals per database: unlimited
Spouse per individual: unlimited
Children per relationship: unlimited
Children and spouses reordered: yes
Field sizes: name (75 characters), location
 (75 characters), notes (65,536 characters)
Event options: can add additional events
 (chosen from a pop-up menu) for each
 individual
Notes options: notes fields are available for
 each individual
Multimedia options: unlimited number of
 photos can be attached to each individual
Program options: information entered in
 place and date fields does not have to be
 in a specified format, can place people
 simply by dragging and dropping them to
 the appropriate spot
Search options: can search for individual
 using name or partial name; browse
 window can be customized (a customized
 list of records can be printed via the
 browse screen)

Reports

View reports before printing: yes
Export data to text: some reports
Worksheet
Individual Report
Family Group Sheet
Browse List (customizable)
Pedigree Chart

Sources

Creation: sources can be entered in the
 individual notes section

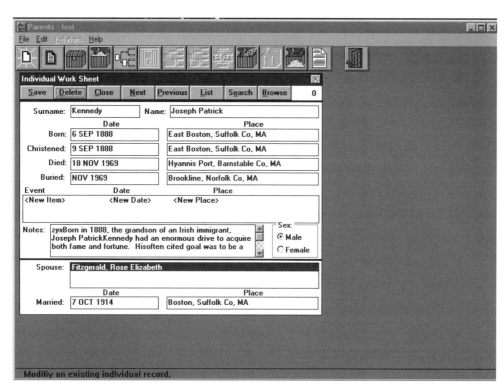

Figure 4.45
Parents
Individual Edit

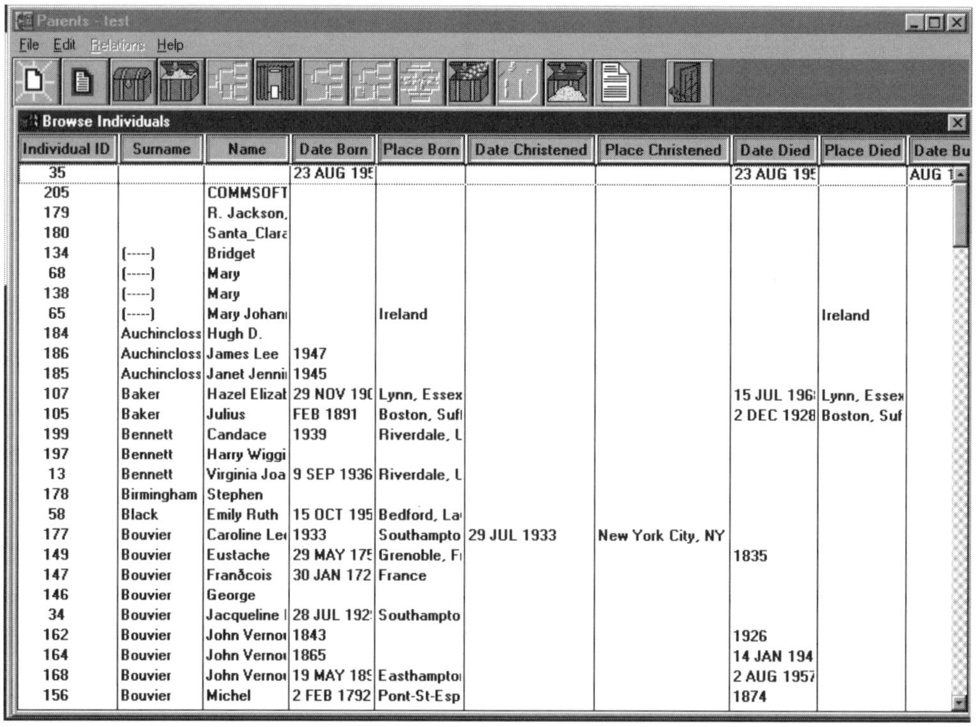

Figure 4.46
Parents Browse
Individuals

Immediate Family of Joseph P. Kennedy

Kennedy, Joseph Patrick
Born: 6 SEP 1888
Place: East Boston, Suffolk Co, MA
Died: 18 NOV 1969
Place: Hyannis Port, Barnstable Co, MA

Kennedy, Joseph Patrick
Born: 6 SEP 1888
Place: East Boston, Suffolk Co, MA
Died: 18 NOV 1969
Place: Hyannis Port, Barnstable Co, MA

Hickey, Mary Augusta
Born: 6 DEC 1857
Place: Winthrop, Suffolk Co, MA
Died: 20 MAY 1923
Place: Boston, Suffolk Co, MA

Kennedy, Edward Moore
Kennedy, Joseph Patrick
Kennedy, Jean Ann
Kennedy, Robert Francis
Kennedy, Patricia
Kennedy, Eunice Mary
Kennedy, Kathleen "Kick"
Kennedy, Rosemary (Rose Marie)
Kennedy, John Fitzgerald
Kennedy, Joseph Patrick

Fitzgerald, Rose Elizabeth

Hannon, Mary Josephine
Born: 31 OCT 1865
Place: Acton, Middlesex Co, MA
Died: 8 AUG 1964
Place: Dorchester, Suffolk Co, MA

Parents Pedigree Chart (4-65)

Kennedy, Joseph Patrick
    Born: 6 SEP 1888 East Boston, Suffolk Co, MA
    Christened: 9 SEP 1888 East Boston, Suffolk Co, MA
    Died: 18 NOV 1969 Hyannis Port, Barnstable Co, MA
    Buried: NOV 1969 Brookline, Norfolk Co, MA

Spouse(s):
Fitzgerald, Rose Elizabeth
    Born: 22 JUL 1890 Boston, Suffolk Co, MA
    Died: 22 Jan 1995
    Married: 7 OCT 1914 Boston, Suffolk Co, MA

Children:
Kennedy, Joseph Patrick
    Born: 25 JUL 1915 Hull, Plymouth Co, MA
    Died: 12 AUG 1944 the air, Suffolk, England

Kennedy, John Fitzgerald
    Born: 29 MAY 1917 Brookline, Norfolk Co, MA
    Died: 22 NOV 1963 Dallas, Dallas Co, TX

Kennedy, Rosemary (Rose Marie)
    Born: 20 FEB 1920 Brookline, Norfolk Co, MA
    Died:

Kennedy, Kathleen "Kick"
    Born: SEP 1918 Brookline, Norfolk Co, MA
    Died: 13 MAY 1948 Ste-Bauzille, Ardeche, France

Kennedy, Eunice Mary
    Born: 10 JUL 1921 Brookline, Norfolk Co, MA
    Died:

Kennedy, Patricia
    Born: 6 MAY 1924 Brookline, Norfolk Co, MA
    Died:

Kennedy, Robert Francis
    Born: 20 NOV 1925 Brookline, Norfolk Co, MA
    Died: 6 JUN 1968 Los Angeles, Los Angeles Co, CA

Kennedy, Jean Ann
    Born: 20 FEB 1928 Boston, Suffolk Co, MA
    Died:

Kennedy, Edward Moore
    Born: 22 FEB 1932 Boston, Suffolk Co, MA
    Died:

The information on this chart may not be correct and is for demonstration purposes only.

Parents Family Group Sheet (4-66)

Personal Ancestral File (PAF)
Version 3.0 for DOS

Basic Information

LDS Church Distribution Center
1999 West 1700 South
Salt Lake City, UT 84110
Voice: 800-537-5950
Voice: 801-240-2584
http://www.genealogy.org/~paf/@whatis.html
Price: $15.00

System requirements: IBM compatible with 286 or higher, MS-DOS 3.3 or higher
RAM: 640KB
Hard drive: 2.5MB space
CD-ROM: not required

Program Information

Individuals per database: 1 million
Spouses per individual: 60; can specify preferred spouse
Children per relationship: 60
Children and spouses reordered: yes
Specify relationship between parent and child: supported (biological, adopted, guardian, etc.)
Multiple parents allowed: supported (5 sets of parents are allowed); can specify preferred set of parents
Name options: titles, honorific, prefixes, and nicknames supported
Field sizes: name (120 characters), location (120 characters), date (35 characters)
Note options: can create notes for individuals or marriages
Program options: Focus command allows you to find all records with a common item (such as all individuals who came from a specific location, all individuals with missing birthplaces, etc.) and view, print, or export the data in those records
Ditto-key entry: supported
Date options: can enter dates in a variety of formats, can specify default format, non-standard dates supported, multiple dates supported, standard date qualifiers supported
Search options: search by given name, surname, sex, birth date, RIN, MRIN, date field, locations, empty fields
Database maintenance and options: duplicate individual merge, duplicate source merge

Reports

View reports printing: yes
Customized reports
- Specify fields to include, items to include
Pedigree chart
- 4, 5, or 6 generations
- Index
- Cascading charts
Family Group Record
- Notes
- Sources
Pedigree Index
Ancestry Chart (pedigree chart with only names, RINs, and birth years)
Ancestry Wall Chart
Descendancy Chart
- Index
Individual Record
- Notes
- Sources
- LDS ordinances
Incomplete Individual Ordinances
Incomplete Marriage Sealings
Name Sorted List (alphabetical list of individuals in database)
Family Group Sorted List (similar to Name Sorted List)
Ahnentafel Chart
- Ancestral File number (AFN)
- ID number
Individuals without Recorded Parents List
Source List
Place Sorted List
Individuals with Notes

List of Possible Record Problems
RIN Sorted List
MRIN Sorted List
Blank charts:
- Pedigree Chart
- Family Group Report

Research Tool Reports
- Correspondence Logs
- Relationship Chart
- Research Log
- Research Process

Sources

Creation: 8 groups of sources for each individual record (general, birth, christening, death, burial, baptism, endowment, sealing to parent), 2 groups for marriage records (marriage and divorce, sealing to spouse)

Source options: 3 parts to each source (description, repository, individual reference)

Comments

The Church of Jesus Christ of Latter-day Saints has produced a companion program that allows PAF to be run in the Windows environment. *Personal Ancestral File Companion 2* has the following features not available in PAF 3.0:

- Cousin Smart option eliminates duplicate entries
- Can run PAF without exiting PAF Companion 2
- Multiple items can be included in any contained search option
- 2 new reports are available: Register Report (Book Format) that exports to any word processor, and a Fan Chart

PAF Companion 2 requires Windows 3.1 or higher, 4MB RAM, 6MB hard drive space, VGA monitor, PAF 3.0 or higher, and is available on disk or CD-ROM. The price for PAF Companion 2 is $10.00; ordering information is the same as for PAF 3.0.

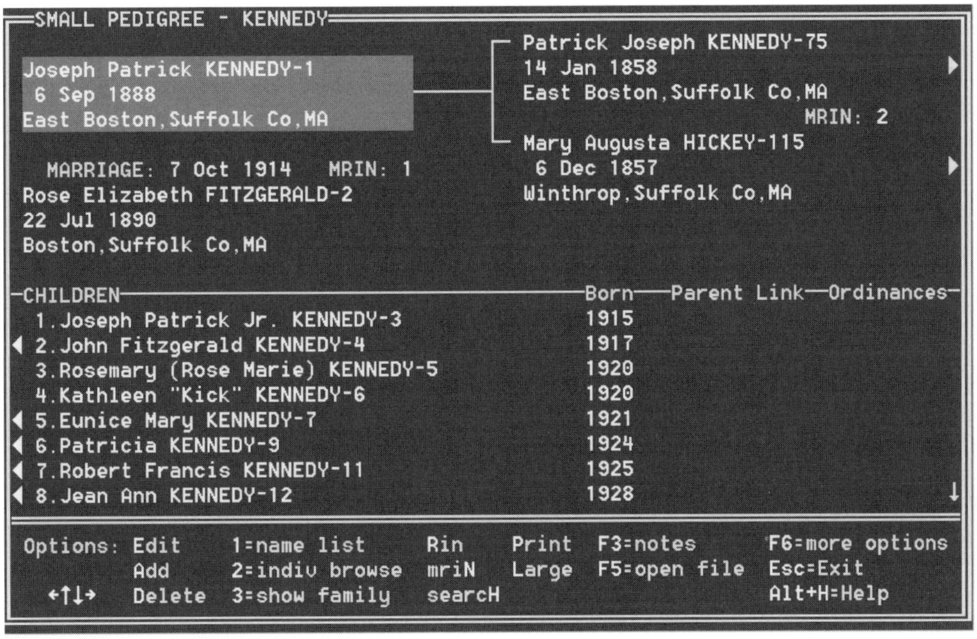

```
=SMALL PEDIGREE - KENNEDY=
                                  ┌ Patrick Joseph KENNEDY-75
 Joseph Patrick KENNEDY-1         │ 14 Jan 1858
  6 Sep 1888                      │ East Boston,Suffolk Co,MA       ▶
 East Boston,Suffolk Co,MA        │                    MRIN: 2
                                  └ Mary Augusta HICKEY-115
   MARRIAGE: 7 Oct 1914  MRIN: 1    6 Dec 1857                      ▶
 Rose Elizabeth FITZGERALD-2        Winthrop,Suffolk Co,MA
 22 Jul 1890
 Boston,Suffolk Co,MA

=CHILDREN=                                    Born─Parent Link─Ordinances─
  1.Joseph Patrick Jr. KENNEDY-3              1915
◀ 2.John Fitzgerald KENNEDY-4                 1917
  3.Rosemary (Rose Marie) KENNEDY-5           1920
  4.Kathleen "Kick" KENNEDY-6                 1920
◀ 5.Eunice Mary KENNEDY-7                     1921
◀ 6.Patricia KENNEDY-9                        1924
◀ 7.Robert Francis KENNEDY-11                 1925
◀ 8.Jean Ann KENNEDY-12                       1928                      ↓

 Options: Edit      1=name list   Rin    Print  F3=notes      F6=more options
          Add       2=indiv browse mriN   Large  F5=open file  Esc=Exit
   ←↑↓→   Delete    3=show family  searcH               Alt+H=Help
```

Figure 4.47
PAF Small
Pedigree View

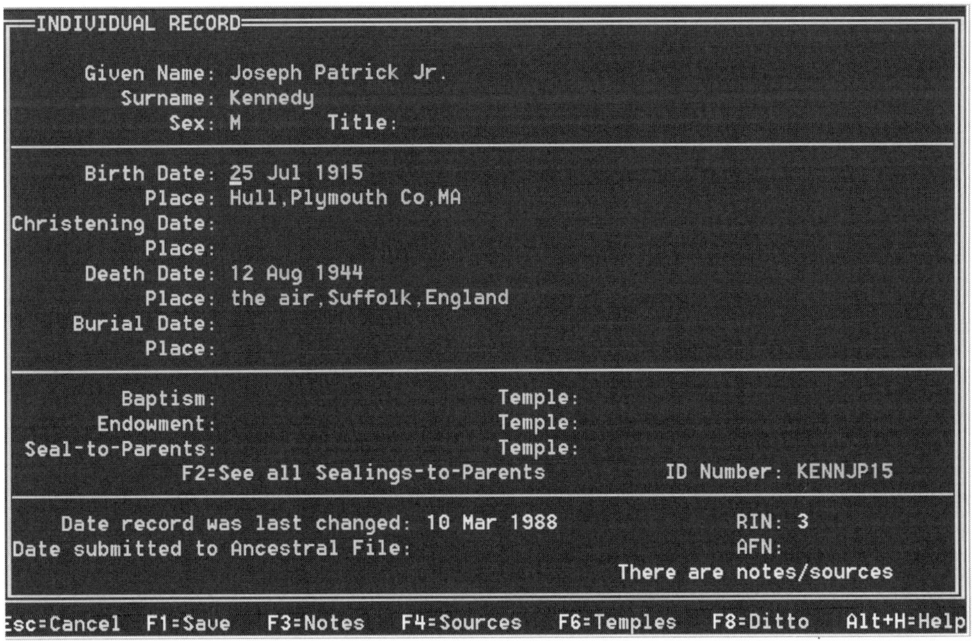

Figure 4.48
PAF Individual
Report View

```
=INDIVIDUAL RECORD=
        Given Name: Joseph Patrick Jr.
          Surname: Kennedy
              Sex: M       Title:

       Birth Date: 25 Jul 1915
            Place: Hull,Plymouth Co,MA
 Christening Date:
            Place:
       Death Date: 12 Aug 1944
            Place: the air,Suffolk,England
      Burial Date:
            Place:

          Baptism:                   Temple:
        Endowment:                   Temple:
  Seal-to-Parents:                   Temple:
           F2=See all Sealings-to-Parents     ID Number: KENNJP15

 Date record was last changed: 10 Mar 1988          RIN: 3
 Date submitted to Ancestral File:                  AFN:
                                        There are notes/sources

 Esc=Cancel  F1=Save  F3=Notes  F4=Sources  F6=Temples  F8=Ditto  Alt+H=Help
```

The information on these charts may not be correct and is for demonstration purposes only.

```
                                                                    16 ----------------------------
                                                                     | RIN:
                                          8 Patrick KENNEDY------------|  BIRTH:
                                          | RIN: 65                   |
                                          | BIRTH:                    17 ----------------------------
                                          |   Ireland                    RIN:
                          4 Patrick KENNEDY-------------|  MARR:   --24              BIRTH:
                          | RIN: 67                     |   Ireland
                          | BIRTH: Abt 1823             | DEATH:                     18 ----------------------------
                          |   Dunganstown,WexCo,Irel    |   Ireland                   | RIN:
                          | MARR: 26 Sep 1849 --25    9 Mary Johanna (-----)--------|  BIRTH:
                          |   Boston,Suffolk Co,MA      RIN: 66                     |
                          | DEATH: 22 Nov 1858          BIRTH:                       19 ----------------------------
       2 Patrick Joseph KENNEDY------|    Boston,Suffolk Co,MA        Ireland             RIN:
       | RIN: 75                     |                                DEATH:                 BIRTH:
       | BIRTH: 14 Jan 1858          |                                  Ireland
       |   East Boston,SuffolkCo,MA|                                                   20 ----------------------------
       | MARR: 23 Nov 1887 --2       |                                                  | RIN:
       |   Boston,Suffolk Co,MA      |                      10 Richard MURPHY-------------|  BIRTH:
       | DEATH: 18 May 1929          |                      | RIN: 68                   |
       |   Boston,Suffolk Co,MA      |                      | BIRTH:                     21 ----------------------------
       |                             5 Bridget MURPHY-------------|                          RIN:
       |                             | RIN: 70                     |  MARR:   --26              BIRTH:
       |                             | BIRTH: 1821                 |
       |                             |   Dunganstown,WexCo,Irel    | DEATH:                     22 ----------------------------
       |                             | DEATH: 20 Dec 1888          |                            | RIN:
       |                             |   Boston,Suffolk Co,MA    11 Mary (-----)---------------|  BIRTH:
       |                                                           RIN: 69                     |
       |                                                           BIRTH:                       23 ----------------------------
       |                                                                                             RIN:
   1 Joseph Patrick KENNEDY---------                               DEATH:                 BIRTH:
   | RIN: 1
   | BIRTH:  6 Sep 1888                                                                   24 ----------------------------
   |   East Boston,SuffolkCo,MA                                                            | RIN:
   | MARR:  7 Oct 1914 --1                                12 Michael HICKEY-------------|  BIRTH:
   |   Boston,Suffolk Co,MA                               | RIN: 112                   |
   | DEATH: 18 Nov 1969                                   | BIRTH:                     25 ----------------------------
   |   HyannisPort,BarnstaCo,MA                           |                                RIN:
   |                               6 James HICKEY----------------|  MARR:   --41              BIRTH:
   | SPOUSE(S):                    | RIN: 114                     |
   | Rose Elizabeth FITZGERALD     | BIRTH: 1836                  | DEATH:                     26 ----------------------------
   |                               |   Cork,CorkCo,MuPro,Irel    |                            | RIN:
   |                               | MARR:   --40              13 Catherine HASSETT-----------|  BIRTH:
   |                               |                             RIN: 113                     |
   |                               | DEATH: 22 Nov 1900          BIRTH:                       27 ----------------------------
   |                               |   Boston,Suffolk Co,MA                                        RIN:
   3 Mary Augusta HICKEY---------|                               DEATH:                 BIRTH:
   | RIN: 115                     |
   | BIRTH:  6 Dec 1857           |                                                        28 ----------------------------
   |   Winthrop,Suffolk Co,MA     |                                                        | RIN:
   | DEATH: 20 May 1923           |                      14 Patrick FIELD--------------|  BIRTH:
   |   Boston,Suffolk Co,MA       |                      | RIN: 109                   |
   |                              |                      | BIRTH:                     29 ----------------------------
   |                              7 Margaret M. FIELD-----------|                          RIN:
   |                              | RIN: 111                     |  MARR:   --39              BIRTH:
   |                              | BIRTH: Abt 1836             |
   |                                                            | DEATH:                     30 ----------------------------
   |                              | DEATH:  5 Jun 1911          |                            | RIN:
                                  |   Boston,Suffolk Co,MA    15 Mary SHEEHY----------------|  BIRTH:
                                                               RIN: 110                     |
                                                               BIRTH:                       31 ----------------------------
                                                                                                 RIN:
                                                               DEATH:                 BIRTH:
```

                                    + means the individual is a child in another family.
         Relationship: (B)=Biological, (A)=Adopted, (G)=Guardian, (S)=Sealing, (C)=Challenged, (D)=Disproved
         Ordinances: B=Baptized, E=Endowed, P=Sealed to Parents, S=Sealed to Spouse, C=Children's ordinances

Personal Ancestral File Pedigree Chart (4-67)

FAMILY GROUP RECORD FOR JOSEPH PATRICK KENNEDY/ROSE ELIZABE FITZGERALD - KENNEDY.PAF - MRIN 1
==
```
HUSBAND Joseph Patrick KENNEDY-1                                    LDS ORDINANCE DATA
------------------------------------------------------------------------------------------------
BIRTH:   6 Sep 1888      PLACE: East Boston,Suffolk Co,MA          B:
CHR.:    9 Sep 1888      PLACE: East Boston,Suffolk Co,MA          E:
MAR.:    7 Oct 1914      PLACE: Boston,Suffolk Co,MA               SS:
DEATH:  18 Nov 1969      PLACE: Hyannis Port,Barnstable Co,MA      SP:
BURIAL: Nov 1969         PLACE: Brookline,Norfolk Co,MA            Parent Link Type: (B)
FATHER: Patrick Joseph KENNEDY-75        MOTHER: Mary Augusta HICKEY-115
OTHER WIVES:                                                       Parents' MRIN: 2
================================================================================================
WIFE    Rose Elizabeth FITZGERALD-2
------------------------------------------------------------------------------------------------
BIRTH:  22 Jul 1890      PLACE: Boston,Suffolk Co,MA               B:
CHR.:                    PLACE:                                    E:
DEATH:                   PLACE:                                    SP:
BURIAL:                  PLACE:                                    Parent Link Type: (B)
FATHER: John Francis "Honey Fitz" FITZGERALD-141    MOTHER: Mary Josephine HANNON-146
OTHER HUSBANDS:                                                    Parents' MRIN: 3
================================================================================================
CHILDREN
================================================================================================
 1. NAME: Joseph Patrick Jr. KENNEDY-3                             Parent Link Type: (B)
--- BIRTH:  25 Jul 1915      PLACE: Hull,Plymouth Co,MA            B:
M   CHR.:                    PLACE:                                E:
    MAR.:                    PLACE:                                SS:
    DEATH:  12 Aug 1944      PLACE: the air,Suffolk,England        SP:
    BURIAL:                  PLACE:
    SPOUSE:
------------------------------------------------------------------------------------------------
 2. NAME: John Fitzgerald KENNEDY-4                                Parent Link Type: (B)
--- BIRTH:  29 May 1917      PLACE: Brookline,Norfolk Co,MA        B:
M   CHR.:                    PLACE:                                E:
    MAR.:   12 Sep 1953      PLACE: Newport,Newport Co,RI          SS:
    DEATH:  22 Nov 1963      PLACE: Dallas,Dallas Co,TX            SP:
    BURIAL: 25 Nov 1963      PLACE: Arlington,Arlington Co,VA
    SPOUSE: Jacqueline Lee BOUVIER-35          MRIN: 4
------------------------------------------------------------------------------------------------
 3. NAME: Rosemary (Rose Marie) KENNEDY-5                          Parent Link Type: (B)
--- BIRTH:  20 Feb 1920      PLACE: Brookline,Norfolk Co,MA        B:
F   CHR.:                    PLACE:                                E:
    MAR.:                    PLACE:                                SS:
    DEATH:                   PLACE:                                SP:
    BURIAL:                  PLACE:
    SPOUSE:
------------------------------------------------------------------------------------------------
 4. NAME: Kathleen "Kick" KENNEDY-6                                Parent Link Type: (B)
--- BIRTH:  20 Feb 1920      PLACE: Brookline,Norfolk Co,MA        B:
F   CHR.:                    PLACE:                                E:
    MAR.:    6 May 1944      PLACE: London,England                 SS:
    DEATH:  13 May 1948      PLACE: Ste-Bauzille,Ardeche,France    SP:
    BURIAL: May 1948         PLACE: Chatsworth,England
    SPOUSE: William John Robert CAVENDISH-202  MRIN: 5
------------------------------------------------------------------------------------------------
 5. NAME: Eunice Mary KENNEDY-7                                    Parent Link Type: (B)
--- BIRTH:  10 Jul 1921      PLACE: Brookline,Norfolk Co,MA        B:
F   CHR.:                    PLACE:                                E:
    MAR.:   23 May 1953      PLACE: New York City,NY               SS:
    DEATH:                   PLACE:                                SP:
    BURIAL:                  PLACE:
    SPOUSE: Robert Sargent Jr. SHRIVER-8       MRIN: 6
------------------------------------------------------------------------------------------------
 6. NAME: Patricia KENNEDY-9                                       Parent Link Type: (B)
--- BIRTH:   6 May 1924      PLACE: Brookline,Norfolk Co,MA        B:
F   CHR.:                    PLACE:                                E:
    MAR.:   24 Apr 1954      PLACE: New York City,NY               SS:
    DEATH:                   PLACE:                                SP:
    BURIAL:                  PLACE:
    SPOUSE: Peter LAWFORD-10                    MRIN: 7
================================================================================================
```

Parent Link Types: (B)=Biological, (A)=Adopted, (G)=Guardian, (S)=Sealing, (C)=Challenged, (D)=Disproved

The informatiton on this chart may not be correct and is for demonstration purposes only.

Personal Ancestral File Family Group Record (4-68)

```
DESCENDANCY CHART FOR JOSEPH PATRICK KENNEDY - KENNEDY.PAF
===================================================================================================
        Name            (Birth/Chr.-Death/Burial)  Birth/Chr. Place
---------------------------------------------------------------------------------------------------
1-- Joseph Patrick KENNEDY-1 (1888-1969)  East Boston,Suffolk Co,MA
 sp-Rose Elizabeth FITZGERALD-2 (1890-    )  Boston,Suffolk Co,MA
    2-- Joseph Patrick Jr. KENNEDY-3 (1915-1944)  Hull,Plymouth Co,MA
    2-- John Fitzgerald KENNEDY-4 (1917-1963)  Brookline,Norfolk Co,MA
     sp-Jacqueline Lee BOUVIER-35 (1929-    )  Southampton,Long Island,NY
        3-- <Unknown>-36 (1956-1956)
        3-- Caroline Bouvier KENNEDY-37 (1957-    )  New York City,NY
         sp-Edwin SCHLOSSBERG-201 (1945-    )
        3-- John Fitzgerald Jr. KENNEDY-38 (1960-    )  Washington,DC
        3-- Patrick Bouvier KENNEDY-39 (1963-1963)  Falmouth,Barnstable Co,MA
    2-- Rosemary (Rose Marie) KENNEDY-5 (1920-    )  Brookline,Norfolk Co,MA
    2-- Kathleen "Kick" KENNEDY-6 (1920-1948)  Brookline,Norfolk Co,MA
     sp-William John Robert CAVENDISH-202 (1917-1944)
    2-- Eunice Mary KENNEDY-7 (1921-    )  Brookline,Norfolk Co,MA
     sp-Robert Sargent Jr. SHRIVER-8 (1915-    )  Westminster,Carroll Co,MD
        3-- Robert Sargent III SHRIVER-21 (1954-    )  Chicago,Cook Co,IL
        3-- Maria Owings SHRIVER-22 (1955-    )  Chicago,Cook Co,IL
         sp-Arnold SHWARZENEGGER-26 (1955-    )
        3-- Timothy Perry SHRIVER-23 (1959-    )  Boston,Suffolk Co,MA
        3-- Mark Kennedy SHRIVER-24 (1964-    )  Washington,DC
        3-- Anthony Paul SHRIVER-25 (1965-    )  Boston,Suffolk Co,MA
    2-- Patricia KENNEDY-9 (1924-    )  Brookline,Norfolk Co,MA
     sp-Peter LAWFORD-10 (1923-1984)  London,England
        3-- Christopher Kennedy LAWFORD-15 (1955-    )  Santa Monica,Los Angeles Co,CA
         sp-Jean Edith OLSSON-19 (1955-    )  Seoul,Korea
        3-- Sydney Maleia LAWFORD-16 (1956-    )  Santa Monica,Los Angeles Co,CA
         sp-James Peter MCKELVEY-20 (1955-    )  Pittsburgh,Allegheny Co,PA
        3-- Victoria Francis LAWFORD-17 (1958-    )  Santa Monica,Los Angeles Co,CA
        3-- Robin Elizabeth LAWFORD-18 (1961-    )  Santa Monica,Los Angeles Co,CA
    2-- Robert Francis KENNEDY-11 (1925-1968)  Brookline,Norfolk Co,MA
     sp-Ethel SKAKEL-40 (1928-    )  Chicago,Cook Co,IL
        3-- Kathleen Hartington KENNEDY-41 (1951-    )  Greenwich,Fairfield Co,CT
         sp-David Lee TOWNSEND-52 (1947-    )  Baltimore,Baltimore Co,MD
            4-- Meaghan Anne Kennedy TOWNSEND-53 (1977-    )  Santa Fe,Santa Fe Co,NM
            4-- Maeve Fahey Kennedy TOWNSEND-54 (1979-    )  New Haven,New Haven Co,CT
            4-- Rose Katherine Kennedy TOWNSEND-55 (1983-    )  Weston,Middlesex Co,MA
        3-- Joseph Patrick II KENNEDY-42 (1952-    )  Boston,Suffolk Co,MA
         sp-Sheila Brewster RAUCH-56 (1949-    )  Bryn Mawr,Montgomery Co,PA
            4-- Joseph Patrick III KENNEDY-58 (1980-    )  Boston,Suffolk Co,MA
            4-- Matthew Rauch KENNEDY-57 (1980-    )  Boston,Suffolk Co,MA
        3-- Robert Francis Jr. KENNEDY-43 (1954-    )  Washington,DC
         sp-Emily Ruth BLACK-59 (1957-    )  Bedford,Lawrence Co,IN
            4-- Robert Francis III KENNEDY-60 (1984-    )  Mt. Kisco,Westchester Co,NY
        3-- David Anthony KENNEDY-44 (1955-1984)  Washington,DC
        3-- Mary Courtney KENNEDY-45 (1956-    )  Boston,Suffolk Co,MA
         sp-Jeffrey Robert RUHE-61 (1952-    )  La Porte,La Porte Co,IN
        3-- Michael LeMoyne KENNEDY-46 (1958-    )  Washington,DC
         sp-Victoria Denise GIFFORD-62 (1957-    )  Bakersfield,Kern Co,CA
            4-- Michael LeMoyne Jr. KENNEDY-63 (1983-    )  Charlottesvlle,Albemarle Co,VA
            4-- Kyle Frances KENNEDY-64 (1984-    )  Washington,DC
        3-- Mary Kerry KENNEDY-47 (1959-    )  Washington,DC
        3-- Christopher George KENNEDY-48 (1963-    )  Boston,Suffolk Co,MA
        3-- Matthew Maxwell Taylor KENNEDY-49 (1965-    )  New York City,NY
        3-- Douglas Harriman KENNEDY-50 (1967-    )  Washington,DC
```

The information on this chart may not be correct and is for demonstration purposes only.

Personal Ancestral File Descendancy Chart (4-69)

PRO-GEN

Version 2.3C for DOS

Basic Information

J. Mulderij & D.J. Scholte in't Hoff
c/o J. Mulderij
Papenveld 1
NL-7475 DD Markelo
The Netherlands
Voice: 011-31-547-362755
mulderij.pro-gen@pi.net
http://www.pi.net/~progen/home.html
Shareware fee: $65.00

System requirements: IBM compatible computers with 640KB memory, MS-DOS 3.0 or higher (runs in Windows 3.1 and Windows 95)
Hard drive: 4.5MB
CD-ROM: not required

Program Information

Individuals per database: 30,000
Multiple parents: not supported
Children and spouses reordered: cannot be reordered without changing dates
Name options: aliases are supported
Field sizes: surname (30 characters), given name (40 characters), place fields (1,000 characters), notes (16,000); can change field lengths if needed
Event options: each event has a source, reference, and source-text field
Note options: notes (Info) field can be searched by filters
Date options: standard date qualifiers are available only with years
Program options: data can be exported to WordPerfect format files, can create a sorted list by any field
Database maintenance and options: data integrity check, backup, and restore functions supported

Reports

View reports before printing: yes
Customized reports
♦ Options: specify items and individuals to include, can edit the list definitions when printing individuals, marriages, ancestor, and descendant reports; can specify in which language reports are printed
Export data to text file: all reports can be generated in WordPerfect, Word, and HTML formats
Blank reports: standard blank forms can be printed and used as worksheets
Persons Index
Marriage Index
Ancestral Index (pedigree box chart)
Individual Report
Ancestral Report
Descendants Report
Histogram
Timeline
Index
♦ Generated by record numbers, Kekule numbers, or descendants numbers

Sources

Creation: sources can be entered for events only

Bells and Whistles

♦ Can generate a mail-merge Wordperfect file containing addresses
♦ Wall charts can be created by printing several graphical Ancestor or Descendant charts

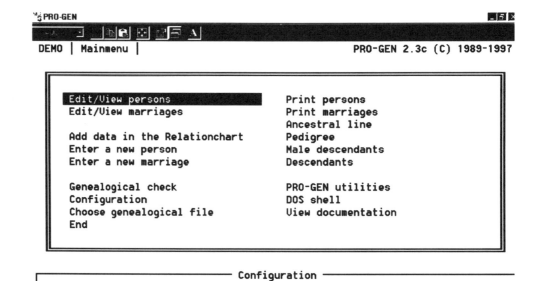

```
⅓ PRO-GEN                                                  _ 5 X
┌───────────────────────────────────────────────────────────────┐
│  ┌─┐  ┌─┐ ┌─┐┌─┐ ┌─┐ ┌─┐┌─┐ A                                   │
├───────────────────────────────────────────────────────────────┤
│ DEMO │ Edit a person  [13] │              PRO-GEN 2.3c (C) 1989-1997│
├┤INDIVIDUAL      13├═════════════╪pg23a-gb├═════╢LAST CHANGE 06/12/1994├
│ Given name: Wilhelmina Frederika Louisa                         │
│ Surname   : van Oranje Nassau                    Sex: F         │
│ Call name : Louise           Alias:              Code:          │
│ Title 1   :            Title 2:              Title 3:           │
│ Father    : van Oranje Nassau, Willem Frederik Karel [6]        │
│ Mother    : van Pruisen, Augusta Wilhelmina Amalia [7]          │
│ Occupation:                                                     │
│ Scratch   :               Info: Van deze weinig gekende    »    │
├┤Address├                                                        │
│ Date  :         Street:                                         │
│ Zip   :         Place:              Country:                    │
│ Phone :                    Info:                                │
├┤Birth├                                                          │
│ Date  : 05/08/1828  Place: Den Haag          Time:              │
│ Source:                            Reference:                   │
│ Text  :                    Info:                                │
├┤Christening├                                                    │
│ Date  :         Place:              Religion:                   │
│ Witn. :                                                         │
│ Source:                            Reference:                   │
│ Text  :                    Info:                                │
├┤Death├                                                          │
└─────────────────────────────────────────────────────────────────┘
 Ctrl-F1=Edit F-keys,Ctrl-A=Special chr.,Alt-keys=jump,Alt-F1=external program
```

Figure 4.49
Pro-Gen
Individual Edit

```
⅓ PRO-GEN                                                  _ 5 X
┌───────────────────────────────────────────────────────────────┐
│  ┌─┐  ┌─┐ ┌─┐┌─┐ ┌─┐ ┌─┐┌─┐ A                                   │
├───────────────────────────────────────────────────────────────┤
│ DEMO │ Mainmenu │                          PRO-GEN 2.3c (C) 1989-1997│
└───────────────────────────────────────────────────────────────┘

    ┌──────────────────────────────────────────────────────┐
    │                                                        │
    │   ▐Edit/View persons▌        Print persons             │
    │    Edit/View marriages       Print marriages           │
    │                              Ancestral line            │
    │    Add data in the Relationchart   Pedigree            │
    │    Enter a new person        Male descendants          │
    │    Enter a new marriage      Descendants               │
    │                                                        │
    │    Genealogical check        PRO-GEN utilities         │
    │    Configuration             DOS shell                 │
    │    Choose genealogical file  View documentation        │
    │    End                                                 │
    │                                                        │
    └──────────────────────────────────────────────────────┘

          ┌──────────────────── Configuration ──────────┐
          │ File        : c:\temp1\pg23\gb\data\DEMO      │
          │ Description : Example file 'Oranje-Nassau'    │
          │ Contents    : 48 persons + 17 marriages       │
          │ Screenlayout: PG23A-GB.DEF                    │
          │ Status      : Read & Write                    │
          └──────────────────────────────────────────────┘
```

Figure 4.50
Pro-Gen
Main Menu

van ORANJE NASSAU Wilhelmina Frederika Louisa x van ZWEDEN BERNADOTTE
Karel XV Lodewijk Eugenius (x Stockholm 19/06/1850)
    * Den Haag 05/08/1828   * Stockholm 03/05/1826
    + Stockholm 30/03/1871   + Malmö 18/09/1872

van ORANJE NASSAU Wilhelmina Helena Paulina Maria x van MECKLENBURG
SCHWERIN Hendrik Wladimir Albrecht Ernst (x Den Haag 07/02/1901)
    * Den Haag 31/08/1880   * Schwerin 19/04/1876
    + Apeldoorn (Het Loo) 28/11/1962   + Den Haag 03/07/1934

van ORANJE NASSAU Willem Frederik Hendrik
    * Soestdijk 13/06/1820
    + Walferdange, Luxemburg 13/01/1879

van ORANJE NASSAU Willem Frederik Karel x van PRUISEN Augusta Wilhelmina
Amalia (x Berlijn 21/05/1821)
    * Berlijn 28/02/1797   * Koningsbergen 01/02/1808
    + Wassenaar 08/09/1881   + Wassenaar 06/12/1870

van ORANJE NASSAU Willem I Frederik x1 van PRUISEN Frederika Louise
Wilhelmina (x Berlijn, Duitsland 01/10/1791)
    * Den Haag 24/08/1772   * Potsdam 18/11/1774
    + Berlijn, Duitsland 12/12/1843   + Den Haag 12/10/1837
van ORANJE NASSAU Willem I Frederik x2 d' OULTREMONT DE WÉGIMONT Henriëtte
Adriana Ludovica Flora (x Berlijn, Duitsland 17/02/1841)
    * Den Haag 24/08/1772   * Maastricht 28/02/1792
    + Berlijn, Duitsland 12/12/1843   + Rahe bij Aken 26/10/1864

van ORANJE NASSAU Willem II Frederik George Lodewijk x van RUSLAND Anna
Paulowna (x St. Petersburg 21/02/1816)
    * Den Haag 06/12/1792   * St. Petersburg, Rusland
                          18/01/1795
    + Tilburg 17/03/1849   + Den Haag 01/03/1865

van ORANJE NASSAU Willem III Alexander Paul Frederik x1 van WÜRTTEMBERG
Sophia Frederika Mathilde (x Stuttgart 18/06/1839)
    * Brussel, België 19/02/1817   * Stuttgart 17/06/1818
    + Apeldoorn (Het Loo) 23/11/1890 + Apeldoorn (Het Loo)
                          03/06/1877
van ORANJE NASSAU Willem III Alexander Paul Frederik x2 van WALDECK
PYRMONT Adelheid Emma Wilhelmina Theresia (x Arolsen 07/01/1879)
    * Brussel, België 19/02/1817   * Arolsen 02/08/1858
    + Apeldoorn (Het Loo) 23/11/1890 + Den Haag 20/03/1934

Generation I

1   **Hendrik Wladimir Albrecht Ernst** (Hendrik) **van MECKLENBURG SCHWERIN**,
born on 19/04/1876 in Schwerin (religion: nh), died on 03/07/1934
in Den Haag at the age of 58. *Hij overlijdt aan een hartaanval.*
Buried on 14/07/1934 in Delft. *De rouwkleur tijdens zijn begrafenis
is wit. Hertog van Mecklenburg, Vorst der Wenden, Schwerin en
Ratzeburg, Graaf van Schwerin, heer van Rostock en Stargard, Prins
der Nederlanden.*
*Evenals Wilhelmina heeft Heinrich een veel oudere vader en een 27
jaar jongere moeder. Van jongs af aan is hij een buitenman, een
verwoed jager en ruiter.*
*Zijn positie als echtgenoot en prins-gemaal blijkt uitermate
moeilijk, omdat deze aktieve prins in feite niets te doen heeft.
Hij is geen intellectueel en zijn belangstelling gaat nu eenmaal
uit naar het buitenleven. Hij zou het liefst een leven als een
Duitse Landjunker leiden.*
*Hij bekleedt funkties bij het Rode Kruis, het Reddingwezen en de
Padvindersbeweging. Ook neemt hij aktief deel aan landontginning en
landbouw.*
*Op zijn enig (wettelijk) kind is hij erg gesteld en hij is voor
haar een hartelijk vader.*
*Volgens sommige bronnen hebben zijn escapades geleid tot
buitenechtelijke nakomelingen.*
*De prins ontvangt eerst een jaargeld uit Mecklenburg, maar na 1918
stopt dit en is hij financieel geheel afhankelijk van Wilhelmina.*
Bron: Van Ditzhuyzen, Oranje-Nassau, een biografisch woordenboek.
Married at the age of 24 on 07/02/1901 in Den Haag. *Het
huwelijksleven tussen deze twee zo verschillende naturen - zij
intelligent, trots en autoritair; hij goedig, eenvoudig en
gulhartig - wordt niet gelukkig en uiteindelijk leiden koningin en
prins geheel van elkaar losstaande levens. De eenzame prins, die
een zeker medelijden opwekt bij de bevolking, heeft behoefte aan
menselijke contacten en gaat veel op reis, waarbij het soms tot
escapades komt.*
Bron: Van Ditzhuyzen, Oranje-Nassau, een biografisch woordenboek to
Wilhelmina Helena Paulina Maria (Wilhelmina) **van ORANJE NASSAU**, 20
years old, born on 31/08/1880 in Den Haag, christened (nh) on
12/10/1880 in Den Haag, died on 28/11/1962 in Apeldoorn (Het Loo)
at the age of 82. *Paleis het Loo*, buried on 08/12/1962 in Delft.
*Evenals haar man, wordt zij in het wit begraven. Koningin der
Nederlanden, Prinses van Oranje Nassau. "Eenzaam, maar niet alleen"
geeft kernachtig de persoonlijkheid samen van deze koningin, die
door haar optreden tijdens de Tweede Wereldoorlog Moeder des
Vaderlands werd genoemd.*
*Vanaf haar achtste groeit zij op in een isolement, met als doel een
hoogverheven vorstin, zelfverzekerd en niet gehinderd door enige
twijfel te worden. Zij heeft een tragische, maar door haar zelf als
onvermijdelijk geaccepteerde jeugd, die de basis legt voor haar
afgeslotenheid, vastberadenheid en karaktersterkte.*
*Mede door haar afstandelijkheid wordt het huwelijk met Hendrik van
Mecklenburg niet gelukkig. De zeer godvruchtige vorstin is*

Wilhelmina Helena Paulina Maria van ORANJE NASSAU * 31/08/1880 Den Haag +
28/11/1962 Apeldoorn (Het Loo) x 07/02/1901 Den Haag Hendrik Wladimir
Albrecht Ernst van MECKLENBURG SCHWERIN * 19/04/1876 Schwerin + 03/07/1934
Den Haag
| Willem III Alexander Paul Frederik van ORANJE NASSAU * 19/02/1817 Brussel,
   België + 23/11/1890 Apeldoorn (Het Loo) x1 18/06/1839 Stuttgart Sophia
   Frederika Mathilde van WÜRTTEMBERG * 17/06/1818 Stuttgart + 03/06/1877
   Apeldoorn (Het Loo) x2 07/01/1879 Arolsen
| Adelheid Emma Wilhelmina Theresia van WALDECK PYRMONT * 02/08/1858 Arolsen
   + 20/03/1934 Den Haag x 07/01/1879 Arolsen
| | Willem II Frederik George Lodewijk van ORANJE NASSAU * 06/12/1792 Den
    Haag + 17/03/1849 Tilburg x 21/02/1816 St. Petersburg
| | Anna Paulowna van RUSLAND * 18/01/1795 St. Petersburg, Rusland +
    01/03/1865 Den Haag x 21/02/1816 St. Petersburg
| | | Willem I Frederik van ORANJE NASSAU * 24/08/1772 Den Haag + 12/12/1843
     Berlijn, Duitsland x1 01/10/1791 Berlijn, Duitsland x2 17/02/1841
     Berlijn, Duitsland Henriëtte Adriana Ludovica Flora d' OULTREMONT DE
     WÉGIMONT * 28/02/1792 Maastricht + 26/10/1864 Rahe bij Aken
| | | Frederika Louise Wilhelmina van PRUISEN * 18/11/1774 Potsdam +
     12/10/1837 Den Haag x 01/10/1791 Berlijn, Duitsland

Ultimate Family Tree

Premier version for Windows 95

Basic Information

Palladium Interactive
900 Larkspur Landing Circle, Suite 295
Larkspur, CA 94939
Voice: 415-464-5500
Fax: 415-464-5530
e-mail: UFTHelp@Palladium.net
http://www.uftree.com
Price: There are 3 versions of UFT available,
UFT ($19.99), UFT Deluxe ($39.99), and UFT
Premier ($59.99)

System requirements: IBM compatible with
   a 386 or higher processor
RAM: 8MB (16MB strongly recommended)
Hard drive: at least 35MB of space (the files
   supplied with the program require about
   5MB space for every 1,000 individuals
CD-ROM: required

Program Information

Individuals per database: unlimited
Spouses per individual: unlimited
Children per individual: unlimited
Children and spouses reordered: yes
Multiple parents: supported
Non-traditional marriages: supported
Name options: titles, aliases, honorific
   titles, suffixes supported
Field sizes: name (52 characters, although
   65,000 characters are available in long
   name field), location (60 characters),
   event (65,000 characters), individual text
   (65,000 characters)
Field options: place information consists of a
   short place name and a place modifier
   (longer location information can be
   entered); a media file can be attached to
   location record
Event options: detailed events feature allows
   you to pick an event from the event

library, add evidence, define event,
associate principal roles, enter new events
for birth, death, marriage, burial, or
extended events (several choices for
extended events), events are automatically
ordered chronologically, can custom
prioritize events, flags can be set (true or
false) for any event, can add roles not
already defined for each associated event,
can preview how a role will appear in
printed report, can add and delete new
event types, add new roles to events;
images can be attached to events for use in
Family Journal Reports
Multimedia options: unlimited number of
   graphics, sound files, or OLE objects can
   be included, 1 image to an individual,
   event, place, or source, can select
   preferred image for individuals, events,
   and locations; can create a slide show of
   multimedia objects
Program options: users may use 1 of 2 modes
   of usage (normal or advanced editing
   modes), 4 program wizards guide new users
   through the process of data entry (new
   individual, new event, new proof, and
   family tree report), information may be
   viewed in a variety of ways (family group,
   family tree, individual summary,
   descendants, kinship, and more),
   individual's medical information can be
   recorded, can set 10 flags per individual,
   can use your own reference numbers
Ditto-key entry: supported
Date options: free-form, structured, and
   other date formats (such as Quaker,
   Jewish, etc.) are supported, dates can be
   sorted if you don't know a date, can
   specify date format; double dates are
   supported
Search options: can search for individuals,
   events, places, sources, multimedia files,
   text, and several other items; can group
   results

Individual's options: individual's signature, nationality, languages spoken, and religion may be noted, URL for a Web site featuring individual

Database maintenance and options: databases can be merged as long as they use the same library files (otherwise you may append 1 database by importing the second database information via GEDCOM), backup and restore function supported, can split database into multiple parts, data integrity check supported, can re-index database

Reports

View reports before printing: yes
Customized Report
- Options: can specify individuals to include, events to include, format, and layout

Photos included: yes
Export data to text file: yes
Sources included: yes
Family Group Sheet
Family Journal
- Register format
- NGS (Modified Register) format

Ancestors Report
- Family Tree (pedigree chart)
- Ahnentafel

Descendants Report
- Indented
- Text
- Direct Drop
- Box Chart

Fan Chart
- 90, 180, or 360 degree circles

Image Report
- Portrait
- Gallery
- Media Tree

Lists:
- Relationship List
- Free-form text
- Footnote (end notes)
- Bibliography
- Index
- Summaries (individual, historical, event, image, place, source, task)
- Calendars

- Tiny Tafel
- Research log

Title Page
Table of Contents
Credits
Timeline

Sources

Creation: sources (evidence) may be entered for a variety of events and are stored in a source library, where they can be accessed and used repeatedly, can preview a source to see how it looks when printed, detailed help and explanations are available to ease the process of entering source citation information, 47 source-type templates available (you can also create your own source templates), can use either structured or free-form sources

Source options: free-form text source type is supported, can copy a source to a bibliography, can conduct a search through source records for 1 particular source (wildcards are supported), can specify the level of consistency, directness, and origin (in Advanced Edit mode only), can enter analysis of evidence and surety level

Bells and Whistles

- A WYSIWYG editor is built in to further customize reports (some reports are excluded from use with the editor)
- A Web page can be generated from database information
- Library Reference Media scanned images can be edited from within the program
- A Spell-check function is included for use in most text fields
- Can create a Tiny Tafel from the database information
- Can create a task list to organize future research projects; can leave electronic sticky notes as reminders on specified windows
- Can import information directly from Roots III data files

Comments

Ultimate Family Tree Deluxe includes the
following bonuses: Family Tutor, Records
Requester, U.S. Gazetteers, and World Photo
Studio. Ultimate Family Tree Premier in-
cludes: immigration and naturalization
tutorial, clip art images, Social Security
Death Index CD-ROM, *The Complete Idiot's
Guide to Genealogy* (CD-ROM version),
PhotoEnhancer software, and NetCard photo
e-mail postcards creator.

The UFT Web page includes both items
available to everyone, and those available
only to registered users. Anyone can view the
SSDI search, GEDCOM Database, submitted
Web pages, basic genealogy info, message
area, and newsletter. Registered users can
upload their Web page, and use a reference
library, online chat areas, tutorials, and an
image archive.

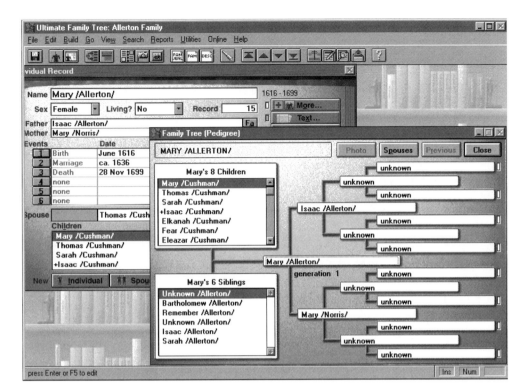

Figure 4.51
Ultimate Family
Tree Pedigree
View

Figure 4.52
Ultimate Family
Tree Role Edit
Screen

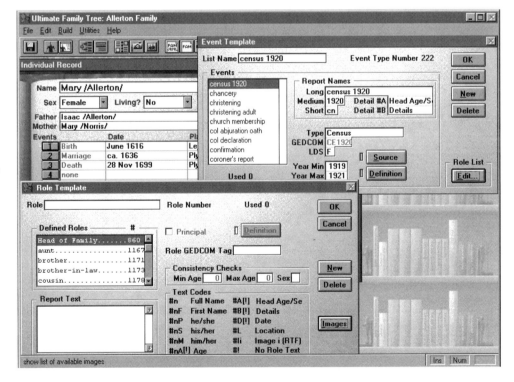

FATHER:	Patrick Joseph Kennedy #44			
	bir:	14 Jan 1858	child	in Boston, MA
	mar:	1887	groom	
	dea:	May 1929	deceased	
	Father:	Patrick Kennedy #46		
	Mother:	Bridget Murphy #47		
MOTHER:	Mary Augusta Hickey #45			
	bir:		child	
	mar:	1887	bride	
	dea:	1923	deceased	
	Father:			
	Mother:			

CHILDREN

1 M	Name:	Joseph Patrick Kennedy #1		
	bir:	6 Sep 1888	child	in Boston, MA
	mar:	7 Oct 1914	groom	in Boston, MA
	to:	Rose Fitzgerald #2		
	dea:	18 Nov 1969	deceased	in Hyannis Port, MA
	bur:		interred	in Holyhood Cemetery,Brookline,MA
2 F	Name:	Loretta Kennedy #67		
	bir:	1892	child	in Boston, MA
3 F	Name:	Margaret Kennedy #57		
	bir:	1898	child	
	mar:		bride	
	to:	Charles Burke #58		

Individual biographical text for Patrick Joseph Kennedy #44

As a young man, Patrick dropped out of school to work on the docks of Boston.   Patrick was able to work his way from being a SaloonKeeper to becoming a Ward Boss, helping out other Irish immigrants. His popularity rose and at the age of thirty he had become a power in Boston politics. In 1892 and 1893 he was elected to the Massachusetts Senate.   Patrick later became a very successful businessman getting into wholesale liquor sales, owning a coal company and becoming the president of a bank.   His personality was mild-mannered, quiet and reserved, and he was viewed as a man of moderate habits.   Meridian St., East Boston, MA Webster St., Boston, MA

Joseph Patrick Kennedy
└─Rose Elizabeth Fitzgerald
  ├─Joseph Patrick Jr. Kennedy
  ├─John Fitzgerald Kennedy
  │ └─Jacqueline Lee Bouvier
  │   ├─
  │   ├─Caroline Bouvier Kennedy
  │   ├─John Fitzgerald Jr. Kennedy
  │   └─Patrick Bouvier Kennedy
  ├─Rosemary (Rose Marie) Kennedy
  ├─Kathleen "Kick" Kennedy
  ├─Eunice Mary Kennedy
  │ └─Robert Sargent Jr. Shriver
  │   ├─Robert Sargent III Shriver
  │   ├─Maria Owings Shriver
  │   ├─Timothy Perry Shriver
  │   ├─Mark Kennedy Shriver
  │   └─Anthony Paul Shriver
  ├─Patricia Kennedy
  │ └─Peter Lawford
  │   ├─Christopher Kennedy Lawford
  │   ├─Sydney Maleia Lawford
  │   ├─Victoria Francis Lawford
  │   └─Robin Elizabeth Lawford
  ├─Robert Francis Kennedy
  │ └─Ethel Skakel
  │   ├─Kathleen Hartington Kennedy
  │   │ └─David Lee Townsend
  │   │   ├─Meaghan Anne Kennedy Townsend
  │   │   ├─Maeve Fahey Kennedy Townsend
  │   │   └─Rose Katherine Kennedy Townsend
  │   ├─Joseph Patrick II Kennedy
  │   │ └─Sheila Brewster Rauch
  │   │   ├─Joseph Patrick III Kennedy
  │   │   └─Matthew Rauch Kennedy
  │   ├─Robert Francis Jr. Kennedy
  │   │ └─Emily Ruth Black
  │   │   └─Robert Francis III Kennedy
  │   ├─David Anthony Kennedy
  │   ├─Mary Courtney Kennedy
  │   ├─Michael Lemoyne Kennedy
  │   │ └─Victoria Denise Gifford
  │   │   ├─Michael Lemoyne Jr. Kennedy
  │   │   └─Kyle Frances Kennedy
  │   ├─Mary Kerry Kennedy
  │   ├─Christopher George Kennedy
  │   ├─Matthew Maxwell Taylor Kennedy
  │   ├─Douglas Harriman Kennedy
  │   └─Rory Elizabeth Katherine Kennedy

1   2   3   4   5   6   7   8   9   10 11 12 13 14 15 16

Ultimate Family Tree Descendants Report (4-74)

Chart 1, generations 1 through 5

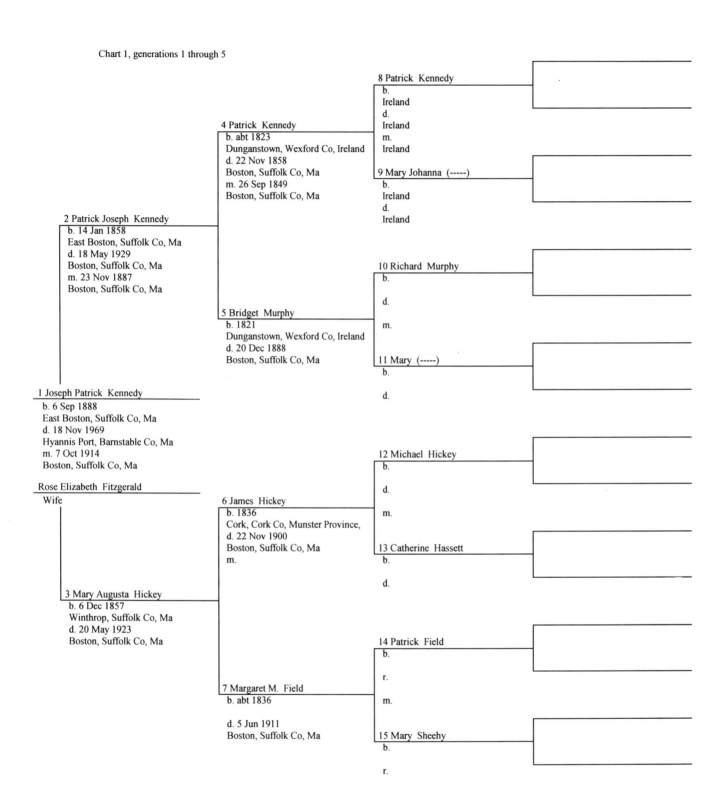

8 Patrick Kennedy
b.
Ireland
d.
Ireland
m.
Ireland

9 Mary Johanna (-----)
b.
Ireland
d.
Ireland

4 Patrick Kennedy
b. abt 1823
Dunganstown, Wexford Co, Ireland
d. 22 Nov 1858
Boston, Suffolk Co, Ma
m. 26 Sep 1849
Boston, Suffolk Co, Ma

2 Patrick Joseph Kennedy
b. 14 Jan 1858
East Boston, Suffolk Co, Ma
d. 18 May 1929
Boston, Suffolk Co, Ma
m. 23 Nov 1887
Boston, Suffolk Co, Ma

10 Richard Murphy
b.

d.

m.

5 Bridget Murphy
b. 1821
Dunganstown, Wexford Co, Ireland
d. 20 Dec 1888
Boston, Suffolk Co, Ma

11 Mary (-----)
b.

d.

1 Joseph Patrick Kennedy
b. 6 Sep 1888
East Boston, Suffolk Co, Ma
d. 18 Nov 1969
Hyannis Port, Barnstable Co, Ma
m. 7 Oct 1914
Boston, Suffolk Co, Ma

Rose Elizabeth Fitzgerald
Wife

12 Michael Hickey
b.

d.

m.

6 James Hickey
b. 1836
Cork, Cork Co, Munster Province,
d. 22 Nov 1900
Boston, Suffolk Co, Ma
m.

13 Catherine Hassett
b.

d.

3 Mary Augusta Hickey
b. 6 Dec 1857
Winthrop, Suffolk Co, Ma
d. 20 May 1923
Boston, Suffolk Co, Ma

14 Patrick Field
b.

r.

m.

7 Margaret M. Field
b. abt 1836

d. 5 Jun 1911
Boston, Suffolk Co, Ma

15 Mary Sheehy
b.

r.

Ultimate Family Tree Pedigree Chart (4-75)

Personal Events	Date	Historical Events/Roles
	Wednesday, November 23, 1887	Birth of Boris Karloff, bogeyman.
	Tuesday, November 29, 1887	Josef Hofmann, famous pianist, makes his US debut at the Met, age 11.
	Tuesday, November 29, 1887	US receives rights to Pearl Harbor, on Oahu, Hawaii.
	Tuesday, January 3, 1888	1st drinking straw is patented.
	Tuesday, January 24, 1888	Birth of Ernst Heinrich Heinkel, built 1st rocket-powered aircraft.
	Friday, January 27, 1888	National Geographic Society founded.
	Saturday, February 25, 1888	Birth of John Foster Dulles, Secretary of State for President Eisenhower.
	Sunday, March 4, 1888	Birth of Knute Rockne.
	Friday, May 11, 1888	Birth of Irving Berlin.
	Sunday, May 13, 1888	The poem "Casey at the Bat" 1st recited in a play in NY.
	Friday, June 1, 1888	1st seismograph installed in California.
	Sunday, June 3, 1888	"Casey at the Bat" is 1st published (by the SF Examiner).
	Thursday, June 28, 1888	Robert Louis Stevenson sails for the South Seas.
	Tuesday, August 7, 1888	1st revolving door installed.
	Tuesday, August 7, 1888	Jack the Ripper killed the 1st of his 6 victims.
	Tuesday, August 21, 1888	Patent issued for the adding machine.
	Tuesday, September 4, 1888	George Eastman patents 1st rollfilm camera & registers "Kodak".
Birth: Joseph was born in East Boston, Suffolk Co, Ma 6 September 1888.	Thursday, September 6, 1888	role: Child
	Friday, September 7, 1888	Jesse James staged his last train robbery.
Christening: He was christened in East Boston, Suffolk Co, Ma, 9 September 1888.	Sunday, September 9, 1888	role: Christened
	Wednesday, September 12, 1888	Birth of Maurice Chevalier, thanked heaven for little girls.
	Wednesday, September 26, 1888	Birth of T.S. Eliot, Anglican.
	Monday, October 1, 1888	1st "National Geographic" magazine was issued.

Ultimate Family Tree Timeline (4-76)

Win-Family
Version 5.01 for Windows

Basic Information

JamoDat
Dr. Dagmarsvej 34
3650 Olstykke
Denmark
Voice: 011-45-47176638
e-mail: Jamodat@jamodat.dk
http://www.jamodat.dk
Shareware fee: $50.00 U.S.

System requirements: IBM compatible 486 or higher, running Windows 3.1, Windows 95, or Windows NT
RAM: 8MB
Hard drive: 4MB space
CD-ROM: not required

Program Information

Individuals per database: unlimited (the program was tested with 60,000 persons)
Spouses per individual: unlimited
Children per relationship: 30
Children and spouses reordered: yes
Multiple parents: supported
Field sizes: name (128 characters), location (128 characters), address (32,000 characters), notes (32,000 characters)
Field options: 5 customizable fields are available for each individual; 1 customizable field is available per marriage
Multimedia options: unlimited photos per individual, images can be attached for each individual and marriage, a preferred photo can be specified, images may be categorized (individual, group, etc.), images can be scanned directly into the program, comments can be entered for images (as well as a year indicator), images can be selected from a master image database
Program options: right click over an individual brings up a menu with delete, edit, navigate, and print options; can drag and drop an individual's information to and from any field
Date options: 8 date formats available, or you may select a free-format date (free-format dates will not be recognized by the statistics function)
Search options: can search for any text in database; you can restrict the search to specfic fields, search results may be printed; individuals can be sorted by a variety of qualifiers (List Sorting feature allows you to select the sort order of all persons)
Merge options: database and individuals
Database maintenance and options: backup and restore function supported, data integrity check supported (results of data check can be printed)

Reports

View reports before printing: yes
Customized reports
* Options: (specify orientation, information to include, number of generations, individuals to include, how names are presented, which events and notes to include, layout, and format)
Photos included: some reports
Export data to text: some reports can be saved as ASCII text
Blank charts: some worksheets available
Ancestor Tree
Descendant Tree
Combination Tree (both ancestors and descendants on 1 chart)
Complete Tree (listing all persons related to a specific individual)
Blood Relatives (no spouses, only ancestors and descendants)
Fixed Book Report
* Cross references
* Index
Ancestor Sun Chart (circular pedigree chart)

Descendant Sun Chart (circular pedigree chart)
Index of Persons
Individual Personal Data Report
Person Worksheet
Missing Person Data Report
Descendants Sheet
Family Group Sheet
Mosaic (overview of all reference information from database)
Place-to-Person Index
Overview of Names Report

Sources

Creation: can enter source information for some events using source field
Source options: no master database of sources is available

Bells and Whistles

- A function allows you to create a Web page from database information
- A comprehensive forms-design function allows you to create your own reports

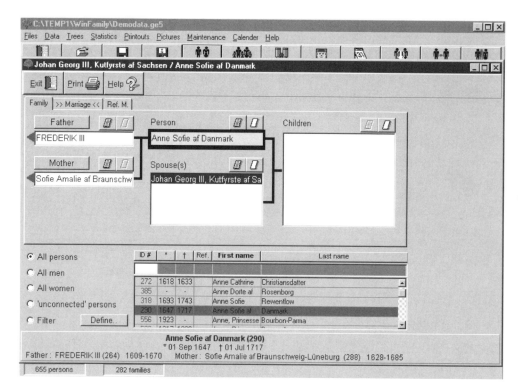

Figure 4.53
Win-Family
Family Screen

Figure 4.54
Win-Family
Individual
Information

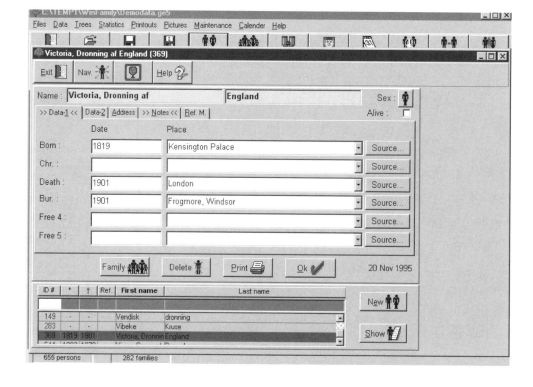

Chapter 5

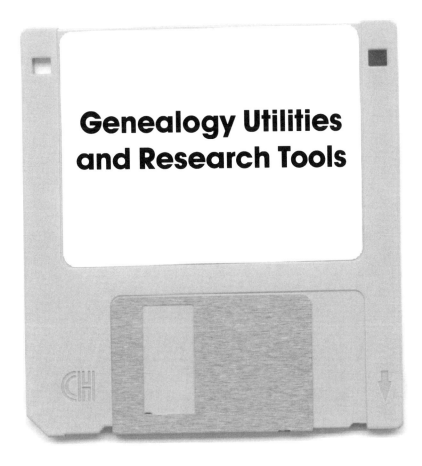

Genealogy Utilities and Research Tools

All About Me

Pat Gulotta
2502 Hickory Road
Homewood, IL 60430
Voice: 708-799-0831
e-mail: pgulotta@wwa.com
http://miso.wwa.com/~dgulotta/pgulotta.html
Shareware fee: $15.00
Demo available for download

System requirements: IBM compatible,
running Windows 95, 486 or higher
processor
RAM: 16MB RAM
Hard drive: 10MB space
Monitor: SVGA

Program features
Program to keep track of events and special
occasions for an individual.
+ Can choose from a list of 50 different
occasions including birth, schooling,
holidays, etc.
+ You can enter other occasions as needed
+ Can add photos, images, and sounds to
events
+ Information is displayed in hierarchical
tree format
+ Can print any of the records

AniMap Plus

The Gold Bug
PO Box 588
Alamo, CA 94507
e-mail: 70303.2363@compuserve.com
http://www.goldbug.com/
Price: $79.00 + $4.50 s/h
Demo available for download

System requirements: IBM compatible with
Windows 3.1 or higher
RAM: 4MB (8MB recommended)
Monitor: VGA or SVGA
CD-ROM: 2x or faster

Program features
Interactive county boundary historical atlas
for the U.S. SiteFinder (a database of U.S.
place names) included on the CD.
+ You can place up to 50 labelled "place
markers" which will stay in position as
you change the years
+ A function allows you to place items from
the SiteFinder databases on the map
+ You can print the maps, or export them
as graphics
+ Can customize your map with overlays
indicating places important in your
research, as well as use the built-in
overlays

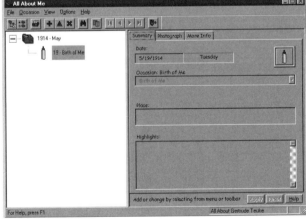

Figure 5.1
All About Me

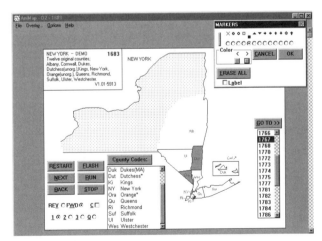

Figure 5.2
AniMap Plus

A-Tools for Windows

T.M. Simpson
20 Palace Green
Berwick upon Tweed, Northumberland
TD15 1HR England
Voice: 011-441-289-304560
e-mail: mike.simpson@btinternet.com
Shareware fee: $10.00
Demo available for download

System requirements: IBM compatible,
    running Windows 3.x or Windows 95

Program features
Contains a series of utilities useful for
researchers.
*   A-Census allows you to keep track of data
    from the UK 1841–1891 censuses
*   A-Locate allows you to select a particular
    parish in England, Wales, or Scotland,
    and print nearby parishes
*   A-Browser is a utility which allows you to
    view and edit any database which can be
    opened by data control (such as Access,
    dBASE, FoxPro, and Paradox)

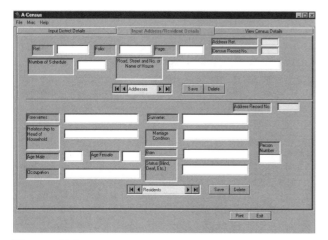

Figure 5.3
A-Census utility from A-Tools

Birdie 32

Drake Software Associates,
1 Wychwood Rise
Great Missenden, Bucks
HP16 0HB England
e-mail: barney@tdrake.demon.co.uk.
http://www.tdrake.demon.co.uk/birdie32.htm
Price: £25

System requirements: unknown

Program features
GEDCOM compatible utility allows you to
manage data downloaded from the IGI (via
the LDS FamilySearch program).
*   You can customize reports by specifying
    fonts, preview reports before you print
*   Can search for text

Cemetery Caretaker

Appleton's Fine Books & Genealogy
Tower Place Mall
8700 Pineville-Matthews Road, Suite #610
Charlotte, NC 28226
Voice: 800-777-3601
Voice: 704-341-2244
Fax: 704-341-0072
BBS: 704-552-1411
e-mail: catalog.request@appletons.com
http://www.appletons.com/genealogy/gene-
app.html
Price: $35.00
Demo available for download

System requirements: IBM compatible,
    running DOS 3.1 or higher

Program features
Program keeps track of where an ancestor is
buried (plot and cemetery), as well as
information on the headstone.
*   You can enter information on unusual
    epitaphs, biographies, and comments
*   A Quick-search function allows you to
    search the entire database
*   Can print a variety of reports from the
    information in the database

Clooz

Ancestor Detective
PO Box 1457
Woodbridge, VA 22193-1457
Voice/Fax: 703-680-6093
e-mail: clooz@ancestordetective.com
http://www.ancestordetective.com

System requirements: IBM compatible,
     running Windows 3.x or higher
CD-ROM: required

Program features
Clooz organizes miscellaneous genealogy
data into an electronic filing cabinet.
*   You can enter your own personal file
    number for each item entered
*   Individuals can be linked to document
    records
*   Can enter basic information for individuals,
    documents, directories, censuses, and
    photos (information entered for most
    documents includes call, roll, and personal
    file numbers, event, source title, and
    author, location, publisher, and
    repository)
*   10 reports can be generated (details for
    selected individuals, census records,
    documents, directories, selected or all
    photos, and lists of all individuals,
    documents, census records, and
    directories for the entire database (can
    print a report to disk in Word format)
*   There is no limit to the number of
    individuals linked to a specific record
*   Using an RTF or ASCII text file, you can
    import a list of individuals into Clooz
*   A manual is included

Corel Family Publisher

Corel
1600 Carling Avenue
Ottawa, ON
K1Z 8R7 Canada
http://www.corel.com/

System requirements: IBM compatible with
     a 386 or better processor, Windows 3.1 or
     higher

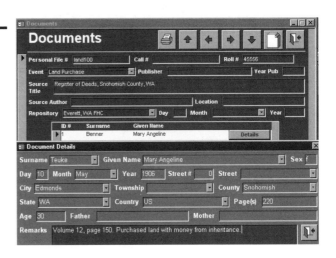

Figure 5.4
Clooz

RAM: 4MB
Hard drive: 4MB space
Monitor: VGA or compatible display
Mouse: required

Program features
Program prints a variety of high-quality
reports and charts from a GEDCOM file.
*   Sort child order
*   Find individuals by name, PIN, or
    reference number
*   Search for text in a number of fields
*   View data in Family Group, Ancestor, or
    Descendants Views
*   Reports can be customized (number of
    generations, events, PIN, siblings, female
    lines, place names, author information,
    and notes)
*   Page layout can be specified (date format,
    box style, paper orientation, and borders
    may be chosen, where applicable)
*   Worksheets with blank spaces for missing
    information can be printed for some
    reports
*   "Cousin Smart" features can be enabled so
    duplicate information will not be printed
    when related individuals marry
*   Reports: Family Group Record, Ancestor
    Chart (pedigree chart), Fan Chart,
    Register Report (book format), and Wall
    Charts (Ancestor or Descendants charts

only); the Register Report (Modified Register or Henry format) is not printed directly to the printer, instead it is saved as a word processing file which you can later modify and print

*   Included viewer feature allows you to freely distribute copies of your family information to friends and family

Cumberland Diary

Cumberland Family Software
385 Idaho Spring Road
Clarksville, TN 37043
Voice: 615-647-4012
e-mail: ira.lund@cf-software.com
http://www.cf-software.com/
Price: $20.00
Demo available for download

System requirements: IBM compatible, running Windows 3.x or higher

Program features

Diary/journal program allows you to search, cut and paste, spell check, and index entries.

*   Text can be imported or exported via ASCII text files, as well as printed (reports can be previewed before printing)
*   You can have as many diary files as you like (each file is limited to 32,000 entries)
*   The diary is divided into 4 sections: Contents, Calendar, Diary, and Index

Daily Journal

Parsons Technology
One Parsons Drive
PO Box 100
Hiawatha, IA 52233-0100
Voice: 319-395-9626
e-mail: info@parsonstech.com
http://www.parsonstech.com/software/
journal.html

System requirements: IBM compatible PC, 486 or better processor, running Windows 3.1 or higher
RAM: 4MB
Hard drive: 2MB space
CD-ROM: required

Program features

Journal program allows you to make journal entries or keep a diary.

*   Can arrange entries by topic
*   Entries may be password protected
*   A backup and restore function is available
*   A spell checker is included
*   You can search and replace text in any entry, as well as import and export text

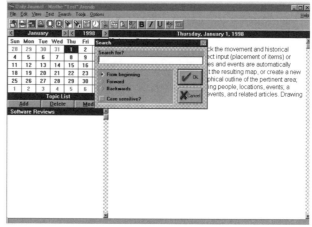

Figure 5.6
Daily Journal

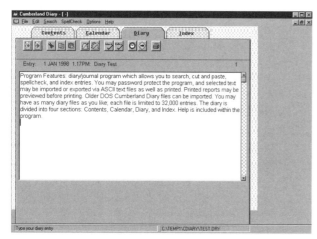

Figure 5.5
Cumberland Diary

DeedMapper

Direct Line Software
71 Neshobe Road
Newton, MA 02168
Voice: 617-527-9566
e-mail: deeds@ultranet.com
http://www.ultranet.com/~deeds/index.shtml
Price: $99.00

System requirements: IBM compatible,
    running DOS 3.3 or higher
RAM: 2MB (4MB if running Windows)
Hard drive: at least 1.2MB space
Monitor: VGA monitor

Program features
Land record software allows you to plot deed
maps.
* Can import/export deed information via
    ASCII format file
* You can export graphics files
* Database can be searched for any phrase
* Descriptions can be entered in "metes and
    bounds" format
* Can print your data in any scale (large
    areas may be printed in multiple pages)
* Optional computerized maps are available
    at additional cost and may be integrated
    into the program

Family Atlas for Windows

Broderbund Software, Inc.
39500 Stevenson Place, Suite 204
Fremont, CA 94539-3103
Voice: 510-494-2754
Fax: 510-794-9152
http://www.parsonstech.com/software/
famatlas.html
Orders accepted online
Price: $19.00

System requirements: IBM or compatible
    PC, 486 or better processor, Windows 3.1
    or higher
RAM: 4MB
Hard drive: 9MB space
CD-ROM: required

Program features
Program creates maps used to track the
movement and historical events of a family or
individual via direct input (placement of
items) or through import of a GEDCOM file.
* Places and events are automatically
    plotted from a GEDCOM; you can edit the
    resulting map or create a new one
* Maps typically consist of geographical
    outline of the pertinent area
* Map items (names or symbols) include
    people, locations, events, a legend,
    graphics depicting historical events, and
    related articles
* Drawing tools allow you to customize
    items (you can also create your own
    legend)
* Related historical articles detail events
    which may be relevant to your research
* U.S. map only is available
* Search function allows you to search for
    locations, geographical features, people,
    and other items
* You can print, copy, edit, delete, merge,
    save, and export created maps

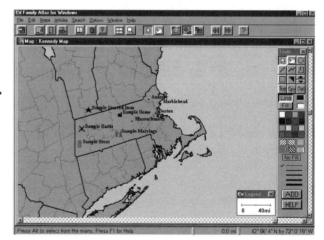

Figure 5.7
Family Atlas

Family Base

Micro Dynamics Electronic Publishing, Inc.
Voice: 801-431-0531
e-mail: info@micro-dynamics.com
http://www.micro-dynamics.com/fbsplash.htm
Price: $39.95

System requirements: IBM compatible, 386
   or higher, Windows 3.1x or higher
RAM: 8MB RAM
Hard drive: 10MB space
Monitor: 64K Colors (16 bit or high color)
CD-ROM: required

Program features
Program allows you to create a scrapbook by
adding photos, text, video and audio clips,
images, graphics, borders, etc.
- A training video is included, as well as
  on-screen instructions and a tutorial
- Search function will search for any word
  in the database
- Can enhance images
- 500+ clip art images, and 30 designer
  fonts

Family Calendar for Windows

Command Line Software
3431 Florida Drive
Loveland, CO 80538
Voice: 970-669-3159
e-mail: east@frii.com or dreast@aol.com
http://www.frii.com/~east/famcal/
famcal.html
Shareware fee: $25.00
Demo available for download

System requirements: IBM compatible 386
   or higher, DOS 5.0 or higher
RAM: 640K
Hard drive: 500K space

Program features
Program has tool to print family-oriented
calendars.
- You can specify font, paper size, and date
  format
- Can use a multi-date scheduler
- You can print a complete list of events
  and a blank data collection form
- The program supports color printers,
  landscape and portrait printing, and
  allows the user to select colors

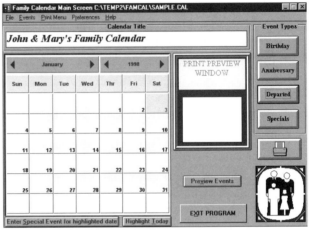

Figure 5.8
Family Calendar for Windows

Family Photo Album

Cumberland Family Software
385 Idaho Spring Road
Clarksville, TN 37043
Voice: 615-647-4012
e-mail: ira.lund@cf-software.com
http://www.cf-software.com/
Price: $20.00
Demo available for download

System requirements: IBM or compatible,
   running Windows 3.x or higher

Program features
Program allows you to create an electronic
photo album which can be shared with others,
or printed as a record of your photos.
- Each album can include 1 million
  chapters
- Each chapter can hold up to 250

scanned images and 64,000 characters of text (the text editor includes a spell-checker)

♦ Each image may be captioned, and you can include a title page and table of contents

♦ You can edit chapters and make changes in photos, captions, chapter headings, or story notes

♦ Chapters can be previewed before printing, and you can save the report as a Windows Meta File (WMF)

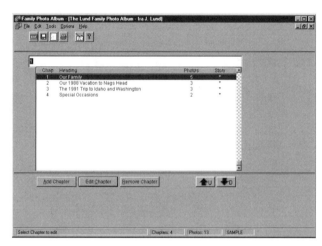

Figure 5.9
Family Photo Album

Family Tree Builder and Family Tree Browser

Ravinder Rao
e-mail: rrao@hotmail.com
http://pw2.netcom.com/~rrao/familytree.html
Shareware fee: none

System requirements: IBM compatible, running Windows 95
RAM: 8MB
Other: Java-enabled Web browser

Program features
Tree Builder utility will create a Web page from information you enter (program does not accept a GEDCOM as a means of inputting data); Tree Browser will display the data file created by Tree Builder.

♦ You can place the output online where it can be read by anyone with a Java-capable Web browser

♦ Program functions allow visitors to browse through relationships and photos, search for family members, and locate them on a map

FixSex 1.01

Ripple Effect Software
PO Box 671
Ellicott City, MD 21041-0671
e-mail: 100041.1315@compuserve.com
http://www.pratt.lib.md.us/~bharding/rippleeffect/FixSex/FixSex.html
Shareware fee: $10.00
Demo available for download

System requirements: IBM compatible, running Windows 95

Program features
Utility which will repair missing or incorrect sex codes in a GEDCOM.

♦ Can automatically assign gender codes based on an individual's name (if the gender cannot be determined by name, it will be determined by spouse's sex)

♦ You can also manually change gender codes

GCFiler

Orelle Corporation
PO Box 643
LaGrange, IL 60525
Shareware fee: $15.00

System requirements: IBM compatible, running DOS 3.1 or higher
RAM: 256K

Program features
Utility converts a standard GEDCOM file to a comma-delimited ASCII file, and vice versa.

GED2HTML

Eugene Stark
14 Landing Lane
Port Jefferson, NY 11777
e-mail: ged2html@gendex.com
http://www.gendex.com/ged2html/
Shareware fee: $20.00
Demo available for download

System requirements: IBM compatible,
running Windows 3.1, Windows 95, or
UNIX

Program features
Utility will convert information from a
GEDCOM into a collection of HTML files.
* Uses the GEDCOM 5.5 standard
* Output is highly configurable
* GENDEX indexing is supported
* You can generate linked pedigree charts, a
  hypertext index, add images, sounds, and
  text
* A version for UNIX is also available
* Alternate character sets are supported
* Can specify a living individual cutoff date

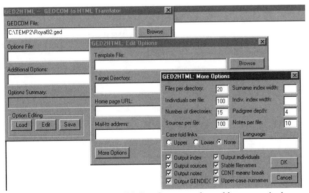

Copyright 1997 Eugene W. Stark, reproduced by permission

Figure 5.10
GED2HTML

GED2WWW

Leslie Howard
e-mail: lhoward@ix.netcom.com
http://pw2.netcom.com/~lhoward/
ged2www.html
Shareware fee: none

System requirements: IBM or compatible,
running DOS, Windows, Windows 95, or
UNIX

Program features
Utility converts a GEDCOM file into a set of
HTML pages.
* The program produces a small number of
  HTML files
* Can produce a gendex.txt file (for
  indexing with the GENDEX project)
* International characters are supported
* Will suppress dates for living individuals
* A summary, index, surname, and data
  pages can be generated
* You can choose text and background
  colors, as well as a background image
* The program is available for DOS or
  UNIX computers

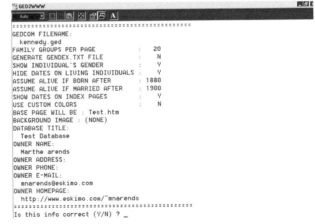

Figure 5.11
GED2WWW

GEDClean

Tom Raynor
e-mail: tomraynor@aol.com
http://members.aol.com/tomraynor2/
gedclean.htm
Shareware fee: none

System requirements: IBM compatible,
   running Windows 3.x, Windows 95 or
   Windows NT

Program features
Utility protects privacy of individuals by
removing living individual's personal information from a GEDCOM file.
◆ Can specify individuals who are living,
   and the program will remove information
   and replace it with the notice "Living
   Individual—Details Withheld"

Ged-Commander 2

Mike Simpson
20 Palace Green
Berwick-upon-Tweed, Northumberland
TD15 1HR England
Voice: 011-441-289-304560
e-mail: Mike.Simpson@btinternet.com
http://www.btinternet.com/~genealogy/
Shareware fee: $10.00

System requirements: IBM compatible,
   running Windows 95

Program features
Utility enables you to manually edit or merge
GEDCOM files.
◆ 2 GEDCOM files can be displayed
   side-by-side
◆ Can conduct an alphabetic surname sort
◆ Can re-number records
◆ Records can be transferred from 1
   GEDCOM to another
◆ Can re-number a file in LDS Ancestral
   File format, merge files
◆ A search function allows you to find and
   replace any text string in either
   GEDCOM
◆ Pattern matching is not supported

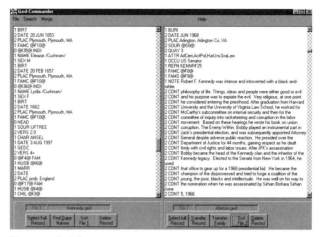

Figure 5.12
GED Commander

Gedcom Viewer

Generic Designs
e-mail: generic@northnet.com.au
http://www.northnet.com.au/~generic/
gedcom/
Demo available for download

System requirements: IBM compatible,
   running either Windows 95 or
   Windows NT

Program features
Utility displays a full pedigree structure from
a GEDCOM file.
◆ Display font and format can be changed
◆ Can check for logical errors
◆ Can print the pedigree
◆ Can calculate inbreeding coefficients

Gedpage

Ron Jacob
e-mail: rjacob@frontiernet.net
http://www.frontiernet.net/~rjacob/
gedpage.htm

System requirements: IBM compatible,
   running Windows 3.1 or higher
RAM: dependent on size of tree
Hard drive: space dependent on size of tree

Program features

Utility will convert a GEDCOM into a series of HTML pages.

*   The standard page is in Family Group Sheet format
*   Can specify background color or graphic, and text color
*   The output is GENDEX compatible

GedPrivy

John Goodwin
6502 Westhaven Lane
Springfield, VA 22150-4260
e-mail: GedPrivy@aol.com
http://members.aol.com/gedprivy
Shareware fee: $10.00
Demo available for download

System requirements: IBM compatible 386 or better CPU, Windows 3.1 or Windows 95

Program features

Utility which marks "private" information on living individuals within a GEDCOM file.

*   The program functions automatically and there is no need to specify living individuals
*   Supports the GEDCOM v5.5 standard

GEN-BOOK

GEN-BOOK
2105 Country Lane
Auburn, CA 95603-9735
Voice: 916-889-8801
e-mail: genbook@foothill.net
http://www.foothill.net/~genbook
Price: $59.95 + $4.00 S/H

System requirements: IBM or compatible computer

Other: must have either PAF, Ancestral Quest, or a GEDCOM file to import data; WordPerfect version 5.0 or later, or Word for Windows 2.0/6.0/7.0 to create the book

Program features

Program will generate a book in either ancestor or descendant format from a GEDCOM, PAF 2.31, Ancestral Quest, or PAF 3.0 file; the resulting book file is in WordPerfect format.

*   Using a word processor, you can make modifications, add photos, maps, etc.
*   Output includes a title page, table of contents, chapter headings, event notes, sources, and an index of names (2 or 3 columns)
*   Output closely resembles the Modified Register System
*   An extensive list of options allows you to customize the output exactly to your specifications
*   Can choose Register, Henry, descendancy, ahnentafel, multi-surname, or sequential-numbering systems
*   Can include or exclude specific individuals or families
*   Can include source notes, blank lines for missing information, footnotes, and RIN numbers
*   Options allow you to change surnames to all capital letters, begin each generation as a new chapter, specify chapter headings, insert an explanation, introduction, and acknowledgment pages
*   You can use LDS temple ordinances, restrict tagged notes, choose page size, use multiple starting points, and cross-reference names via page numbers
*   5 versions of the program are available: GEN-BOOK version 7.0 for PAF 2.31 (DOS); version 7.0 for PAF 3.0 (DOS); version 7.0 for PAF 2.31 (Windows); version 7.0 for PAF 3.0 (Windows); version 7.0 for GEDCOM

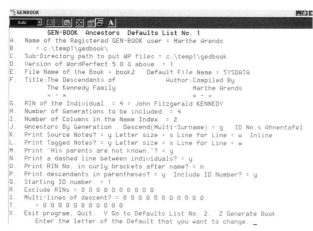

Figure 5.13
GEN-BOOK

GenBox

Thoughtful Creations
ATTN: William T. Flight
GENBOX Registration
PO Box 19406
Cincinnati, OH 45219
Shareware fee: $45.00

System requirements: IBM compatible,
running DOS, Windows 3.1, or Windows 95

Program features
Utility produces box charts from a GEDCOM
file.
* 5 chart types are available (Descendant,
Ancestry, Related, Everyone, and
Custom Box Charts)
* Reports can be previewed before printing
* You can choose font style and size, and
print modes
* A font editor is included with the
program

GenBrowser

Ripple Effect Software
PO Box 671
Ellicott City, MD 21041-0671
Shareware fee: $20.00
e-mail: 100041.1315@compuserve.com
http://www.pratt.lib.md.us/~bharding/
rippleeffect/GenBrowser/GenBrowser.html
Demo available for download

System requirements: IBM compatible,
running Windows 95
Hard drive: 1MB or more
Other: access to Internet

Program features
A Web browser created specifically for genealogists, GenBrowser has the unique function
of generating a GEDCOM from information
found on a Web page using GEDPAGE,
GED2HTML, or Indexed GEDCOM Method
(IGM) format.
* Can search online for an individual or
group of individuals automatically at
several genealogy-specific and general
search engine sites
* Program also has the ability to
display only those pages which have
changed since you last searched

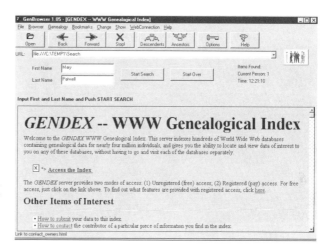

Figure 5.14
GenBrowser

The Genealogical Companion

David J. Harrier
e-mail: harrier@geocities.com
http://www.geocities.com/SiliconValley/2399/
tgc.htm
Shareware fee: none
Demo available for download

System requirements: IBM compatible 486 or
higher, running Windows 95 or NT
RAM: 16MB or more

Hard drive: 18.5MB
Monitor: EGA or higher monitor
Other: In order to use the most of the functions, you need to have Family Origins data files

Program features
Program fills in the gaps of the Family Origins program.

* Can conduct broken chains analysis
* Census manager feature does not require Family Origins file
* Can create correspondence, To-Do, and a Research Log
* Can generate a Fact Type Report, Families Without a Source Report, Soundex Summary
* Can create a set of Web pages from the Family Origins information
* An older version for Windows 3.1 is also available

Figure 5.15
The Genealogical Companion

GenMap UK

Stephen Archer
90 St. Albans Road
Dartford, Kent
DA1 1TY England
Voice: 011-441-322-291509
e-mail: 100142.2542@compuserve.com.
http://ourworld.compuserve.com/homepages/
steve_archer/GENMAP.HTM
Price: $40.00

System requirements: IBM compatible, running Windows 3.1 or Windows 95, 486 or higher processor
RAM: 8MB (16MB recommended)

Program features
Utility which will display and print U.K. maps of historical or genealogical data.

* You can plot the movement of surnames through time and location
* Can use either Dot-Distribution or County-Floodfill mapping styles
* Individual records can be edited
* GEDCOM is supported
* Resulting maps can be printed

HTML Genie

GeneaWare
95 Kimberly Street
Fredericton, NB
E3A 5V6 Canada
e-mail: geneaware@deltastar.nb.ca
http://www.deltastar.nb.ca/GeneaWare/
Shareware fee: $19.95
Demo available for download

System requirements: unknown

Program features
Utility creates a series of HTML files from a GEDCOM file.

* You can generate output in 4 report formats: Descendancy List, Modified Register Report, Family Record Report, and an Ahnentafel List
* You can search a GEDCOM file and display individual data
* A GENDEX file can be generated
* Options allows a variety of customized output

IGIRead

TWR Computing
Clapstile Farm, Alpheton
Sudbury, Suffolk
CO10 9BN England
Voice/Fax: 011-441-284-828271
e-mail: TWRcomputing@clapstile.
dungeon.com
http://www.dungeon.com/~clapstile/
software.htm
Price: £10

System requirements: IBM comptatible,
    running DOS 2.0 or later
RAM: 256K
Monitor: CGA/EGA/VGA

Program features
Utility will read files generated from the IGI
(part of the FamilySearch Program which can
be found at Family History Centers).
* Can read IGI output in the form of
    GEDCOM 2.1, 3.0, Text 1988, and Text
    1993
* You may create a single resulting file
    from 1 or more input files, with no limit
    on the size, or number of input or output
    files
* Can convert information from a SSDI
    GEDCOM file

JavaGED

Chris Shearer Cooper
14 Lena Lane
Milford, MA 01757
Shareware fee: $20.00
http://www.kersur.net/~ccooper/
javamain.shtml
Demo available for download

System requirements: IBM compatible,
    running Windows 95 or NT
Other: Netscape Communicator 4.0, Netscape
    Navigator 3.01, or Microsoft Internet
    Explorer 3.0–4.0

Program features
Program converts a GEDCOM file into a
Java-based Web document.
* The companion program Java2GED will
    pre-process a GEDCOM file

Kinship Archivist

Singularity Solutions, Inc.
Kinship Archivist Registration
3808 110th Avenue East
Edgewood, WA 98372
e-mail: evjendan@frugal.com
http://www.frugal.com/~evjendan/
ancestry.html
Shareware fee: $20.00
Demo available for download

System requirements: IBM compatible 386,
    486, or Pentium, running Windows 3.1 or
    higher
RAM: 4MB
Monitor: VGA or SVGA monitor
Hard drive: required
Other: Web browser

Program features
Utility will create a series of Web pages from
a GEDCOM file or from your direct input.
* You can specify which tags to use, and
    HTML page defaults
* Can add information to individuals,
    include notes, etc.

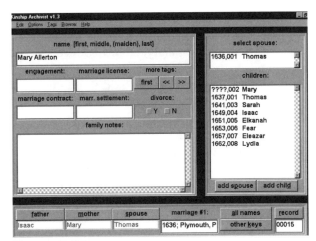

Figure 5.16
Kinship Archivist

KinWrite Plus

LDB Associates, Inc.
143 S. Oakwood
Wichita, KS 67218
Voice: 316-651-0200
e-mail: ldbond@compuserve.com
Price: $59.00

System requirements: IBM compatible,
running DOS 3.1 or higher
RAM: 640K
Hard drive: required
Other: Must also have data stored in PAF
version 2.0, 2.1, 2.2, or 2.3 structure;
some features require the use of
WordPerfect 5.0 (or higher), or a word
processor which will convert WordPerfect
files

Program features

The program produces a narrative structure
report in book format using PAF data files.
GEDCOM is not supported.

* You can select either generation or
  family line reports for a specific
  individual
* Output is available in Modified Register,
  KinWrite, or KinDraft formats
* A comprehensive manual gives details and
  examples on using the program, as well as
  a brief section on using WordPerfect and
  Word with the output
* A 1 or 2 column name index may be
  generated
* You can print directly to the printer, a
  text file, or WordPerfect file
* Can print blank spaces for missing
  information; specify page headers; create
  custom book or report title; specify
  multiple date formats; add supplemental
  data such as a forward, footnotes,
  ancestor charts; can include allied
  families information; specify the number
  of generations
* Options allow you to carry children to the
  next generation, and include both families
  when cousins marry, and more
* A KinWrite upgrade is planned (Windows
  only) to support PAF version 2.x, as well
  as PAF version 3.0

Life History Disk

Star·Com Microsystems
Windsor Park East
25 West 1480 North
Orem, UT 84057
Voice: 801-225-1480
Price: $19.95

System requirements: IBM compatible (DOS
or Windows), Macintosh, or Apple II
computer
Other: A word processor must be present to
read the text file; files are available in
ASCII, WordPerfect, and Word formats

Program features

Life history format guides you through
writing personal histories for yourself or
other individuals.

* A life history may be generated on the
  computer by simply filling in the blanks
  of a history outline, or it can be printed
  and used to conduct interviews
* Chronological and subject-formatted
  chapters cover: ancestry and heritage
  (4 generations); early childhood;
  elementary, junior, and high school years;
  college years; special service; military
  service; marriage and family; adult years;
  life lessons/religious affiliations
* A manual is included on disk
* Full details on conducting interviews are
  given, as well as hints and tips on what to
  do once you have a narrated life history
* Also included is advice on keeping a
  personal journal, instructions on making
  a video life history, and a graphics title
  page border

My Life

JamoDat-USA
3705 Lookout Drive
Huntsville, AL 35801
e-mail: weywadt@hiwaay.net
http://www.jamodat.dk/Mylifemain.htm
Shareware fee: $40.00

System requirements: IBM compatible 486
    or higher, running Windows 95
RAM: 8MB
Hard drive: 4MB space

Program features
Utility will create a diary of events in an
individual's or family's life.
*   Each page covers 6 months
*   Can add text, images, graphics, and
    timelines, and print the resulting diary in
    book form

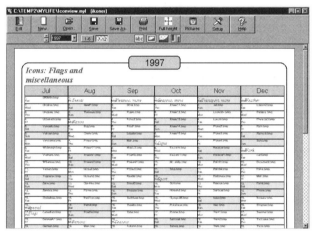

Figure 5.17
My Life

PAF*Mate

Progeny Software, Inc.
5518 Prospect Road
New Minas, NS
B4N 3K8 Canada
Voice: 902-681-1131
Fax: 902-681-2747
e-mail: progeny@fox.nstn.ca
http://www.progeny2.com
Price: $39.99

System requirements: IBM or compatible 386
    or better, Windows version 3.1 or higher
RAM: 4MB
Hard drive: minimum 4MB space
Monitor: VGA or compatible display
Other: PAF version 2.0 or higher

Program features
PAF utility will print a variety of high
quality genealogy charts from PAF data files.
*   No GEDCOMs are required
*   Reports include Register Report (book
    format), Family Group Record, Ancestor
    Chart (Pedigree Chart), Ancestor Chart
    with Siblings, Descendants Chart, Fan
    Chart, and Wall Charts (large-scale
    Ancestor, Descendants, and Fan Charts)
*   You can customize the charts by selecting
    which individuals to include, box style,
    font, choice of events to include, date
    format, place names, unlimited
    generations, and more
*   Register Report can be saved in text
    format, as well as Word, WordPerfect,
    Lotus AmiPro, and Microsoft Works
    formats
*   Blank Family Group Records can be
    printed as worksheets
*   Cousin Smart feature eliminates duplicate
    ancestors when related individuals marry

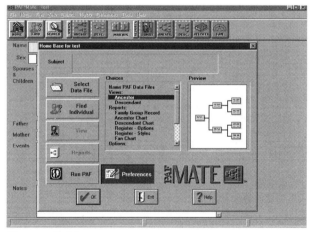

Figure 5.18
PAF*Mate

Progenitor

Crestline Enterprises
e-mail: giammot@access.digex.net
http://www.access.digex.net/~giammot/webged/
Shareware fee: $20.00
Demo available for download

System requirements: IBM compatible,
running Windows 95
Other: Java-capable Web browser

Program features
Utility will convert information from a
GEDCOM to a series of HTML files.
- The program uses a Java applet which
  creates a name-index file whenever a
  visitor views the pages
- Supplemental searches can be conducted
  either alphabetically or in Soundex
  format
- Options include additional text
  information, individual and marriage
  notes, birth year threshold (dates after
  the specified year will have information
  removed for privacy), a non-Java surname
  index, and a GENDEX index file
- Other options allow you to further
  customize the output

Research Shop

Amy Giroux
6491 Yellowstone Street
Orlando, FL 32807
e-mail: agiroux@compuserve.com
http://www.geocities.com/~agiroux
Shareware fee: $20.00
Demo available for download

System requirements: IBM compatible,
running Windows 3.1 or higher

Program features
Program organizes research projects via
research session events.
- Letters, microfilm, books, phone calls,
  negative responses, and user-defined
  events can be added

- You can associate an unlimited number of
  events with a research session
- Can create a To-Do list
- Reminder function will warn of overdue
  items
- Generates blank data-gathering forms
  (Research Notes, Pedigree Charts, Family
  Group Sheets, and Census Extracts)
- Creates an invoice for professional
  research services

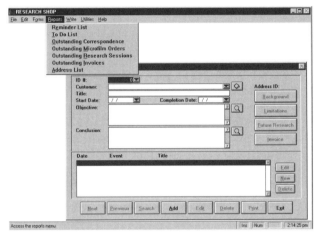

Figure 5.19
Research Shop

Sky Filer

Sky Software
4675 York One Road
Lineboro, MD 21088
Voice: 800-776-0137
Fax: 410-374-3484
http://www.sky-software.com
Price: $35.00
Demo available for download

System requirements: IBM or compatible
PC, 386 or higher, running Windows
3.1 or higher
RAM: 4MB
Hard drive: 3MB space

Program features
Flexible organizer uses a filing cabinet meta-
phor to organize research and data.
- Can arrange information in alphabetical
  or chronological order

- ◆ Can track correspondence
- ◆ Options include indexing CDs, organizing a filing cabinet, catalog books, etc.
- ◆ You can attach notes (called "contents") to each item, drawer, or folder; a maximum of 30,000 characters of text is allowed per note
- ◆ The manual contains a short tutorial
- ◆ Can search the entire database for up to 60 characters of text
- ◆ Can import and export text in comma- and quote-delimited ASCII format
- ◆ 2 printed reports are allowed: a hierarchical listing, and an index of items
- ◆ Other features: databases can be merged, items can be duplicated, folder labels (for filing cabinets) can be printed
- ◆ 3 template databases are included as examples

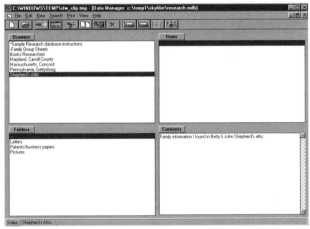

Figure 5.20
Sky Filer

Sky Index

Sky Software
4675 York One Road
Lineboro, MD 21088
Voice: 800-776-0137
Fax: 410-374-3484
http://www.sky-software.com
Price: $99.00 + $5.00 s/h
Demo available for download

System requirements: IBM or compatible PC, 386 or higher, running Windows 3.1 or higher

RAM: 4MB
Hard drive: 3MB space

Program features
Program creates indexes for any type of material: books, newspapers, periodicals, records, etc.

- ◆ Manual contains a short tutorial
- ◆ Each topic has 1 main heading and up to 2 levels of sub-topics (sub-headings), and a page number (each field is allowed 255 characters)
- ◆ Features include append, flip and insert (exchange the contents of the topic and sub-topic fields), duplicate prior field, automatic maiden name, search and replace, merge indexes, generate a proof-reading report, ignore duplicates, ASCII delimited file import and export, dBASE III+ file import, a choice of sorting methods (ASCII, letter-by-letter, word-by-word)
- ◆ You can specify headers, footers, font, character format, and number of columns
- ◆ Can generate Rich Text Format (RTF) output, as well as an ASCII file
- ◆ Up to 10 macros may be assigned for ease of data entry
- ◆ Repair and compacting functions are supported
- ◆ You must use a word processor to print the generated index via RTF or ASCII output file

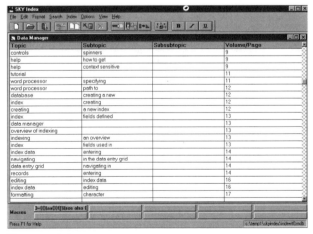

Figure 5.21
Sky Index

Tree Draw for Windows

SpanSoft
11 Rowan Terrace
Cowdenbeath, Fife
KY4 9JZ Scotland
Voice/Fax: 011-441-383-510597
e-mail: SpanSoft@compuserve.com
http://ourworld.compuserve.com/homepages/
SpanSoft/
Shareware fee: $34.00
Demo available for download

System requirements: IBM compatible 286
or higher, Windows 3.1 or higher
Hard drive: 1.5MB space
Other: a GEDCOM file or the Kith and Kin
program

Program features
Utility creates high-quality, drop-line charts.
♦ Can add maps, photos, clip art, diagrams,
  etc. to the chart

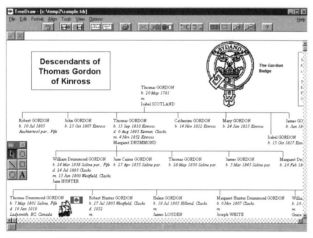

Figure 5.22
Tree Draw for Windows

uFTi

Oughtibridge, Ltd.
42 Stoops Lane
Doncaster, Yorkshire
DN4 7RY England
Voice: 011-441-302-531290
e-mail: oughtibridge@compuserve.com
http://ourworld.compuserve.com/homepages/
oughtibridge/ufti.htm
Shareware fee: none, although a $20.00 per
site alternative license is available if you
want to edit the generated pages
Demo available for download

System requirements: IBM compatible,
running Windows 95 or higher (for the 32
bit version; the 16 bit version requires
Windows 3.1 or higher)
RAM: 8MB (12–16MB recommended)
Hard drive: 10MB space
Monitor: VGA

Program features
Utility converts information from a
GEDCOM file to a series of HTML Web
pages.
♦ Can add text notes
♦ Program supports a wide range of events
♦ Can include sources and source quality
♦ Can generate an index of surnames
♦ Tables of ancestors can be added
♦ Can specify graphic backgrounds, frames,
  and more

Chapter 6

Macintosh and Other Genealogy Software

Most of the genealogy databases listed in the following pages support GEDCOM import and export. I was not able to review the programs listed in this chapter due to equipment restrictions; all information about the software is from the program's documentation or the author. Databases are listed first, followed by utility programs.

Please note that, while the information present was accurate at the time of writing, new versions of software may change, add, or eliminate functions. Contact the vendor or author for information on current versions.

Macintosh Genealogy Databases

Family Heritage File

Star·Com Microsystems
Windsor Park East
25 West 1480 North
Orem, UT 84057-8323
Voice: 801-225-1480
Price: $99.00
Demo available for download

System requirements: Macintosh compatible
RAM: 512K
Hard drive: required (or second floppy disk drive)
Printer: required

Program features
Individual options: 3 given names and titles are supported, 30 children per relationship allowed, can designate primary spouse, reorder children, and specify no children for a family
Note options: unlimited History Notes for each individual, can access a directory of individuals who have History Notes
Program options: data file access (work with multiple databases, can export data in ASCII or GEDCOM format, user preferences include LDS and Jewish options, LDS ordinance fields optional
Search options: search by individual, parent, spouse, child, marriage, name, or date
Bells and whistles: built-in spell checker
Reports
- Pedigree Chart
- Descendants Chart
- Family Group Record
- Individual Information Summary
- Lists (a variety of lists are available)

Family Tree Maker

Broderbund Software, Inc.
Banner Blue Division
39500 Stevenson Place, Suite 204
Fremont, CA 94539-3103
Voice: 510-494-2754

Fax: 510-794-9152
http://www.familytreemaker.com
Price: $99.99
Demo available for download
Orders accepted online

System requirements: PowerPC processor, System 7.1.2 or higher
RAM: 16MB (8MB with virtual memory)
Hard drive: 15MB space
CD-ROM: required

Program features
Individual options: 2 million individuals allowed, can enter information on names, dates, notes, stories, nicknames and special titles, medical information, addresses, adoptions, divorces, and re-marriages, graduations, baptisms, and burials
Bells and whistles: access to Family Archives CDs is supported
Reports
- Ancestor Tree
- Descendants Tree
- Kinship Report
- LDS Report
- Birthday and Anniversary Calendars
- Custom Report
- Family Group Sheet

Comments
The Macintosh version of FTM is very similar to version 3.02 for Windows, but with no scrapbook capability

Gene

Diana and David Eppstein
8 Owen Court
Irvine, CA 92612
Voice: 714-854-6594
e-mail: eppstein@ics.uci.edu
http://www.ics.uci.edu/~eppstein/gene/
Shareware fee: $15.00
Demo available for download

System requirements: 3 versions available for older 68000 machines, power PCs, and 1 version for people who want to run the same program on both types of machines

Program features

Individual options: photos can be attached to individuals, can enter events for individual and family

Program options: GEDCOM compatible, can specify date format

Bells and whistles: Web page can be generated

Reports

+ Ancestor Families Report
+ Ancestor Report
+ Calendar
+ Descendant Families Report
+ Descendants Report
+ Family Group Sheet
+ File summary
+ Single card

Heritage

TAG Software
14049 232nd Avenue SE
Issaquah, WA 98027
206-865-2239
e-mail: grandine@eskimo.com
http://www.eskimo.com/~grandine/heritage.html
Shareware fee: $15.00
Demo available for download

System requirements: 68020 (or better) CPU, MacOS 7.0 (or later)

RAM: 4MB

Hard drive: 300K space

Program features

Individual options: free-form biographical information supported, family notes are supported, date ranges are supported

Program options: GEDCOM compatible, images may be tracked and displayed,

Bells and whistles: foreign language version available in French, Danish, and German

Reports

+ Ancestor Report
+ Descendant Report

+ Family Group Sheet
+ Biographical Sketch
+ Alphabetized Surname Reports

Reunion for Macintosh

Leister Productions
PO Box 289
Mechanicsburg, PA 17055
Voice: 717-697-1378
Fax: 717-697-4373
e-mail: info@LeisterPro.com
http://www.leisterpro.com/
Price: $99.00
Demo available for download

System requirements: Any Macintosh or Power Macintosh (except Plus, SE, Classic, PB100, original MacPortable), System 7.1 or later

RAM: 4MB minimum

Hard drive: 3MB space (family file size will be an additional 400K per 1,000 people)

Program features

Individual options: A variety of information can be entered such as names, dates, places, notes, facts, custom fields, mailing address, and marital status; images, video and sound can be linked to an individual; images can be placed into reports and charts

Program options: GEDCOM compatible, multiple-criteria searches are supported, pop-up lists of often used information supported, source documentation uses a master list

Reports

+ Descendants Report (graphic tree chart)
+ Pedigree Report (graphic tree chart)
+ Cascading Pedigree Chart
+ Family Group Sheet
+ Book-style Reports (narrative Ahnentafel, Register, and Family History Report)
+ Person Sheets
+ Questionnaires
+ Custom Lists
+ Birthday and Anniversary Lists
+ Blank charts

Ultimate Family Tree

Palladium Interactive
900 Larkspur Landing Circle, Suite 295
Larkspur, CA 94939
Voice: 415-464-5500
Fax: 415-464-5530
e-mail: UFTHelp@Palladium.net
http://www.uftree.com/
Price: $59.95

System requirements: System 7.0.1 or
   higher, 68040 or PowerMac
RAM: 8MB (16MB strongly recommended for
   better performance)
Hard drive: 22MB space
CD-ROM: 2x speed

Program features
The Macintosh version of Ultimate Family
Tree Deluxe has the same features as the
Windows version. For details on features, see
the Windows review on page 176.

Macintosh Utility Programs

Family Base

Micro Dynamics Electronic Publishing
Voice: 801-431-0531
e-mail: info@micro-dynamics.com
http://www.micro-dynamics.com/fbsplash.htm
Price: $39.95

System requirements: 68020 or higher,
   System 7
RAM: 8MB
Hard drive: 10MB space
Monitor: 64K Colors (16 bit or high color)
CD-ROM: required

Program features
Software allows you to create a scrapbook by
adding photos, text, video and audio clips,
images, graphics, borders, etc.
* A training video is included
* Search function will search for any word
  in the database
* Can enhance photos
* 500+ clip art images, and 30 designer
  fonts are included

Family History Composer

Cygnal Software
1225 Vienna Drive #986
Sunnydale, CA 94089
408-734-4130
e-mail: cygnalsoft@aol.com

http://members.aol.com/CygnalSoft/Private/
Cygnal_Software.html
Price: $49.00
Demo available for download

System requirements: System 7
Hard drive: required
Other: a word processor which can read RTF
   files, and a GEDCOM

Program features
Transforms information from a GEDCOM
into a family history.
* Event information is composed into
  sentences and merged with text you have
  written
* You can customize the output by
  selecting how much information to
  include, which individuals to feature, etc.
* You can generate a title page, table of
  contents, bibliography, and name index
* Sources, footnotes, and column-formatted
  text are supported

Gedpage

Ron Jacob
e-mail: rjacob@frontiernet.net
http://www.frontiernet.net/~rjacob/
gedpage.htm

System requirements: unknown

Program features
Utility converts a GEDCOM into a series of HTML pages.
- The standard page is in Family Group Sheet format
- Can specify background color or graphic, and text color
- The output is GENDEX-compatible
- Can customize the text

Genealogy Pro

Micro Evolution Technologies
58 Chapman Street
Sunshine VIC 3020
Australia
Voice: 011-61-3-9310-1370
e-mail: mevolve@pobox.com
http://www-personal.monash.edu.au/~pcf/GenealogyPro.html
Shareware fee: none
Demo available for download

System requirements: 256K enhanced ROM or greater (Genealogy Pro does not currently support the Macintosh SE, Macintosh Plus, or earlier models), System 6.07 or later

Program features
Utility draws family tree charts.
- You can produce vertical, horizontal, and wheel formats, each of which supports a variety of formats
- You can show or hide various fields
- Can specify the style and order of fields
- Custom fields can be added
- Over 5,000 individuals can be stored in the database, and each individual is allowed 32K of notes
- GEDCOM support is included
- Charts printed include Direct Line Chart (Pedigree Chart), Horizontal Direct Line Chart, Vertical Direct Line Chart, Concentric Circular Direct Line Chart (Wheel Chart), Horizontal Family Chart, and Vertical Family Chart

MacPAF Report Utility

Nexial Systems
Joe M. Oglesby
2075A Lakewood Club Drive South
Saint Petersburg, FL 33712
Voice: 813-866-9281
http://members.aol.com/nexialist/index.html
Shareware fee: $20.00
Demo available for download

System requirements: unknown

Program features
Program extracts data and generates text reports from the Macintosh version of PAF
- Reports include Ahnentafel, Descending Charts, and a variety of lists (Name Frequencies, Individual Extract, Reference Note Summary, Soundex)

Sparrowhawk 1.0

Brad Mohr
6501 Ravenna Avenue NE, #207
Seattle, WA 98115
e-mail: bmohr@tjp.washington.edu
Shareware fee: $20.00

System requirements: System 7.0 or higher

Program features
Sparrowhawk is a GEDCOM-to-HTML conversion program for the Macintosh, based on version 2.5a of Gene Stark's GED2HTML program for Windows.

Older Macintosh Genealogy Programs

The following programs are older, and may no longer be supported by the authors. For more information, contact the author or vendor.

FamilyRecords

(HyperCard program)
(freeware)
Ben G. Walker
e-mail: BenW7@aol.com

Genealogy Explorer 2.0

Food for Thought Software
9235 Fern Lane
Des Plaines, IL 60016
Voice: 708-298-0295

HeartWood

(HyperCard program)
HeartWood Software, Inc.
PO Box 5190
Bayview Station
Bridgeport, CT 06610
Voice: 203-374-7481

MacGene

Applied Ideas, Inc.
PO Box 3225
Manhattan Beach, CA 90266
Voice: 213-545-2996

Roots & Branches

(HyperCard program)
Douglas A. White
PO Box 1113
Fairfield, IA 52556
Voice: 515-472-6461

SunriseGEN

(HyperCard program)
ComputerWare
2800 West Bayshore Road
Palo Alto, CA 94303
Voice: 800-326-0092

Genealogy Software for Other Operating Systems

Amiga

DGen
(utility to convert Scion files to HTML pages)
Cr. T.M. Nichols JP
PO Box 228
Pannawonica WA 6716
Australia
e-mail: spinne@networx.net.au
http://www.networx.net.au/~spinne/#DGEN
Price: unknown

Origins II
The Puzzle Factory
PO Box 986
Veneta, OR 97487
Voice: 503-935-3709
Price: unknown

Apple Newton

Relations
Peter Mitchell
Mitchell System Designs
9558 83 Street
Edmonton, AB
T6C 3A1 Canada
Voice: 403-465-3943
e-mail: pmitchell@kagi.com
http://www.ccinet.ab.ca/pmitchell/
Relations2.html
Price: $20.00

Psion

Gedfried
Rolf Aeschbacher
Erlenstrasse 79
CH-8408 Winterthur
Switzerland
e-mail: Rolf.Aeschbacher@village.ch
http://www.village.ch/~aeschbacher/
gedfried.html
Price: free

Geni
Martin Dunstan
1 Cupar Mills
Cupar, Fife
KY15 5EH Scotland
e-mail: mnd@dcs.st-and.ac.uk
http://www-theory.dcs.st-andrews.ac.uk/
~mnd/export/geni/
Price: £15

kGene
Kevin Groves
e-mail: kgroves@cix.co.uk
http://www.compulink.co.uk/~kgroves/
Price: free

Unix

Lifelines
Tom Wetmore
e-mail: info@bartonstreet.com
http://bartonstreet.com/software/lines/
Price: free

 # Appendix A

Database Comparison Chart

Features	A-Gene	Ancestors & Descendants	Ancestral Quest	BirthWrite
Price	£20	$87.00	$44.95/39.95	$30.00
Demo available	Yes	No	Yes	Yes
Platform	Windows	DOS	Windows	Windows
# individuals per database	Unlimited	9,999	30,000	2 billion
Reorder children	Yes	Yes	Yes	No*
Source master list	No	Yes	No	No
# multimedia items per person	3	None	Unlimited	30
Generate Web Page (HTML files)	No	No	No	No
Customizable Reports	Yes	Yes	Yes	Yes
Data backup function	Yes	Yes	Yes	No

Notes:
*children are ordered by birth date or order of entry.

Features	Brother's Keeper	Cumberland Family Tree	EZ-Tree	FamilyBase For Windows
Price	$49.00	$50.00–74.00	$30.00	£15
Demo available	Yes	Yes	Yes	Yes
Platform	Windows	Windows	DOS	Windows
# individuals per database	1 million	1 million	Varies*	1,000
Reorder children	Yes	Yes	No	Unknown
Source master list	No	Yes	No	No
# multimedia items per person	Multiple	250	None	None
Generate Web Page (HTML files)	No	No	No	No
Customizable Reports	Yes	Yes	No	Yes
Data backup function	Yes	Yes	Yes	Yes

Notes:
* The number of individuals per database varies according to the amount of data included.

Features	Family Heritage	Family Matters	Family Origins	Family Scrapbook
Price	$49.95	$25.00	$29.00	$ Unknown
Demo available	No	Yes	Yes	Yes
Platform	Windows	Windows	Windows	DOS
# individuals per database	Unlimited	Unlimited	Unlimited	999,999
Reorder children	Yes	Yes	Yes	Unknown
Source master list	Yes	Yes	Yes	No
# multimedia items per person	Multiple	3 per family	Multiple	No
Generate Web Page (HTML files)	Yes	No	Yes	No
Customizable Reports	Yes	Yes	Yes	Yes
Data backup function	Yes	Unknown	Yes	Unknown

Features	Family Tree In A Window	Family Tree Maker	Generations	Genius Family Tree
Price	$29.95	$19.99–99.99	$49.95	$39.00–48.00
Demo available	Yes	Yes	No	Yes
Platform	Windows	Windows*	Windows	Windows
# individuals per database	Unknown	Unlimited	30,000	5,000
Reorder children	Unknown	Yes	Yes	Yes
Source master list	No	Yes	Yes	No
# multimedia items per person	Multiple	2,000	Multiple	No
Generate Web Page (HTML files)	No	Yes	No	No
Customizable Reports	Yes	Yes	Yes	Yes
Data backup function	Unknown	Yes	Yes	Yes

Notes:
*Macintosh version also available. See Chapter 6 for information.

Features	Genus Senior	Kindred Konnections	Kith and Kin	Legacy
Price	$115.00–147.00	Free	$48.00	$49.95
Demo available	Yes	Yes	Yes	Yes
Platform	Windows	Windows	Windows	Windows
# individuals per database	Unlimited	8 million	16,383*	Unlimited
Reorder children	Unknown	Yes	Unknown	Yes
Source master list	No	No	No	Yes
# multimedia items per person	5	None	Multiple	Unlimited
Generate Web Page (HTML files)	No	No	No	Yes
Customizable Reports	Yes	No	Yes	Yes
Data backup function	Unknown	Yes	Yes	Yes

Notes:
* Allows 16,383 people and families combined.

Features	The Master Genealogist	My Family History	Parents	Personal Ancestral File (PAF)
Price	$59.00–99.00	$59 (AUD)	$25.00–44.95	$15.00
Demo available	Yes	No	Yes	No
Platform	Windows	Windows	Windows	DOS
# individuals per database	Unlimited	3,000	Unlimited	1 million
Reorder children	Yes	Yes	Yes	Yes
Source master list	Yes	No	No	Yes
# multimedia items per person	Unlimited	Unlimited	Unlimited	None
Generate Web Page (HTML files)	Yes	No	No	No
Customizable Reports	Yes	Yes	Yes	Yes
Data backup function	Yes	Unknown	Unknown	Yes

Features	PRO-GEN	Ultimate Family Tree	Win-Family	
Price	$65.00	$19.99-59.99	$50.00	
Demo available	Yes	No	Yes	
Platform	DOS	Windows 95*	Windows	
# individuals per database	30,000	Unlimited	Unlimited	
Reorder children	No	Yes	Yes	
Source master list	No	Yes	No	
# multimedia items per person	None	Unlimited	Multiple	
Generate Web Page (HTML files)	No	Yes	Yes	
Customizable Reports	Yes	Yes	Yes	
Data backup function	Yes	Yes	Yes	

Notes:
*Macintosh version also available. See Chapter 6 for information.

 # Appendix B

Genealogy Software Vendors

Genealogy Software Vendors

The following companies sell software, books relating to software and computers, or both.

AGLL, Inc.
PO Box 329
Bountiful, UT 84011-0329
Voice: 800-760-AGLL
Fax: 801-298-5468
e-mail: custserv@heritagequest.com
http://www.agll.com/elect/el.html

Ancestor Trails
5755 Cohasset Way
San Jose, CA 95123
Voice: 408-227-1645
FAX: 408-226-7303
e-mail: ancestor@ancestor.com
http://www.ancestor.com/scripts/
WebCatalog/$WebCat.exe/Ancestor/
default.tmpl

Ancestry Genealogy Shoppe
Ancestry, Inc.
266 West Center Street
Orem, UT 84057
Voice: 801-426-3500 or 800-262-3787
Fax: 801-426-3501
e-mail: sales@ancestry.com
http://www2.viaweb.com/ancestry/

Appleton's Books & Genealogy
Tower Place Mall
8700 Pineville-Matthews Road #610
Charlotte, NC 28226
Voice: 800-777-3601 or 704-341-2266
Fax: 704-341-0072
BBS: 704-552-1411
e-mail: catalog.request@appletons.com
http://www.appletons.com

Automated Research, Inc.
1160 South State Street, Suite 170
Orem, UT 84097-8237
Voice: 801-222-9774
Fax: 801-221-1106
e-mail: johnfw@aricds.com
http://www.aricds.com/guide/
genprogs.html

Genealogical Services
PO Box 1227
West Jordan, UT 84084-1227
Voice: 801-280-1554
e-mail: info@genservices.com
http://www.genservices.com/cgi-bin/
jerry/web_store/web_store.cgi

Global Genealogy Supply
158 Laurier Avenue
Milton, ON
L9T 4S2 Canada
Voice: 800-361-5168
Fax: 905-875-1887
e-mail: sroberts@globalgenealogy.com
http://www.globalgenealogy.com/
software.htm

Global Heritage Center
Sterling Ledet & Associates
2176 Heritage Drive
Atlanta, GA 30345
Voice: 404-325-3338
Fax: 404-636-8477
e-mail: sjledet@netcom.com
http://www.ledet.com/genealogy/
ghc.html

Golden Branches
PO Box 11468
Spring, TX 77391-1468
Voice: 281-251-GOLD
e-mail: golden@flex.net
http://www.goldenbranches.com/

Gould Books
PO Box 126
Gumeracha, South Australia 5233
Voice: 011-61-8-8389-1611
Fax: 011-61-8-8389-1599
e-mail: gould@adelaide.on.net
http://www.gould.com.au/

Hearthstone Bookshop
5735A Telegraph Road
Alexandria, VA 22303
Voice: 888-960-3300
Fax: 703-960-0087
e-mail: info@hearthstonebooks.com
http://www.hearthstonebooks.com/

Lineages
Lineages, Inc.
PO Box 417
Salt Lake City, UT 84110-0417
Voice: 801-531-9297
Fax: 801-531-6819
e-mail: info@lineagesnet.com
http://www.lineagesnet.com/catalog/
SoftwareDisplay.asp?Display=Topical

Lost In Time
PO Box 634
Burtonsville, MD 20866
Fax: 301-890-1669
e-mail: lit@radix.net
http://www.lostintime.com/catalog/
products.htm

The Memorabilia Corner
1312 McKinley
Norman, OK 73072-6535
Voice: 405-321-8366
Fax: 405-321-3444
http://members.aol.com/TMCorner/
index.html

Pandect Services
178 Loughborough Road
Mountsorrel
Loughborough, Leics
LE12 7AX England
Voice: 011-441-509-415101
Fax: 011-441-509-620442
e-mail: pandect@compuserve.com
http://ourworld.compuserve.com/
homepages/pandect/

S & N Genealogy Supplies
Greenacres, Salisbury Road
Chilmark, Wilts
SP3 5AH England
Voice/Fax: 011-441-722-716121
e-mail: genealogy_Supplies@compuserve.com
http://ourworld.compuserve.com/homepages/
Genealogy_Supplies/whatsonm.htm

 # Appendix C

Looking for an Old File?

Genealogy File Archives

There are a variety of genealogy-specific file archives available on the Internet, and some genealogy BBSs. You can find the archives by using the URLs below, or entering a filename in a search engine.

For the most part, the files you will find in the archives are dated; in addition to software, there are some helpful text files, GEDCOMs, and other data files available.

You can download any of the files in the archives listed via your Web browser, or an FTP program. Most text files are unarchived; most programs are archived. As always, when downloading an unknown file, be sure to run a virus detector before executing any file.

Genealogy-Specific URLs

http://ftp.quest-net.com/CDH/
GENE_01.htm
A large collection of older genealogy programs and data text files (IBM compatible)

ftp://ftp.cac.psu.edu/pub/genealogy
A large collection of (mostly) older genealogy programs and data files (IBM, MAC, other OS)

http://web.ukonline.co.uk/Members/
n.bayley/FILES.HTM
Small collection of shareware, demos, and some data files (IBM compatible)

ftp://ftp.genealogy.org/pub/genealogy/
software/util/PAF/pafutils/
PAF Utilities for Macintosh and DOS

General Archives with Genealogy Programs

http://www.shareware.com/
Shareware.com (IBM, MAC, other OS)

http://www.softseek.com/
SoftSeek.com (IBM compatible)

http://www.hotfiles.com/
ZDNet Software Library (IBM and MAC)

http://www.filez.com/
Filez (shareware/freeware/demo file search engine)

Looking for an Old File?

If you are looking for an older program you may find it online at one of the genealogy file archives. The following are files which were (January 1998) stored at the Penn State FTP site at ftp://ftp.cac.psu.edu. Warning: most of these files are no longer supported by the authors, and may not work on newer systems; use them at your own risk! Always protect your data and use only backups when running an unfamiliar program.

From the ftp://ftp.cac.psu.edu/pub/genealogy/windows directory

Filename	Description	File Size (in bytes)	Date Uploaded
aq_demo1.exe	Demo of Ancestral Quest	504898	Aug 1, 1995
aqdemo1a.zip		420338	Mar 1, 1995
bkwin02.zip	Brother's Keeper	1447281	Apr 22, 1996
eucalypt.zip		294856	Jun 8, 1995
famtres1.zip	Family Treasures 3.x Part 1/2	254552	Sep 14, 1995
famtres2.zip	Family Treasures 3.x Part 2/2	276562	Sep 14, 1995
fm3211.zip	Family Matters 3.21 1 of 4	1817131	Aug 3, 1997
fm321up.zip	Upgrades old Family Matters to 3.21	1806148	Aug 3, 1997
fmtrw106.zip	Family Tree in a Window	339683	Apr 22, 1996
fow6_16.exe	Family Origins v6 demo 32 bit	1924979	Aug 30, 1997
fow6_32.exe	Family Origins v6 demo 32 bit	2089798	Aug 30, 1997
genius.exe	GENIUS for Windows	723072	Aug 8, 1996
genmst.zip		549160	May 16, 1995
gj115gb.zip	GENUS Junior Gen. Prgm demo v1.15	459453	Jan 18, 1995
gntr97en.zip	GENTREE - Genealogical Navigation software - English Version latest version	1268792	May 10, 1997
gs21gb.zip	GENUS Senior for Windows demo	1140013	Jan 18, 1995
kk300.zip	Kith and Kin for Windows v3.0	412092	Oct 5, 1995
pan104.zip	Pantheon v1.04	157190	Apr 22, 1996
parwn306.zip	Parents v3.06	96425	Sep 14, 1995
tgc30.zip	The Genealogical Companion v3.0	9703950	Dec 15, 1997
trd111.zip	TreeDraw: Windows	370570	Jan 30, 1996
ufti16.zip	uFTi v 1.2 for Windows 3.1	3456474	Dec 16, 1996
ufti32.zip	uFTi v 1.2 for Windows 95 and NT	3654310	Dec 16, 1996
wingen06.zip	WinGen v0.600: Genealogy database	255832	Apr 22, 1996
wipaf091.zip	Windows Into PAF	628953	Jul 15, 1996

From the ftp://ftp.cac.psu.edu/pub/genealogy/utils directory

Filename	Description	File Size (in bytes)	Date Uploaded
awk320.zip	AWK for DOS	98194	Oct 29, 1993
b2t1-2.lzh		13934	May 10, 1992
chart.zip		44094	Sep 29, 1991
chrnos.zip		116833	Oct 29, 1991
cola40.zip		101389	Oct 6, 1991

From the ftp://ftp.cac.psu.edu/pub/genealogy/utils directory

Filename	Description	File Size (in bytes)	Date Uploaded
datecalc.lzh		9508	May 9, 1992
dbase3		7699	Jan 26, 1992
dfoot3.zip		26963	Jan 12, 1992
dmhstcal.lzh		76118	May 10, 1992
fcg101.zip		41069	Oct 22, 1991
ged2t9.zip		73472	Oct 2, 1991
genkit16.zip		59392	Oct 29, 1992
hebrewmc.zip		9521	Nov 5, 1991
named130.zip		45783	May 10, 1992
namev300.zip		90955	Aug 7, 1992
platchek.lzh		103267	May 9, 1992
rcal.zip		10614	May 26, 1992
roots2ged		6887	Jan 26, 1992
srch132s.zip		48105	Aug 7, 1992
ttgen12.zip		25640	Jan 22, 1992
xtract41.zip	Search utility for us1800 1% Federal and UKC 2% censuses	320514	Feb 29, 1996

From the ftp://ftp.cac.psu.edu/pub/genealogy/programs directory

Filename	Description	File Size (in bytes)	Date Uploaded
ae_1_7a.exe	ArbrEdite-French Genealogy program	271669	Jun 15, 1994
cdiary13.zip		216408	Feb 14, 1994
cem063.arj		198578	May 4, 1993
census20.zip	Genealogy: EZCensus - 1880/90	177872	May 4, 1993
chron16.exe		3414885	Aug 29, 1996
clan202.zip		154856	May 4, 1993
crd541s.zip		318366	Sep 7, 1993
crdlt30s.exe		289761	May 4, 1993
crt74s1.exe		313269	May 4, 1993
cstory12.zip		247853	Feb 14, 1994
disgen.zip		654598	May 4, 1993
dropln11.zip		234743	May 17, 1994
fcg102.zip	Fan Chart Generator	45213	Jun 25, 1993
fhh130.zip	Family History Help-research tutorial	63103	May 4, 1993
fname10.zip		33161	Sep 16, 1993
frll101.zip		50399	May 4, 1993
gacp200.zip	Great American Census Program	95952	May 9, 1995
ged.zip		78479	May 4, 1993
gen-fv.zip		59014	Jan 6, 1995
gene-db.lzh		180224	May 4, 1993
genlink.lzh		133295	Jun 23, 1993
gentiq11.zip	Geneatique II+ 1.1g	495910	Jan 25, 1994
gim_316.zip	GIM 3.16:	696411	Jan 6, 1997
gm_21a.zip		135625	Feb 24, 1994

From the ftp://ftp.cac.psu.edu/pub/genealogy/programs directory

Filename	Description	File Size (in bytes)	Date Uploaded
gng2-2.zip		196616	Apr 24, 1995
hazadata.arj		482173	Oct 19, 1994
herit105.zip		281426	May 4, 1993
igi25545.zip	Builds a database from Family Search "text" diskettes	255640	May 11, 1995
jgscemet.zip		49815	Dec 12, 1993
myfmly20.zip	My Family Genealogy program	233349	May 4, 1993
readigi.zip		79312	May 11, 1995
ry_v5_1.zip		319500	Feb 26, 1995
ry_v5_2.zip		287716	Feb 26, 1995
ry_v5_3.zip		298903	Feb 27, 1995
ry_v5_4.zip		299570	Feb 27, 1995
soundex.unix	Unix shell script to calculate Soundex codes	1657	May 4, 1993

From the ftp://ftp.cac.psu.edu/pub/genealogy/mac directory

Filename	Description	File Size (in bytes)	Date Uploaded
ExtrasHandler.sea	4 new Extras for Mac PAF 2.3.1	100352	Oct 15, 1996
GenTree20b8.sea.hqx	Swedish Genealogy program	247463	Nov 4, 1994
Reu4Mac.sea	Reunion for Macintosh demo	459904	Jun 9, 1995
af2mp11.sit.hqx	Ancestral File to MacPAF 1.1	350136	Jan 23, 1996
famdata2.sea.hqx	FamilyData 0.2 freeware	305255	Jan 23, 1996
family-record.hqx	Family Record (Hypercard)	29428	Nov 18, 1991
fhc10.sit.hqx	Family History Composer 1.0	164428	Dec 4, 1995
fhf31demo.sea.hqx	Family Heritage File 3.1 demo	668325	Nov 22, 1995
fp2tour.sit.hqx	Farmer's Plotter 2.0 Tour	170449	Nov 17, 1995
ged2tt10.sit	GEDCOM to Tiny Tafel generator	43776	Mar 1, 1995
gedfam11.sit.hqx	GEDCOM Families 1.1	118266	Dec 4, 1995
gedtra.sit	GED Transfer (GEDCOM to ASCII)	65664	Mar 1, 1995
gene41.sit.hqx	Gene v.4.1 shareware program	872288	Jan 23, 1996
genealogyprodemo2.1.sit.hqx		84792	Jan 30, 1996
genuti10.sit.hqx	Gene Utilities 1.0	77950	Dec 4, 1995
hayom2.sit.hqx	HaYom 2.0 Hebrew calendar	113463	Nov 17, 1995
heartwood2.0.sit.hqx	HeartWood 2.0 Demo	665327	Nov 22, 1995
heritage311.cpt.hqx	Heritage shareware program	904111	Aug 30, 1997
intercal13.sit.hqx	InterCal 1.3 Julian/Gregorian calendar	461039	Jan 23, 1996
macgen10.sit	MacGene to GEDCOM converter	55808	Mar 1, 1995
macpaf11.sit	MacPAF Utility 1.1	201728	Mar 1, 1995
whatday.sea.hqx	WhatDay? date converter	38861	Nov 17, 1995

 # Appendix D

Internet Software Resources

Genealogy Computer Interest Groups

The list below is not complete; it is intended to give you information about the larger and better-known Computer Interest Groups (CIGs) available. A comprehensive list of CIGs can be found at http://www.genealogy.org/~gwsc/gwsccig.htm.

U.S.

Amateur Computer Group of New Jersey Genealogy Special Interest Group
e-mail: gensig@hr.bellcore.com
http://www.castle.net/~kb4cyc/gensig.html

Arizona Genealogy Computer Interest Group
4411 S. Rural Road, Suite #104
Tempe, AZ 85282
e-mail: gfoster@futureone.com
http://www.getnet.com/non-profit/agcig/

Cajun Clickers Genealogy SIG (Louisiana)
e-mail: cars@intersurf.com
http://www.intersurf.com/~cars/

Central Kentucky Computer Society Family History SIG
1300 New Circle Road, Suite 105
Lexington, KY 40505 USA
Voice: 606-255-CKCS (2527)
Contact: Barry Bingham
e-mail: rbbingham@som-ky.campus.mci.net
http://www.ckcs.org/sig.html

Central Texas PC Users' Group Genealogy CIG
Contact: James Hollas
Voice: 817-280-1415
e-mail: james.hollas@1201.ima.infomail.com
http://www.ctpcug.com/sigs.htm

Colorado Genealogical Society Computer Interest Group
PO Box 9218
Denver, CO 80209-0218
Voice: 303-571-1535

e-mail: genealogist@cogensoc.org
http://www.cogensoc.org/cgs/cgs-cig.htm

CompuServe Genealogy Forum
http://directory.compuserve.com/Forums/ROOTS/Abstract.asp

Computer Genealogy Society of Long Island (New York)
e-mail: walter@tnp.com
http://members.macconnect.com/users/v/vitev/genesocli/

Elkart, IN PC Users Group Genealogy SIG
e-mail: stevens@skyenet.net
http://www.skyenet.net/~stevens/gensig1.htm

Genealogical Computing Association of Pennsylvania
Michael A. Miller, GENCAP Treasurer
51 Hillcrest Road
Barto, PA 19504
http://www.libertynet.org/~gencap/

GENCOM PC Users Group of Shreveport, Louisiana
9913 Dagger Point
Shreveport, LA 71115-3239
e-mail: Tohr50@softdisk.com
http://www.softdisk.com/comp/gencom/

Genealogical Computer Society of Georgia
e-mail: noahsark@mindspring.com
http://www.mindspring.com/~noahsark/gcsga.html

Grass Roots Genealogical Group
Nevada County Genealogical Society
PO Box 176

Cedar Ridge, CA 95924
http://www.nccn.net/leisure/crafthby/
genealog.htm

HAL-PC Genealogy SIG
e-mail: jeans@hal-pc.org
http://www.hal-pc.org/~jeans/gene.shtml

Minnesota Genealogical Society Computer Interest Group
Computer Interest Group
PO Box 16069
Saint Paul, MN 55116-0069
e-mail: mgsray@mtn.org
http://www.mtn.org/mgs/branches/
computer.html

Personal Computer Club of Charlotte, North Carolina Genealogy Special Interest Group
PO Box 114
Paw Creek, NC 28130-0114
http://www.chem.uncc.edu/pccc/gensig/

The Roots Users Group of Arlington, Virginia
RUG Membership
PO Box 82
Arlington, VA 22210-0082
http://genealogy.org/~rug/

San Mateo County Genealogical Society Computer Interest Group
SMCGS Membership
PO Box 5083
San Mateo, CA 94402
e-mail: smcgs@genealogy.org
http://genealogy.org/~smcgs/charter.html

Sonoma Valley, California Computer Group
Contact: KJ Aanestad and Jeanette Woods
e-mail: aanestad@wco.com
http://www.vom.com/svcg/SVCGnews.html

The Wichita Genealogical Society
PO Box 3705
Wichita, KS 67201-3705

e-mail: Mike.Ward@digital.com
http://kuhttp.cc.ukans.edu/kansas/wgs/
online.html

Australia
Victorian GUM (Genealogists Using Computers) Inc.
252 Swanston Street, 5th Floor
Melbourne VIC 3000
Australia
e-mail: info@vicgum.asn.au
http://www.vicgum.asn.au/

Belgium
PRO-GEN User Group
Contact: Ivo Gilisen, Neremstraat 12,
B-3840 Borgloon, Belgium
Voice: 011-32-12-74-24-38
e-mail: PRO-GEN.LIMBURG@ping.be
http://ping4.ping.be/~ping2011/index-
E.html#PRO-GEN users' group
LIMBURG

Vlaamse Vereniging voor Familiekunde-Genealogie & Computer
e-mail: pavp@uia.ua.ac.be
http://win-www.uia.ac.be/u/pavp/
vvfgc.html

Canada
Alberta Family Histories Society
PO Box 30270
Station B
Calgary, AB
T2M 4P1 Canada
Voice: 403-214-1447
e-mail: rempelj@cadvision.com
http://www.freenet.calgary.ab.ca/afhs/
sigs.html

British Columbia Genealogical Society Computer Group
PO Box 88054
Lansdowne Mall
Richmond, BC
V6X 3T6 Canada

Voice: 604-502-9119
e-mail: bcgs@npsnet.com
http://www.npsnet.com/bcgs/bcgscgrp.htm

Norfolk, Ontario Historical Society GenCIG
e-mail: doverw@nornet.on.ca
http://alpha.nornet.on.ca/gencig/

England
Society of Genealogists CIG
Society of Genealogists
14 Charterhouse Buildings
Goswell Road, London
EC1M 7BA England
e-mail: cig@gold.ac.uk.
http://scorpio.gold.ac.uk/~cig/
meetings.htm

New Zealand
Computer Interest Groups of The New Zealand Society of Genealogists
Wellington Contact: Brian Jenkin
Voice: 011-64-4-526-4172
e-mail: bjenkin@ibm.net
http://www.voyager.co.nz/~pycroftb/
cgcgpag4.html

Kapiti Genealogical Computer Group
Contact: Bill Carter
Voice: 011-64-4-298-8576
e-mail: 100232.1526@compuserve.com
http://users.iconz.co.nz/marks/

New Plymouth Genealogy Computing Group
Contact: Gail Raynor
122 Wairau Road
Oakura, New Zealand
http://www.geocities.com/Athens/Delphi/
9288/npgcg.html

South Africa
Genealogical Society of South Africa Computer Interest Group
Contact: Johan van Deventer
Voice: 011-12-348-3220

e-mail: jcvd@intekom.co.za
http://www.geocities.com/Athens/7783/

Sweden
Computer Genealogy Society of Sweden
Gamla Link ping
582 46 Link Ping
Sweden
Voice: 011-46-13-14-90-43
e-mail: dis@dis.se
http://www.dis.se/disengl.htm

PAF Groups

As with the genealogy CIGs, there are a great number of groups devoted to PAF; too many to list here. The Utah Valley PAF Users Group, listed below, maintains a list of PAF User Groups around the world at their Web site at http://www.genealogy.org/~uvpafug/allpafug.html

Utah Valley PAF Users Group
Jay P. Markham, President
490 E 600 South
Orem UT 84058
Voice: 801-224-1167
http://www.genealogy.org/~uvpafug/

Software Mailing Lists and Newsgroups

A mailing list is a topic-specific discussion which is carried out through e-mail and sent to subscribers. A newsgroup is a topic-specific message area found on the Usenet section of Internet. In addition to the mailing lists below, you can find discussion areas, bulletin boards, and message conferences on many software company sites.

Popular Mailing Lists and Newsgroups

General Lists

Genealogy Computing
GENCMP (gatewayed with the Usenet newsgroup soc.genealogy.computing)
To subscribe, send an e-mail with the message SUBSCRIBE, to:
gencmp-l-request@rootsweb.com
To post: gencmp-l@rootsweb.com

Product-Specific Lists

Brother's Keeper
BK5forum
To subscribe, send an e-mail with the message SUBSCRIBE, to:
bkforum-request@rootsweb.com
To post: bk5forum@rootsweb.com

Brother's Keeper
BK5-L
To subscribe, send an e-mail with the message SUBSCRIBE, to:
bk5-l-request@genealogy.emcee.com
To post: bk5-l@genealogy.emcee.com

Cumberland Family Tree Products
CFT-WIN
To subscribe, send an e-mail with the message SUBSCRIBE, to:
cft-win-l-request@rootsweb.com
To post: cft-win-l@rootsweb.com

Family Origins
FAMILY-ORIGINS-USERS
To subscribe, send an e-mail with the message SUBSCRIBE, to: family-origins-users-l-request@rootsweb. com

To post: family-origins-users-l@rootsweb.com.

Family Tree Maker
FTMTECH-L
To subscribe, send an e-mail with the message SUBSCRIBE, to:
ftmtech-l-request@lists.best.com
To post: ftmtech-l@lists.best.com

LifeLines
LINES-L
To subscribe, send an e-mail with the message SUBSCRIBE Lines-L firstname lastname, to:
listserv@vm1.nodak.edu
To post: lines-l@vm1.nodak.edu

Personal Ancestral File (PAF)
PAF
To subscribe, send an e-mail with the message SUBSCRIBE PAF, to:
majordomo@rehtori.kasanen.fi
To post: paf@rehtori.kasanen.fi.

Reunion
ReunionTalk
To subscribe, send an e-mail with the subject SUBSCRIBE, to:
ReunionTalk@List.LeisterPro.com   or visit http://www.leisterpro.com/doc/ListForm.html

The Master Genealogist/Family Roots
FR2TMG-L
To subscribe, send an e-mail with the message SUBSCRIBE, to:

fr2tmg-l-request@rootsweb.com
To post: fr2tmg-l@rootsweb.com

The Master Genealogist
TMG-L
majordomo@doit.com To subscribe, send
an e-mail with the message SUBSCRIBE
TMG-L, to: tmg-l@doit.com

Other Mailing Lists
The following programs also have mailing
lists available. Contact the program
author for information on subscribing.

Family Tracker
http://www.surfutah.com/web/famtrak/

Family Treasures
http://www.famtech.com/fa00001.htm

Kith and Kin
http://ourworld.compuserve.com/
homepages/SpanSoft/kk.htm

Mailing List Sites

Genealogy Resources on the Internet
http://users.aol.com/johnf14246/
gen_mail_software.html

Genealogy Software Review Web Sites

Genealogy Software Springboard
(mostly IBM compatible)
http://www.toltbbs.com/~kbasile/
software.html

Macintosh Genealogy Software FAQ
http://www.cyberenet.net/~gsteiner/
macgsfaq/

 # Appendix E

Programs Not Reviewed

There are a few programs missing from the reviews in Chapters 4 and 5. They were omitted for a variety of reasons; either I was unable to obtain a copy, I was unable to get the program to work on my system, or the program was not yet released. For your convenience, the programs are listed below with contact information and price (where known).

Family History System

September 1997 Version
Phillip E. Brown
834 Bahama Drive
Tallahassee, FL 32311-7363
e-mail: pbrown@fhs.tallahassee.net
http://fhs.tallahassee.net
Price: $35.00

Family Ties

Individual Software, Inc.
4255 Hopyard Road, Suite 2
Pleasanton, CA 95488
Voice: 800-331-3313
Fax: 510-734-8337
e-mail: messageto@individualsoftware.com
http://www.individualsoftware.com/
Price: $19.95

Softkey's Family Tree for Windows 3.1 and Windows 95

The Learning Company, Inc.
One Athenaeum Street
Cambridge, MA 02142
Voice: 800-845-8692
http://www.learningco.com
Price: $12.99

Genealogical Information Manager

Version 3.17 for DOS
David "Blaine" Wasden
4692 Bentley Place
Duluth, GA 30136-6126
e-mail: dblaine@mindspring.com
http://www.mindspring.com/~dblaine/gimhome.html
Price: $20.00

GENSOL

Version R03V10 for DOS
John Graham
63 Luculia Avenue
Baulkham Hills, NSW 2153
Australia
e-mail: johngrah@ozemail.com.au
http://www.ozemail.com.au/~johngrah/
Price: not available at time of inquiry

Our Family Tree

Alpha Software
168 Middlesex Turnpike
Burlington, MA 01803-4483
Voice: 781-229-2924
Fax: 781-272-4876
e-mail: info@alphasoftware.com
http://www.alphasoftware.com/oft/index.html
Price: $49.95

Pedigree for DOS

TWR Computing
Clapstile Farm, Alpheton
Sudbury, Suffolk
CO10 9BN England
Voice/Fax: 011-441-284-828271
e-mail: twr@clapstile.dungeon.com
http://www.dungeon.com/~clapstile/pedigree.htm
Price: £60

TREE-O

Version v.1.2.3 for Windows
Genealogical Computer Services
Price: $40.00
Available at TheGameBoard BBS:
905-689-3982 or 905-689-9409

 # Appendix F

The Mystery of GEDCOM

GEDCOM Explained

GEDCOM: you hear it mentioned in sentences, like "If it doesn't have GEDCOM support, don't buy it," and "The latest GEDCOM specifications can be found on my Web site at ...," and "Feel free to download my 60,000 name GEDCOM." Many people new to computers (and some old hands) are confused: is GEDCOM a file or a specification? Actually, it's both! GEDCOM is the acronym for **GE**nealogy **D**ata **COM**munication, and was created by The Church of Jesus Christ of Latter-day Saints to allow genealogy data to be exchanged between different types of software. A GEDCOM is simply a specially-formatted text file, listing information such as name, dates, locations, relationships, events, etc. The latest version of GEDCOM is 5.5, but new standards are being developed.

Why use GEDCOM?

Most genealogy programs store data in proprietary data forms which cannot be read by other programs. This would be no problem if everyone used the same software, but they don't. If I wanted to share my Family Origins data with a friend who used Family Tree Maker, I'd be out of luck unless both programs supported the import and export of data in GEDCOM format (which they do). Thus I can export my Family Origin data into a GEDCOM file, which my friend can then load into her Family Tree Maker program, and, voila! A data exchange has taken place. With GEDCOM you can view others' research, incorporate it into your own file, print it out, and add or subtract to it *without* having to re-enter the data by hand.

What are the limitations?

Unfortunately, there are times when data is not stored in a GEDCOM properly — not all the software uses the very latest specification of GEDCOM — and sometimes data can be lost, or garbled. Source notes seem particularly vulnerable.

What exactly does a GEDCOM file look like?

Each GEDCOM file consists of a Level (each level 1 line refers to the previous level 0 line, level 2 lines refer to the previous level 1 line, etc.), a Tag (such as **INDI** for individual, **HUSB** for husband, **BIRT** for birth), and a Value (the actual data). There are 6 basic sections to a GEDCOM file: header, submitter, individuals, families, sources, and a trailer.

The following is part of a GEDCOM exported from a genealogy database program (comments are in italics):

0 HEAD	*Denotes the beginning of the file*
1 SOUR Program_Name	*Source of the GEDCOM*
2 VERS 2.02	*Version*
1 DEST PAF	*Destination format of the GEDCOM*
1 CHAR IBMPC	*IBM characters*
1 FILE gert.ged	*File name*
1 DATE 14 Jan 1996	*Date file was created*
0 @S1@ SUBM	

1 NAME Marthe Arends	*Name and address information*
1 ADDR PO BOX 1571	
2 CONT Snohomish, WA 98291-1571	
0 @I4@ INDI	*This is the individuals section*
1 NAME KENNETH WARDEN /NEESE/	*First person in the database*
1 SEX M	
1 BIRT	
2 DATE 8 Jan 1909	*Birth date*
2 PLAC NANAIMO,B.C.	*Birthplace*
1 DEAT	
2 DATE 26 Aug 1983	*Death date*
2 PLAC EDMONDS,SNOHOMISH CO.,WA	*Death place*
1 BURI	*Burial date*
2 PLAC EDMONDS,SNOHOMISH CO.,WA	*Burial place*
1 OCCU CARPENTER	*Occupation*
1 EDUC Grade School	*Education*
1 RELI Presbyterian (?)	*Religion*
1 COMM MEMBERSHIP: Masonic order	*Memberships*
1 FAMS @F3@	*This person is Spouse in family #3*
1 FAMS @F5@	*He is also Child in family #5*
1 NOTE Ken was rescued from an	*Notes*
explosion of a ship loaded with dynamite in Nanaimo when	
2 CONT he was about 4 years old. He suffered a fracture of his skull and	
2 CONT remembers being delusional.	
[stuff deleted]	
0 @F3@ FAM	*This is the family section family #3*
1 HUSB @I6@	*Husband is individual #6*
1 WIFE @I7@	*Wife is #7*
1 CHIL @I8@	*Child #1 is individual #8*
1 CHIL @I4@	*Child #2 is individual #4*
1 MARR	
2 DATE 15 Feb 1932	*Marriage date*
2 PLAC SEATTLE,KING CO.,WA	*Marriage location*
1 DIV N	*No divorce*
1 NOTE Ken and Gertrude eloped to the Smith Tower in Seattle (then the tallest building).	
[stuff deleted]	
0 TRLR	*The last line signifies the end of the GEDCOM*

Does it do any tricks?

You bet! There are many shareware and freeware programs out there that will do everything from "prune the branches" on a GEDCOM to merge files, print specialized charts, and make Web pages.

The following files are available via an anonymous ftp at the sites listed below.

Windows files
Available at ftp://ftp.simtel/pub/simtelnet/win3/genealgy
ged2ht24.zip   Stark's GEDCOM to HTML program

DOS files
Available at ftp://ftp.simtel/pub/simtelnet/msdos/genealgy/
msg2paf.zip   Genealogy data ASCII to PAF
gedsimpl.zip   A simple explanation of GEDCOM
genbx202.zip   Prints box charts from GEDCOM files
55gedcom.zip   GEDCOM Standard 5.5/WP 5.1 format

Macintosh files
Available at ftp://wuarchive.wustl.edu/systems/mac/umich.edu/util/organization/
af2macpaf.sit.hqx Takes a GEDCOM that was created by the LDS "Ancestral File"
                   program and "cleans it up" by translating the little inconsistencies
                   where Mac PAF and AF disagree on how a GEDCOM file should
                   appear.
gtott1.0.sit.hqx   Reads genealogy databases in GEDCOM Version 2 format and
                   produces files in the data comparison Tiny Tafel 1.6 format.

The following DOS and Windows files are available via an anonymous ftp from
ftp://ftp.cac.psu.edu/pub/genealogy/gedcom

demo.zip   GEDCOM manipulation utilities
eged10.zip   Specifications for CommSoft's event-driven GEDCOM (draft)
enft2ged.zip   Enhanced Family Tree to GED
fa22c.zip   Family Attic (set of GEDCOM tools)
famvie20.zip   GEDCOM file viewer w/graphics capability
fhsged.zip   GEDCOM for Family History System
ftetcged.zip   Family Tree, Etc. to GEDCOM
gcf11.zip   GCFiler (converts GEDCOM to ASCII text)
ged2ex11.zip   GEDCOM into Excel 5.0a
ged2ht20.zip   GEDCOM to HTML translation programs
ged2tth1.zip   GEDCOM to Tiny Tafel
gedcht16.zip   Make pedigree family tree chart from GED file (LJ3/PS)
gedcom.zip   Draft Release 5.3 of the GEDCOM Standard
gedcomma.zip   Insert/remove GEDCOM commas
gedfx2.zip   Repairs GEDCOM files
gedlab.zip   GEDCOM utilities
gedmrg.zip   Merge 2 GEDCOM files
gedread5.zip   v.0.5 Statistics about GEDCOM file
gedsrt13.zip   Sort GEDCOM files
gedtr1.zip   GEDCOM Treasure demo (includes browse)
gedvw105.zip   GEDCOM file viewer/interpreter
geneal2.zip   PostScript charts from GEDCOM

gensrch.zip	Gensrch, find common ancestors between GEDCOM files; freeware
gipsi22.zip	Process GEDCOM files from the IGI
gp10.zip	Display and print data in a GEDCOM file
howrel.zip	How Are We Related? determines relationships from GEDCOM files
pedgre23.zip	Prints quality pedigrees from GEDCOM
sdiprt.zip	Social Security Death Index Print from GEDCOM
wallde.zip	Wall chart from GEDCOM (demo)
wallped4.zip	Wall pedigree chart from GEDCOM
xltged.zip	XLate converts GEDCOMs from non-DOS by adding LF

Internet GEDCOM Resources

GenWeb Project	http://demo.genweb.org/gene/genedemo.html
GenDex Project	http://www.gendex.com
GEDCOM Mailing List	to subscribe, send an e-mail with the message SUBSCRIBE GEDCOM-L, to listserv@listserv.nodak.edu

 # Appendix G

Computer Genealogy Publications

Print Publications—Books

Genealogy Via the Internet:Tracing Your Family Roots Quickly and Easily: Computerized Genealogy in Plain English
Ralph Roberts
(Alexander, NC: Alexander Books, 1997)

Genealogy Online: Researching Your Roots Web Edition
Elizabeth Powell Crowe
(New York: McGraw-Hill, 1997)

The Internet for Genealogists: A Beginner's Guide
Barbara Renick and Richard S. Wilson
(La Habra, CA: Compuology, 1997)

Netting Your Ancestors
Cyndi Howells
(Baltimore: Genealogical Publishing Co., 1997)

Searching for Cyber-Roots
Laurie and Steve Bonner
(Salt Lake City: Ancestry Inc, 1997)

Virtual Roots: A Guide to Genealogy and Local History on the World Wide Web
Thomas Jay Kemp
(Wilmington, DE: Scholarly Resources Inc., 1997)

Your Family Tree
Jim Oldfield, Jr.
(Grand Rapids, MI: Abacus Books, 1997)

Print Publications—Periodicals

Computers In Genealogy
The Director
Society of Genealogists
14 Charterhouse Buildings, Goswell Road
London EC1M 7BA
England
Quarterly publication
e-mail: cig@gold.ac.uk
http://scorpio.gold.ac.uk/~cig/
Welcome.html#top

Everton's Genealogical Helper
PO Box 368
Logan, UT 84323-0368
e-mail: catalog@everton.com
http://www.everton.com
Price: $24.00 (6 issues per year)

Family Chronicle Magazine
PO Box 1201
Lewiston, NY 14092
Voice: 416-696-5488
Fax: 416-696-7395
e-mail: magazine@familychronicle.com
http://www.familychronicle.com/
Price: $21.00 (6 issues per year)

Genealogical Computing
PO Box 476
Salt Lake City, UT 84110
e-mail: gceditor@ancestry.com
http://www.ancestry.com
Price: $25.00 (4 issues per year)

NGS/CIG Digest
(published bi-monthly in the National
Genealogy Society's Newsletter)
National Genealogical Society
Computer Interest Group
4527 17th Street, North
Arlington, VA 22207-2399
Voice: 800-473-0060
Fax: 703-525-0052
http://www.genealogy.org/~ngs//
ngscig.html
Price: free with NGS membership
(individual membership is $40.00)

Online Pioneers
PO Box 1571
Snohomish, WA 98291-1571
e-mail: mnarends@eskimo.com
http://www.eskimo.com/~mnarends
Price: $24.00 (12 issues per year)

Online Publications

Digital Digest
http://jb.com/~carla/

**Eastman's Online Genealogy
Newsletter**
http://www.ancestry.com/home/
eastarch.htm

Journal of Online Genealogy
http://www.onlinegenealogy.com/

**Online Edition of Everton's
Genealogical Helper**
http://www.everton.com/ghonline.html

 # Glossary

Ahnentafel
(German for Ancestor Table) Numbered format which displays information about the ancestors of an individual by generation. Information includes name, dates and places of birth, marriage, and death events.

ASCII
(American Standard Code for Information Interchange) Lowest common denominator of text, it is text without any formatting codes. ASCII text can be read by any computer platform.

BBS (Bulletin Board System)
Program that lets remote users (users who are not on the host computer) access the system. BBSs generally have message areas, file transfer areas, and online games. Traditionally, BBSs were accessed via terminal software and a phone line; now many BBSs are available on Internet and can be reached by Telnet.

database
Software which allows you to organize and manipulate information.

download
Transferring a file from a remote computer to a user's computer.

e-mail
Electronic message sent from one person to another.

event
An occurrence to which you can assign a date and title, such as Birth, Death, Marriage, Baptism, etc.

Fan Chart
Pedigree chart which displays information in a circular format.

field
The place where you enter information in a program.

freeware
Software which may be used freely without compensation to the author.

FTP (File Transfer Protocol)
Transfer of files between a user's computer and a host computer.

GEDCOM
(GEnealogical Data COMmunication) The standard by which genealogical data is transferred from one genealogy program to another.

HTML
(HyperText Markup Language) Coded text which allows you to use links to other documents on the World Wide Web.

Kinship Report
Report which shows how one individual is related to others in the database.

label
Name of an event, such as Birth, Death, Marriage. Some programs allow you to customize labels.

multimedia
Graphics, sound, and video files.

PAF (Personal Ancestral File)
Program created by The Church of Jesus Christ of Latter-day Saints.

Pedigree Chart
Chart which shows the ancestors of an individual in pedigree format.

peripherals
Hardware which may be added onto a basic computer system; a scanner, printer, and removable media drives are all examples of peripherals.

Register Report
(aka Modified Register, Henry Style Report) Numbered style of report generally used in printed books, which displays detailed information about an individual and descendants.

RIN (Record Identification Number)
Identifying number assigned by a program.

shareware
Software which is free to use for a limited time; after that you must pay (register) to continue using the program. Some shareware is fully functional, other programs have limited use.

SSDI
Social Security Death Index.

Soundex
Code to index similar sounding names which are spelled differently.

TT (Tiny Tafel)
File which displays a specially formatted, abbreviated Ahnentafel report.

utility
Program which has a special function or abilities, but is not a database.

upgrade
The new version of an existing program is often referred to as "upgrading." Some upgrades are free, others may have a charge.

upload
Transfer a file from a user's computer to a host computer.

URL (Uniform Resource Locator)
The Internet address of a Web page.

user-defined
Ability of the user to specify information about an item in a program, such as a user-defined field.

version number
The identifying number given to each release of software.

Wall Chart
Multiple pages of a chart which, when assembled, create 1 giant chart. Wall charts can also be printed on large paper using specialty plotters.

Web page
Document on the World Wide Web which may contain graphics and text.

wildcard
A character which stands in for missing characters, generally used in a search function. The search phrase Benn*r would search for the name Bennar, Bennir, Benner, Bennor, etc.

 # Index